RESURRECTION:

Faith or Fact?

RESURRECTION:
Faith or Fact?

A SCHOLARS' DEBATE
BETWEEN A SKEPTIC AND A CHRISTIAN

Carl Stecher and Craig Blomberg

with contributions by Richard Carrier and Peter S. Williams

Pitchstone Publishing
Durham, North Carolina

Pitchstone Publishing
Durham, North Carolina

Library of Congress Cataloging-in-Publication Data

Names: Stecher, Carl, author. | Blomberg, Craig L., 1955- author. | Carrier, Richard, 1969- author. | Williams, Peter S., author.
Title: Resurrection : faith or fact? A scholars' debate between a skeptic and a Christian / Carl Stecher and Craig Blomberg ; with contributions by Richard Carrier and Peter S. Williams.
Description: Durham, North Carolina : Pitchstone Publishing, [2019] | Includes bibliographical references.
Identifiers: LCCN 2018049179 (print) | LCCN 2018054116 (ebook) | ISBN 9781634311755 (ePub) | ISBN 9781634311762 (ePDF) | ISBN 9781634311779 (mobi) | ISBN 9781634311748 (pbk. : alk. paper)
Subjects: LCSH: Jesus Christ—Resurrection. | Jesus Christ—Historicity. | Christianity and atheism.
Classification: LCC BT482 (ebook) | LCC BT482 .S74 2019 (print) | DDC 232/.5—dc23
LC record available at https://lccn.loc.gov/2018049179

Contents

Introduction

Carl Stecher, Ph.D.

Was Jesus miraculously raised from the dead? For almost 2,000 years traditional Christians have positively answered this question—"He has risen indeed." For these Christians, Jesus' resurrection has been the foundational doctrine of the faith. In Paul's words, ". . . if Christ was not raised, your faith has nothing to it . . . If it is for this life only that Christ has given us hope, we of all people are most to be pitied" (1 Corinthians 15:17–19).

The purpose of this volume is to explore the evidence: is Jesus' resurrection a fact of history? The debate brings together the eminent Christian scholar Craig Blomberg, author of more than twenty books on Christianity, and myself, a college professor with a strong background in history and a special interest in Christianity. For several decades I have focused on the resurrection question, discovering to my great surprise that despite the voluminous scholarship devoted to this question, including thousands of pages of scholarly books and journal articles and dozens of debates pitting Christian scholars against skeptical scholars, some very strong arguments against the resurrection as a fact of history have not been made.

Specifically, the case for the resurrection as fact rests upon the belief of some of Jesus' original disciples that He had appeared to them, alive, three days after his execution by the ruling Romans. What has not received significant attention are the multiple possible natural explanations for the disciples' resurrection belief, all of them based upon common, well-documented human behavior. My argument is that the Gospel accounts provide the only substantive evidence for resurrection, and that consequently we cannot know with any certainty what happened 2,000 years ago. The unexamined natural explanations are all plausible, conform to normal human behavior, and have been the subject of many university studies and experiments.

The debate in this volume is divided into five parts and structured to give maximum opportunity to test these natural explanations. The first part consists of statements by the four participating scholars in this debate. We share our worldviews and how we came to the beliefs we hold as individuals. Because our perceptions of reality are so fundamentally at variance, and because these differences so affect our perception of evidence, we agreed that these differences should be made clear from the beginning.

The second part begins with my case against the resurrection as a fact of history, followed by Craig Blomberg's rebuttal and my rejoinder to Craig's rebuttal.

The third part begins with Craig's positive case for the resurrection's historicity, followed by my rebuttal and Craig's rejoinder. This organization is designed to facilitate as much back and forth as possible.

The fourth part is devoted to commentary upon the two previous chapters of debate by first, Richard Carrier, a distinguished atheist scholar and author of several books defending naturalist explanations of history and the world, and by Peter S. Williams, a prominent British scholar and author of several books defending traditional Christian beliefs.

In the book's fifth and final part, Craig and then I respond briefly to the assessments of Peter and Richard and make our final statements.

At the end of the book, we offer our suggested readings on the subject, with each participant nominating ten books for further study.

At times this debate will touch upon other, related questions. After all, Christian orthodoxy generally preaches that Jesus' resurrection is central to the faith, because it is God's sacrifice of his only Son. As a result, those who have the correct faith in Jesus and his sacrifice will receive eternal joy in Heaven, and those who do not have this faith will experience eternal torment in Hell (or else, as some think, annihilation). So context is important, and our debate will also at times touch upon the Christian teachings that God is all-powerful., omniscient, and morally perfect. The resurrection question finds its significance in this context.

Our purpose in this book is to test an essentially new challenge to the traditional case for Jesus' resurrection as a fact of history, and to do this with mutual respect and an honest attempt by all four participants to find common ground when possible, and when it is not, to come to a better understanding of how our minds seem to work differently, and how sometimes what appears a clear truth to some seems clearly false to others.

I have collaborated previously with both Peter S. Williams and Craig Blomberg, and I consider them both to be good friends, despite our different beliefs. Having read several of Richard Carrier's many books and watched his debates on YouTube, I am delighted that he has accepted our invitation to participate in this project; his contributions have been invaluable and many faceted. And to reflect the respect and collegial feelings of the four participants, we will often refer to each other by our first names.

Additional Acknowledgments: We are grateful to our two editors, Sharon Broll and Davida Rosenblum, for their many valuable suggestions and for their help in producing a clean manuscript. Without their help this project would never have come to completion.

PART ONE: HORIZONS

Living Without Gods

Carl Stecher, Ph.D.

I am often asked how I came to my present skepticism about the claims of traditional Christianity. From kindergarten through high school I lived in Sheboygan, Wisconsin, with my parents, my sister, who is two years my senior, and my brother, twelve years my junior. We attended as a family the local Congregational church every other Sunday; alternate weekends we spent with our grandparents in Milwaukee. The Harvard-educated minister of the Sheboygan church often cited Paul Tillich. I remember something about "the ground of all being." I don't think of either of my parents as being religious—we didn't say grace at the dinner table or discuss religion. My mom later worked as a church organist and choir director and my father served as a deacon, despite being, according to my sister, a nonbeliever. Curiously, although I was close to my parents, I don't remember ever discussing God or religion with them.

Nor do I remember discussing religion with my sister during these years; it was only later that I discovered that she was a Christian believer. After she graduated from college she married an Episcopalian and for more than fifty years she has been a devout low-church evangelical Episcopalian with a close personal relationship with Jesus and a strong commitment to live her faith in service of others. I love her very much and I am immensely proud of her, but over the years we have discussed our religious beliefs with great caution and deference, fearing that our very different views might become a barrier between us. My brother shares my skepticism about the God of Christianity but has for decades practiced meditation. He was attracted to Transcendental Meditation at the beginning of the movement, but abandoned it when claims were made that those who believed could miraculously levitate.

The onset of my skepticism was sudden and unexpected. The first time I gave the question of God's existence serious consideration, I was a high school sophomore. I had recently completed the mild indoctrination of my parents' Congregational church and had been confirmed a fifteen-year-old Christian. I was saying my dutiful bedtime prayer (". . . and God bless Mom and Dad and . . .") when it suddenly occurred to me that nobody was listening: *I was praying to a God I did not believe in.* There was a gigantic gulf between the world I perceived and the fundamental assertions of Christianity: that an invisible, all powerful, morally perfect spirit is everywhere, listening to and watching over all human beings simultaneously. The idea seemed contrary to the world as I experienced it and all common sense. In fact, God seemed no more real than Santa Claus. The one perplexing fact was that so many otherwise normal adults, having outgrown Santa Claus, still seemed to believe in God.

This realization was not the result of any philosophical analysis, nor was it the result of unanswered prayer or teenage angst or rebellion, and it had nothing to do with my sense of right or wrong. Rather, my bare recitation of Christian beliefs suddenly seemed self-evidently untrue. This God—or any personal god, for that matter—was no more real to me than Jupiter, Wotan, or the Tooth Fairy. My disbelief was not a choice. It was a discovery. And to this day I find it impossible to believe in the God of Christianity.

By now my wife has long been an essential part of my world. She too grew up in Sheboygan and received a much more rigorous indoctrination into conservative Christian faith in a Calvinistic Dutch Reformed church. During her childhood she attended Saturday Bible school and Sunday church service and Sunday school. She has a bachelor's and a master's degree and a Phi Beta Kappa key from the University of Wisconsin, and she is an exceptionally kind and caring person. We started dating when we were sophomores in high school and I have been in love with her for 60 years. She reports that despite the years of church school, she can never remember actually believing.

Fast-forward two decades. When our two children were in grade school, my wife and I decided that they should be exposed, as we had been, to the dominant Christian faith of our culture; we therefore attended a Congregational church while they went to its Sunday school. I sang in the (quite dreadful) church choir and accepted an invitation to teach a Lenten study course, which I titled "Why I Am Not a Christian." After this I decided to reopen the questions of God and belief that I had closed years before, embarking upon extensive reading. I found the questions surprisingly engrossing and, as a tenured English professor at Salem State College, I was able to teach undergraduate and graduate courses on the Bible as literature and a course of my own design called "The Search for God," for which I assigned readings from a great variety of sources, including many texts from world religions. In the process I became more and more immersed in questions related to religious belief. Not only did I begin corresponding with several Christian scholars but I also wrote essays for periodicals such as *The Humanist* and *Skeptic*. In 2000, while vacationing in Great Britain, I came across *The Case for God*, a highly praised 425-page book by Peter S. Williams, a British philosopher of religion. In it Peter wrote, "There are enough critics of belief in God to make for a good debate . . . debating with someone else introduces new perspectives which the lone armchair philosopher might not consider . . . I have therefore sought to interact with the arguments and opinions of non-believers."

Taking Peter at his word, I mailed him a rather long letter in which I detailed why I thought his case for God fell short. For months nothing happened. Then one day I received a thick packet from Great Britain. In it was a response to my letter—98 pages long, single-spaced, with hundreds of footnotes. I responded, and an extensive correspondence ensued, which eventually I spent a sabbatical editing: the result was *God Questions,* a book-length manuscript published online by the British Christian site, bethinking.org. This is available online for free (just search for "Stecher & Williams, *God Questions*.") Peter and I both think we had the stronger arguments but are willing to let our readers decide; the one limitation of the site is that it allows for no feedback.

My involvement with questions of Christian beliefs expanded with the publication of N. T. Wright's *The Resurrection of the Son of God* in 2003. My curiosity aroused about the evidence for this central belief of Christianity, I ordered it through Amazon and, upon its arrival, trudged through all 817 pages. Hundreds of pages of Wright's tome provide background about ancient pagan and Jewish beliefs about life after death and related topics, which left hundreds of pages of discussion on the evidence for the physical resurrection of Jesus. Wright comes to the conclusion that Jesus' disciples discovered the tomb to be empty, and beginning from three days after his execution by the Romans, "various 'meetings' took place not only between Jesus and his followers (including at least one initial skeptic) but also . . . between Jesus and people who had not been among his followers." Wright regarded "this conclusion as coming in the same sort of category, of historical probability so high as to be virtually certain, as the death of Augustus in AD 14 or the fall of Jerusalem in AD 70" (Fortress Press, p. 710). Unconvinced by Wright's arguments, I wrote a review essay, published by *Skeptic Magazine* ("Faith, Facts, and the Resurrection of Jesus" 11, no. 4 [2005]: 73–78). I sent Bishop Wright a copy of the article, accompanied by a deferential letter, but he declined to respond to this or to my follow-up phone call (at which time his secretary told me that he was too busy to speak with me).

The first evidence that I had that at least one person had read *God Questions* was an invitation from the president of the Oregon State University Socratic Club to debate the question of whether Jesus' resurrection was a fact of history; my opponent was to be the eminently qualified Craig Blomberg. Our debate can be viewed on YouTube, as "OSU Socratic Club Debate: The Resurrection of Jesus: An Article of Faith or a Fact of History?" Building on the ideas I had developed in my essay review of Wright's *The Resurrection of the Son of God*, I built a 25-minute argument against the historicity of the resurrection; I have been refining that argument since that time.

I found a new challenge to that argument with the publication of Michael Licona's *The Resurrection of Jesus: A New Historiographical Ap-*

proach (IVP, 2010). Licona's contribution to the evangelical case for the resurrection as history is a "mere" 718 pages (or about three pounds, according to my scale). Licona's principal contribution to the debate is a discussion of historical method and an attempt to consider the evidence for the resurrection in the context of that discussion. I entered into an email correspondence with Licona about the resurrection question and the positions he had taken in his book, sending him the debate preparation I had assembled in anticipation of a rematch with Craig Blomberg. At first Michael (our exchanges quickly switched to a first-name basis) expressed great interest, but he later warned that he had considerable time constraints and might take some time to get to my case against the resurrection as history. A full year passed before Michael turned to my arguments; he wrote a few entirely irrelevant paragraphs dismissive of my analysis and stated he was not interested in pursuing the question with me. My view is that I raised challenges to the historicity of Jesus' resurrection that Licona would rather not engage.

I've recently read polls indicating that as many as 80 percent of Americans believe in angels, with a very high percentage of people also believing in Satan and demons. This greatly surprised me. I have no recollection of any talk about angels or demons (or hell) in either Congregational church I have attended. From the time I no longer believed in Santa Claus, probably in the first or second grade as best as I can remember, I had thought of all such beings as imaginary, like trolls and fairies and the Wicked Witch of the West. (Or was it the Wicked Witch of the *East*, as my wife remembers? But this is just a question of which witch is which.) The angel sat on the right shoulder of Sylvester the cat, while the devil sat on his left shoulder. I thought of angels, to the extent that I thought about them at all, as the probably imagined beings in Bible stories with wings or at least a supernatural glow about them; I certainly never expected to encounter one or have anyone else relate such an encounter. Casper, the cartoon ghost, was make-believe, like every other ghost, and for me in the same category as angels and demons.

In his book *Can We Still Believe the Bible? An Evangelical Engagement with Contemporary Questions* (Brazos, 2014), Craig wrote about an exorcism that his wife observed in their church. "The woman started speaking in a deep, bass, growling voice and recoiling when the pastor prayed in Jesus's name over her . . . As others around prayed more fervently, our pastor spoke even more forcefully . . . Suddenly the demon left, and the woman grew limp" (p.182). Previously I had thought of the movie, *The Exorcist,* as an entertainment and probably an embarrassment to most educated Catholics. In the Congregational churches of my experience—and, I suspect, my sister's Episcopalian church—an exorcism is about as likely as a Voodoo ritual or an animal sacrifice on the sanctuary altar. I assumed, quite mistakenly it seems, that only a small minority of adults actually believed in angels and demons, much less exorcisms. When Peter Williams published his book, *The Case for Angels,* I'm afraid I thought this too weird to be taken seriously.

Interacting as I have with Peter and Craig, two conservative Christian scholars with impeccable credentials, has been instructive; I think we have made a good start understanding our differing perceptions of reality. We live in different worlds, or at least we perceive the world we live in very differently. The three of us see that it would take a fundamental shift in our worldviews for us to agree on the interpretation of such events as resurrections and exorcisms. For them, these types of strange episodes present clear evidence of the supernatural, while for me, they have natural causes, even in those cases when an odd occurrence defies easy explanation. Indeed, there are plenty of things I don't understand that do seem to be miraculous. How does the ugly caterpillar become the beautiful butterfly? How does a voice come out of the sky telling me to turn left on Challmer Street? Quite clearly neither requires the active intervention of a supernatural being.

So I am, by long habit of mind, a skeptic about the supernatural, and specifically about Christian teachings about Jesus' resurrection. I have thought hard, read extensively, and debated at length two first-rate Christian scholars on the topic of Christian doctrines, including, specifically, the question of the historicity of Jesus' resurrection. I do not discount the possibility that I am mistaken, but I have yet to see compelling evidence either for the truth of traditional Christian theology or for Jesus' resurrection from the dead. Our focus in this debate will be on this last question.

My purpose is not to convert Craig, Peter, my sister, or anyone else to my way of thinking, but to continue to explore God questions, to understand better the world as it appears to conservative Christian believers, to test my conclusions against the best that can be said in favor of traditional Christian belief, and to support others who cannot accept traditional Christianity but have not had the opportunity to study God questions as carefully as I have.

A Journey of Christian Faith

Craig Blomberg, Ph.D.

Like Carl, I was raised in the upper Midwest, in Rock Island, Illinois, in a mainline Protestant church. In my case it was a Lutheran church (LCA). My family attended most Sundays, and I attended Sunday school the hour before the worship service. I was generally a compliant child, but I was helped enormously by being allowed to draw or write during the pastor's sermons, which did not ever seem to be geared toward children. The church was liturgical, so the service every week was almost identical, except for the once-a-month Communion services when the liturgy changed a little. I could say or sing everything I was supposed to from rote, leaving my mind free to wander to anything I wanted to think about.

Like Carl, I, too, went through the motions of confirmation class during junior high, along with about eight other boys and two or three girls. As far as I could tell, I took the process as seriously as any of them, but that isn't saying much. Our pastor did not have a disciplining bone in his body, it seemed, nor did he know how to write on the blackboard in our confirmation classroom without turning his back completely on the dozen of us, so that there were several boys who used that time to throw spit wads at each other or see how much other mischief they could get up to quietly. We were supposed to be studying a simplified version of Luther's small catechism, which we did some of the time, but our pastor, probably trying to be relevant, was more likely to stop and discuss the latest Simon and Garfunkel hit song than to teach us biblical content.

As was the case for many young people confirmed in the mainline Protestant world in or around that turbulent year of 1968, confirmation became the ticket to leave church. It was supposed to be our initiation into the adult life of the church, but thirteen-year-olds in the late 1960s usually didn't qualify for that label, nor was there anything for us to do differently once we were confirmed. The only way my father convinced me to go to church in ninth grade was by agreeing to let me join him in the church office after the offering was taken to help count the money. Math was always my favorite subject, so at least this was more interesting than our pastor's sermons, which were tangentially related to one of three Scripture passages read out of a lectionary each week, but more memorable for their quotations from great literature than for explaining or applying anything in the Bible.

During my sophomore year in high school, everything changed. My best friend was involved in a club called Campus Life (a ministry of the parachurch organization Youth for Christ) that met one evening a week in various students' homes. Within a few weeks of the start of the school year, he invited me to come and, for the first time in my life, I discovered kids my own age who talked about having a personal relationship with Jesus. And it wasn't just talk; they behaved differently. I had always been what would be called a nerd and a geek, pretty scrawny on the playground and not that good looking, but an exceptional student. So since I had no hope of being a jock or attracting the good-looking girls, I reveled in what I could do well—academics. I went on to be my high school's valedictorian out of a class of over 700. I was also pretty tactless at times in showing off what I could do academically so, not surprisingly, I had very few close friends. But the Campus Life kids (club meetings usually brought in 30–40 high schoolers) were consistently different. They took a genuine interest in me, just like they took a genuine interest in the handful of poorer black kids willing to associate with the majority of us slightly better-off white ones. (This was the age of race riots, two of which closed our school for three days my junior year, with it reopening the following week with armed state troopers in every hallway.)

Campus Life typically started off with some fun if not downright crazy "icebreaking" activities. The one paid leader, a thirtyish man, who had to raise his own support, would then lead a discussion on a topic of interest to teens in those days, largely just asking questions and allowing as many to talk as wanted to and trying to draw everyone into the discussion at one time or another. Topics ranged from drugs to the Vietnam War to rock music to hippie life to teen suicide to the Cold War to dating and sex to race relations and so on. We almost always had at least a half-dozen or so non-Christian friends who would come and keep the conversations lively. Then for the last fifteen or twenty minutes of the formal part of the evening, the club leader would give a "wrap-up," in which he would present a low-key Christian perspective on the topics we had discussed. Over the three years of my involvement a number of friends became believers.

By the late winter of tenth grade (February 1971), I realized I needed and wanted what so many of my friends had. I was still reciting a memorized bedtime prayer my mother had taught me from when I was a youngster that was pretty immature for my age now, but I had watched some of my friends pray "extemporaneously," as if they were having a conversation with someone and not just reading preprepared prayers as we always did in church. So I prayed one evening words to the effect of, "Dear Jesus, I've been praying to you daily the same brief prayer for years, thinking I was one of your followers, but now I'm not at all sure. If there's more I have to do, please show me. I want you to be my Lord, the person in charge of every aspect of my life, in ways I know I haven't let you be this far. Please forgive my sins. Help me to be more loving and kind, like so many of my new friends at Campus Life, and less conceited."

Nothing changed overnight but I believe God was gradually helping me to mature. Then, a year later, my world was rocked. A girl I had grown up with in my neighborhood tried to take her life. She had come to Campus Life a few times before this but wasn't a regular. Three of the student leaders in the club spontaneously organized what they called a prayer meeting for Pat on a Wednesday evening at one of their homes. I asked my best friend what this was all about. He explained that whoever wanted to come was welcome, and we would just sit around and people could pray silently or out loud for Pat and anything else the Spirit would lead us to pray for.

I came to the meeting of about a dozen or so of us and that's exactly what we did. If the silence between prayers got really long, one of the student leaders would read a verse or two from somewhere in the Bible that seemed directly to address what we were praying about. Then he or she would focus our attention on another aspect of our concerns and we'd pray about that for a while. We went on for nearly an hour. What impressed me even more than all the spontaneous prayers was my friends' ability to range widely throughout the Scriptures and quote all these passages that were so relevant. I wasn't aware that any of the adults, much less kids, in my church could do that. I figured there must be a reference work somewhere that had all these passages listed in them that I wanted to learn about. I asked each one, independently of each other, how they were able to quote all these passages. As if they had conspired to give me the same answer, each said something like, "I try to read my Bible every day and when I come across particularly meaningful passages I highlight them. From time to time, I try to memorize some of these key verses." I knew our Campus Life leader had talked about regular private prayer and Bible reading as a good practice, but this was the first time I realized some of the kids actually did it.

I realized immediately this is what I wanted to do. This embarked me on the practice of regularly reading a portion of the Bible, whether short or long, and meditating on it, which I have followed more days than not over the last 47 years. My best friend suggested I start with the little letter near the back of the New Testament called 1 John and re-read it for six straight days, looking for and highlighting different things each time: main points one day, commands another, warnings a third, promises to claim a fourth, examples to follow a fifth, verses I wanted to memorize a sixth. I did it, and I was amazed how much I learned, how the Bible came alive and how it seemed God was speaking directly to me. I proceeded over the next couple of years to do the same thing with each of the other New Testament books, though the longer the book the fewer times I read it. But I did read every book at least twice. In college I finished the Old Testament this way as well. In many ways, my real conversion dates to when I started to be a regular Bible reader and student of its teaching.

For college, I went to a liberal Lutheran college in my hometown, not because it was Lutheran but because I didn't have enough money to move away from home and it was one of the academically highest-ranked liberal arts colleges in the Midwest. We had to take three classes in religious studies in our liberal arts core and I quickly discovered a very different approach to the Bible that I had not encountered either in church or Campus Life. I quickly was taught that the only really scholarly American Ph.D. programs in New Testament were at Harvard, Yale, Princeton, Chicago, and Berkeley and that scholars from those schools believed that only about 20 percent of the New Testament Gospels reflected what Jesus actually said or did. The rest was the invention of the early church. Curiously, my professor and the other four full-time members of the religion department were ordained Lutheran pastors, but they all accepted a modification of Gerhard Lessing's "ugly ditch": the accidental truths of history could not form the basis of the necessary truths of religion. Faith operated in one realm of life, history in another, and the two never had to intersect at all!

In those days, local conservative Christian bookstores, unlike today, actually stocked large numbers of academic as well as popular-level works, and I devoured them. I also located excellent works in my college library that were not on any professor's reading lists. Time after time I discovered convincing replies to each intellectual challenge that I encountered in the classroom. I was stunned that whenever I asked my professors about how they would answer the scholarship I had read, they had never even heard of the works or the arguments they contained. But these books interacted with all the scholars my professors were citing in class!

Though I didn't realize it at the time, the course of my life became set when one of my professors threw down the gauntlet and stated with a Cheshire-cat-like grin that it was impossible to maintain one's intellectual integrity and be an evangelical or theologically conservative Christian who believed the Bible was a reliable account of God's actions in history on behalf of humankind. I already had learned enough from my studies to know my professor was wrong. But I didn't yet realize the *strength* of the evidence for historic Christian beliefs. After spending a year teaching high-school math, which had been my original college major (I later added religion and Spanish to create a triple major), I felt God strongly leading me to go into teaching biblical studies at a tertiary level.

I enrolled in what at that time was widely viewed as the academically strongest evangelical seminary in the country, Trinity Evangelical Divinity School, got an M.A. in New Testament studies, met and married my wonderful wife, Fran, and then proceeded to doctoral studies at the University of Aberdeen in Scotland. Although my thesis was in the area of the interpretation of Jesus' parables, I always kept my interest in the question of how much of the Gospels reflected the actual life of the historical Jesus. I was involved in an international six-year, six-volume "Gospels Project" under the auspices of the Tyndale Fellowship, related to the University of Cambridge, which produced cutting-edge high-level scholarship on precisely this issue from 1980 to 1986. I contributed articles to three of the volumes and became a coeditor of the final one. So I was thrilled when Fran and I were offered a fellowship to pay all our expenses to live for an academic year in Cambridge and produce the projected semi-popularizing one-volume summary and supplement to the six technical volumes, *The Historical Reliability of the Gospels* (InterVarsity Press). It came out in 1987, surprised me by how well it did, and shocked me that it stayed in print long enough for me to produce a second edition in 2007 for the twentieth anniversary of its initial publication.

In the 47 years since I truly owned my faith for myself, I have always made it a priority to be involved in a church that stressed systematic Bible teaching and preaching, loved people, and cared about issues of social justice. I have been blessed to meet the most wonderful people I have encountered anywhere, who have practiced what they preached, had their lives remarkably transformed from horrible upbringings, seen miraculous healings on occasion and answers to prayer more consistently, and have presented the most intellectually satisfying answers to all the hard philosophical questions of life that I have encountered everywhere. Of course, I have met lots of other kinds of people in those churches, too, and I have visited lots of other kinds of churches. But I have seen enough positive models, including those of friends dying prematurely of cancer and undergoing some agonizing suffering, that I know that true Christianity works. I have seen people come to faith in the last weeks of their life after a lifetime of unbelief and watched as they died with a peace they had never previously had. I have studied church history, warts and all, but seen the amazing good that Christians do all over the world, including providing a disproportionately large percentage of the foundations for Western science, medicine, law, education, relief work, and humanitarian aid of many kinds. I am also old enough to have seen the effects of pure, ideological atheism created in Khrushchev's Soviet Union and Mao's China. I have made three extended ministry trips in recent years to Albania, the one nation in which it was officially illegal to believe in God under Communism, and seen the hunger and thirst for Christian teaching since the fall of the Iron Curtain.

While my academic career has spanned both undergraduate and graduate-level teaching, both in the United States and around the world, and while I have been privileged to author, coauthor, or edit more than 25 books and 150 journal articles or essays in multiauthor works, the topic I have kept coming back to most often and the topic I have been invited to speak on in churches, universities, civic clubs, and elsewhere more than any other has been the reliability of Scripture. In 2001, I published *The Historical Reliability of John's Gospel* (with InterVarsity Press); in 2014, *Can We Still Believe the Bible? An Evangelical Engagement with Contemporary Questions* (with Brazos Press of Baker Book House); and in 2016, *The Historical Reliability of the New Testament* (B & H Academic). The more I have studied, the more I have become aware of the vast quantity of corroborating material that exists. But I also recognize that there are always multiple spins one can put on the evidence and that none of it individually or cumulatively is so overwhelming as to compel belief. I have also never wanted to replicate the approach my undergraduate religion professors took—teaching only one side of an issue and declaring it to be the only intellectually viable one. That is why I have appreciated the opportunities I have had over the years for dialogue and debate with others who hold quite different perspectives on important religious topics. This is why I was quick to accept invitations to participate in two different debates with Carl over a three-year period at Oregon State University and why I appreciate his vision for this book.

It is interesting to see how similar our upbringings were before our spiritual paths diverged. But I see in Carl's courtesy, in his love for his sister, in his willingness to let those with faith rely on it especially in times of crisis, and in his eagerness to participate in discussion and debate with those who hold views that are opposite from his own (rather than just dismissing them out of hand), what looks to me like the remnants of his upbringing and church-going years. At the very least they disclose to me the stamp of God's image on his life as on every human being (Genesis 1:26–28).

Autobiographical Thoughts on the Wisdom of Faith

Peter S. Williams, M.Phil.

Like any history, this autobiographical chapter is *partial*, both in the sense that it's incomplete and that it's designed to set out my background in view of our subject.

For as long as I can remember, I've been a member of that majority of humanity to whom the proposition "God exists" is intuitively plausible. I chime with the Psalmist:

> The heavens are declaring the glory of God,
> and their expanse shows the work of his hands.
> Day after day they pour forth speech,
> night after night they reveal knowledge.
> There is no speech nor are there words—
> their voice is not heard—
> yet their message goes out into all the world,
> and their words to the ends of the earth. (Psalm 19:1–4, ISV)[1]

Intuition plays a key role in philosophy, and so in all intellectual pursuits. As C. S. Lewis observed: "You cannot produce rational intu-

---

1. See: Peter S. Williams, "Psalm 19," peterswilliams.podbean.com/mf/feed/69yukf/Psalm_19.mp3.

ition by argument, because argument depends upon rational intuition. Proof rests upon the unprovable which just has to be 'seen.'"[2] This is one reason it doesn't do to see reason and faith (that is, *trust* or *allegiance*) as opposed to one another by nature.[3] Rationality requires faith, and faith should be exercised wisely.

While some intuitions (e.g., intuitions of the laws of logic) are indubitable, others carry varying degrees of *prima facie* warrant, such that "if one carefully reflects on something, and a certain viewpoint intuitively seems to be true, then one is justified in believing that viewpoint in the absence of overriding counterarguments (which will ultimately rely on alternative intuitions)."[4]

From childhood, the intuitive *appearance of things to me* included not only the reality of God, but also the interlinked objective values of truth, goodness, and beauty (and their parasitical shadows of falsehood, evil, and ugliness), of meaningful purpose and a physical world full of intricate complexity and grandeur, all experienced from the irreducibly first-person perspective of an embodied but more than bodily self, a self with a degree of freedom and the consequent responsibility to think and to act well.

Of course, I realize that (beyond indubitable intuitions) such phenomenological appearances are the beginning of a conversation rather than the end of the discussion. Nevertheless, I think it's important to recognize that this is the beginning of the conversation; and that the discussion proceeds on the basis of such intuitive, properly basic, principled credulity.

Moreover, "an appeal to intuitions does not rule out the use of additional arguments that add further support to that appeal."[5] I think the arguments for accepting the above description of reality are stronger

---

2. C. S. Lewis, "Why I Am Not a Pacifist," in *The Weight of Glory and Other Addresses* (HarperOne, 2001), 67.

3. See: Peter S. Williams, "Hebrews 9:11–15," peterswilliams.podbean.com/mf/feed/arau6z/Hebrews_9.mp3.

4. J. P. Moreland and William Lane Craig, *Philosophical Foundations for a Christian Worldview* (IVP, 2003), 422.

5. Ibid.

than those against.[6] Concerning ultimate reality, I think there are sound and mutually reinforcing cases against naturalism/materialism[7] and for theism.[8]

It's not that I haven't had, or don't have, questions. I think questions are essential to any serious spirituality—that is, any "way of life" that seeks to integrate one's head, heart, and hands. As Timothy Keller says,

> A faith without some doubts is like a human body without any antibodies in it. People who blithely go through life too busy or indifferent to ask hard questions about why they believe as they do will find themselves defenceless against either the experience of tragedy or the probing questions of a smart skeptic. A person's

6. See: Peter S. Williams, *A Faithful Guide to Philosophy* (Wipf and Stock, 2019).

7. See: Peter S. Williams, YouTube playlist, "Problems with Materialism/ Metaphysical Naturalism," www.youtube.com/playlist?list=PLQhh3qcwVE Wg0lWsfZnhQvzNfRT_jHLJA (August 18, 2018); William Lane Craig and J.P. Moreland, eds., *Naturalism* (Routledge, 2014); Daniel C. Dennett and Alvin Plantinga, *Science and Religion* (Oxford University Press USA, 2011); Stewart Goetz and Charles Taliaferro, *Naturalism* (Eerdmans, 2008); J. P. Moreland, *The Recalcitrant Imago Dei* (SCM, 2009); Angus Menuge, *Agents Under Fire: Materialism and the Rationality of Science* (Rowman & Littlefield, 2004); Thomas Nagel, *Mind and Cosmos* (Oxford University Press, 2012); Victor Reppert, *C. S. Lewis' Dangerous Idea* (IVP, 2003); Richard Swinburne, *Mind, Brain, and Free Will* (Oxford University Press, 2013); Williams, *A Faithful Guide to Philosophy*.

8. See: Peter S. Williams, YouTube playlist, "Natural Theology," www.youtube. com/playlist?list=PLQhh3qcwVEWiDA8QN4h8wLrrbm49fLzPN (August 18, 2018); YouTube playlist, "Debating God," www.youtube.com/playlist?list=PLQ hh3qcwVEWiY3UmTAiRdj2OW4SBG0y_W (November 29, 2017); Paul Copan and Paul K. Moser, eds., *The Rationality of Theism* (Routledge, 2003); Corey Miller and Paul Gould, eds., *Is Faith in God Reasonable?* (Routledge, 2014); R. Douglas Geivett and Brendan Sweetman, eds., *Contemporary Perspectives on Religious Epistemology* (Oxford University Press, 1992); J. P. Moreland, *Consciousness and the Existence of God* (Routledge, 2009); J. P. Moreland and William Lane Craig, *Philosophical Foundations for a Christian Worldview*, 2nd ed. (IVP, 2017); Jerry L. Walls and Trent Dougherty, *The Plantinga Project: Two Dozen (or So) Arguments for God* (Oxford University Press, 2018); Peter S. Williams, *C. S. Lewis vs. the New Atheists* (Paternoster, 2013) and *A Faithful Guide to Philosophy*.

faith can collapse overnight if she has failed over the years to listen patiently to her own doubts, which should only be discarded after long reflection.[9]

I know what it is to wrestle with doubts, and critical reflection has sometimes led to a change in my views. However, my pursuit of the truth has, thus far, never seemed to me to require ditching any of the key worldview commitments listed above. Indeed, I sincerely believe that a commitment to the true, the good and the beautiful ultimately requires the rest of the worldview that I affirm. Readers looking for an introduction to such matters might read my book, *A Faithful Guide to Philosophy: A Christian Introduction to the Love of Wisdom*. Such is the horizon I bring to the study of the historical Jesus and his purported resurrection.

Having been born to Christian parents who raised me within the community of a Baptist church in the south-coast English city of Portsmouth, my spiritual maturation was (and is) a process of ratcheting understanding and recommitment to "the faith that God has once for all given to his people" (Jude 3, CEV). My parents were both science teachers who encouraged me to think about everything, not least the relationship between science and theology,[10] so I didn't take Christianity lightly. I knew other people have different beliefs and ways of life. However, I was impressed by the Bible from an early age. For me, it had what J. B. Philips called "the ring of truth,"[11] though I recognized that truth was communicated in different ways by different types of literature.

As a child, my untutored reaction to the opening of Genesis was,

9. Timothy Keller, *The Reason for God* (Dutton, 2008), xvi–xvii.

10. See: YouTube Playlist, "Christianity and Science," www.youtube.com/play list?list=PLQhh3qcwVEWjeYJfOKB1YYXsInZ5GIPL (August 27, 2017); Robert C. Koons, "Science and Theism: Concord Not Conflict," robkoons.net/media/ 69b0dd04a9d2fc6dffff80b3ffffd524.pdf; John Lennox, *God's Undertaker: Has Science Buried God?* 2nd ed. (Lion, 2009); Del Ratzsch, *Science & Its Limits* (IVP, 2000); Keith Ward, *God, Chance & Necessity* (OneWorld, 1996); Williams, *A Faithful Guide to Philosophy*.

11. J. B. Philips, *The Ring of Truth: A Translator's Testimony* (Waterbrook, 2000).

"What a lovely poem." Today, as a Bible reader and preacher,[12] I continue to seek what Augustine called the "literal"—that is, the nonallegorized *reading according to literary genre*—meaning of biblical texts,[13] and I consequently reject the woodenly literalistic young-earth reading of the biblical creation myth (not only in Genesis 1:1–2:3 but also in passages like Psalm 104).[14] Of course, by "myth" I do *not* mean the "fictitious story" of colloquial usage: "myth, in the technical sense, is concerned with ultimate realities, not fiction."[15] As William Lane Craig explains,

> Whereas 19th century scholars looked at ancient creation myths as a sort of crude proto-science, contemporary scholars tend more to the view that such stories were taken figuratively, not literally, by the people who told them.[16]

Genesis 2:4 to Genesis 11 seem to be mytho-historical in nature.[17]

---

12. For podcasts of my sermons, see: podcast.peterswilliams.com/?s=sermon.

13. See: Gavin Ortlund, "Did Augustine Read Genesis 1 Literally?" henrycenter. tiu.edu/2017/09/did-augustine-read-genesis-1-literally. See also: J. H. Taylor, S. J. ed., excerpt from Augustine's "The Literal Meaning of Genesis," www. christianmind.org/history/augustine1.htm.

14. See: YouTube playlist, "Young Earth Creationism," www.youtube.com/pl aylist?list=PLQhh3qcwVEWitFuSuMLz5fmhRGBHR8-_O (August 26, 2018); Peter S. Williams, "Psalm 104," podcast.peterswilliams.com/e/sermon-psalm-104/; Paul Marston, "Understanding the Biblical Creation Passages," www.asa3.org/ASA/topics/Bible-Science/understanding_the_biblical_ creation_passages.pdf; J. Daryl Charles, *Reading Genesis 1–2: An Evangelical Conversation* (Hendrickson, 2013); Charles Halton, ed., *Genesis: History, Fiction, or Neither?* (Zondervan, 2015); J. B. Stump, ed., *Creation, Evolution, and Intelligent Design* (Zondervan, 2017); John H. Walton, *The Lost World of Genesis One* (IVP Academic, 2009).

15. James K. Hoffmeier, "Genesis 1–11 as History and Theology," in *Genesis: History, Fiction, or Neither?* ed. Charles Halton (Zondervan, 2015), 27. See: Peter S. Williams, "Mythology," in *Dictionary of Christianity and Science*, ed. Paul Copan et al. (Zondervan, 2017).

16. William Lane Craig in Gregg D. Caruso, eds., *5 Questions: Science & Religion* (Automatic Press, 2014), 39.

17. See: Charles Halton ed., *Genesis: History, Fiction, or Neither?* (Zondervan, 2015), 81-88. See also: John H. Walton, *The Lost World of Adam And Eve*

Turning to the more straightforwardly historical narratives that follow[18] (although we are of course dealing here with ancient historiography), I saw in the Bible a collection of literature that was brutally honest about the failings of its most elevated heroes, such as Moses (murderer), King David (adulterer), Peter (who denied knowing Jesus having promised to stick by him), and Paul (who persecuted Christians before becoming one). The same could be said with respect to the Bible's depiction of the Jewish nation, the disciples, and the early church. Such honesty signals a concern for truth. I have subsequently spent a lot of time investigating the Bible and writing about the historical Jesus.[19]

As a teenager, I came to appreciate the psychological realism of biblical passages such as Romans 7:15–25:

> I do not understand what I do . . . Although I want to do good, evil is right there with me. For in my inner being I delight in God's law; but I see another law at work in me, waging war against the law of my mind and making me a prisoner of the law of sin at work within me. What a wretched man I am! Who will rescue me from this [sinful self] that is subject to death? Thanks be to God, who delivers me through Jesus Christ our Lord! (NIV)

As to *how* God delivers through Jesus, Keith Ward argues,

> The crucifixion of Jesus, in so far as it is an act of God as well as the self-offering of a human life, is the particular and definitive his-

---

(IVP Academic, 2015).

18. See: K. A. Kitchen, *On the Historical Reliability of the Old Testament* (Eerdmans, 2003); Craig L. Blomberg, *The Historical Reliability of the Gospels*, 2nd ed. (Apollos, 2007).

19. See: Peter S. Williams, *Getting at Jesus: A Comprehensive Critique of Neo-Atheist Nonsense about the Jesus of History* (Wipf & Stock, 2019); *Digging for Evidence* (Christian Evidence Society, 2016), www.peterswilliams.com/publications/books/digging-for-evidence; "The Epistle of James vs. Evolutionary Christology," *Theofilos* 9, no. 1 (2016); *Understanding Jesus: Five Ways to Spiritual Enlightenment* (Paternoster, 2011) and "New Testament Criticism and Jesus the Exorcist," *Quodlibet Journal of Christian Theology and Philosophy* 4, no. 1 (2002).

torical expression of the universal sacrifice of God in bearing the cost of sin. Sin is a harm done to God, inasmuch as it causes God to know, and to share, the suffering and reality of evil. The 'ransom' God pays is to accept this cost, to bear with evil, in order that it should be redeemed, transfigured, in God . . . The patience of God, bearing the cost of sin, takes the life and death and resurrection of Jesus as its own self-manifestation, and makes it the means by which the liberating life of God is made available in its essential form to the world.[20]

This makes intuitive sense to me, for what is forgiveness but the willingness of a wronged individual to absorb the wrong done to them for the sake of relationship with the person who wronged them? The crucifixion of Jesus is a figurative display of God's willingness to forgive repentant sinners who give him their allegiance:[21]

No one is declared righteous before [God] by the works of the law, for through the law comes the knowledge of sin. But now apart from the law the righteousness of God (which is attested by the law and the prophets) has been disclosed—namely, the righteousness of God through the faithfulness of Jesus Christ for all who [put their faith in him]. For there is no distinction, for all have sinned and fall short of the glory of God. But they are justified freely by his grace through the redemption that is in Christ Jesus. God publicly displayed him at his death as [a sacrifice of atonement] accessible through faith. This was to demonstrate his righteousness. . . in the present time, so that he would be just and the justifier of the one who lives because of Jesus' faithfulness. (Romans 3:20–26, NET)[22]

Jesus' crucifixion was also a performative action that created what

---

20. Keith Ward, *What the Bible Really Teaches* (SPCK, 2004), 109–110.

21. See: Joel B. Green and Mark D. Baker, *Recovering the Scandal of the Cross*, 2nd ed. (IVP, 2011); Richard Swinburne, *Responsibility and Atonement* (Clarendon, 1998); Williams, *Understanding Jesus*.

22. See: C. H. Dodd, *The Epistle of Paul to the Romans* (Hodder and Stoughton, 1941), 49–61; Joel B. Green and Mark D. Baker, *Recovering the Scandal of the Cross* (Paternoster, 2000), 104.

he called "the new covenant in my blood" (see 1 Corinthians 11:25 and Luke 22:20), a new mode of relationship with God:

> Paul doesn't see Christ's death and resurrection as the salve for a troubled conscience . . . he regards Christ's death as dealing with sin as part of the human (indeed: cosmic) condition. The participatory strand in Paul's theology takes sin to be a problem of our *identity*. The atonement does not merely adjust our 'moral standing' but instead [if we respond to it positively] inaugurates a change in the kind of beings we are.[23]

Writing in the mid 50's of the first century, Paul describes "the way" of Christian spirituality as *a participation in Jesus' death and resurrection:*[24]

> Do you not know that all of us who have been baptized into Christ Jesus were baptized into his death? We were buried therefore with him by baptism into death, in order that, just as Christ was raised [up out of] the dead by the glory of the Father, we too might walk in newness of life. For if we have been united with him in a death like his, we shall certainly be united with him in a resurrection like his . . . Christ, being raised from the dead, will never die again . . . For the death he died he died to sin, once for all, but the life he lives he lives to God. So you also must consider yourselves dead to sin and alive to God in Christ Jesus . . . present yourselves to God as those who have been brought from death to life . . . just as you once presented your members as slaves to impurity and to lawlessness leading to more lawlessness, so now present your members as slaves to righteousness leading to sanctification . . . For the wages of sin is death, but the free gift of God is eternal life in Christ Jesus our Lord. (Romans 6:3–23, ESV)

This spiritual communion doesn't earn, but appropriates and un-

---

23. Tim Bayne and Greg Restall, "A Participatory Model of the Atonement," consequently.org/papers/pa.pdf.

24. See: Peter S. Williams, "Christian Identity," podcast.peterswilliams.com/e/christian-identity-1515598142.

packs the communal new-covenant relationship of salvation and sanc-
tification (i.e., spiritual renovation),[25] which God makes available "in
Christ" for all humans to accept or reject (see 1 Timothy 2:4–7 and Hebrews 11:39–40).[26]

James doesn't contradict "the gospel of God's grace" (Acts 20:24,
ISV) when he writes that "faith without deeds is useless" (James 2:20,
NIV). James is here using the complex Greek word *pistis* (faith) to mean
a merely intellectual assent devoid of the religiously relevant allegiance
or trust which naturally reveals itself in deeds. James' point is that a
commitment-free "faith that" isn't the same as a saving "faith in": "What
good is it . . . if someone claims to have faith but has no deeds? Can such
faith save them? . . . [such] faith without deeds is dead" (James 2:14 &
26, NIV). The deeds (works) James has in mind flow from saving faith
(a point made by Jesus' depiction of judgment in Matthew 25:31–46[27]),
but saving faith trusts God for forgiveness without thinking forgiveness can be earned. Hence, James affirms that "Mercy triumphs over
judgment" (James 2:13) and that it is those who are "rich in faith" who
"inherit the kingdom [God] promised those who love him" (James 2:5,
NIV). As Jesus phrased the point: "This is the only work God wants
from you: Believe [*pisteuēte*—i.e., place your allegiance and trust] in the
one he has sent" (John 6:29, NLT).

The historical lynchpin of this gospel (i.e., "good news") of grace is
of course the claim that Jesus "died" and was "buried" and was "raised
up out of the dead," being "declared to be the Son of God in power according to the Spirit of holiness by his resurrection from the dead, Jesus

---

25. See: Dallas Willard, *The Great Omission: Reclaiming Jesus's Essential Teachings on Discipleship* (HarperOne, 2014).

26. See: Peter S. Williams, "The Particular and Exclusive Christ," peterswilliams.podbean.com/mf/feed/zr36r9/Exclusivism_2017.mp3; William Lane Craig, *On Guard for Students* (David C. Cook, 2015); Clark H. Pinnock, ed., *The Grace of God and the Will of Man* (Bethany House, 1989); John Sanders, *No Other Name: Can Only Christians Be Saved?* (SPCK, 1994); Jerry L. Walls, *Heaven: The Logic of Eternal Joy* (Oxford University Press, 2002); Jerry L. Walls and Joseph R. Dongell, *Why I Am Not a Calvinist* (IVP, 2004); Dallas Willard, *Knowing Christ Today* (HarperOne, 2009).

27. See: R. T. France, *Matthew* (IVP Academic, 2008), 357–362.

Christ our Lord" (Romans 1:4, YLT and ESV).[28]

My parents read C. S. Lewis's *Narnia* books to me as a child. As I matured, I read many of Lewis' nonfiction writings, which piqued my interest in reading philosophy. Here, besides a host of non-Christian thinkers, I've been deeply influenced by luminaries such as Aquinas, Augustine, Descartes, and Pascal; by British scholars of the early and mid-twentieth century, such as C. S. Lewis, C. E. M. Joad, W. R. Sorley, A. E. Taylor, and F. R. Tennant; and by Christians in the post-positivist renaissance among analytical philosophers (e.g., William Lane Craig, Steven T. Davis, Stephen C. Meyer, J. P. Moreland, Thomas V. Morris, H. P. Owen, Alvin Plantinga, Richard Swinburne, Keith Ward, Dallas Willard, etc.).[29]

I was further stimulated to explore the intellectual dimension of faith by a friend from college. A student of the natural sciences as well as an excellent musician, David Bacon was, as we say, "a bright cookie." Together we helped lead the college Christian Union and formed a band, mainly playing covers of Pink Floyd. Having studied at Cambridge University, Dr. Bacon is now a Senior Lecturer and Reader in Cosmology at the University of Portsmouth and a fellow congregant of the Church of England.

In the last session of a course for people considering baptism, I gave my minister a "definite maybe" as to whether I'd go through with it,

---

28. See: Williams, *Getting at Jesus*. See also: Peter S. Williams, YouTube playlist, "Debating the Resurrection," www.youtube.com/playlist?list=PLQhh3 qcwVEWhAPCkcpFsSwEXrYKuBhoaq (November 8, 2018); YouTube playlist, "The Resurrection of Jesus," www.youtube.com/playlist?list=PLQhh3qcwVE WjF0VbpQ9sPUUivlyF5n0wB (September 26, 2018); Paul Copan, ed., *Will the Real Jesus Please Stand Up? A Debate between William Lane Craig and John Dominic Crossan* (Baker, 1998); Stephen T. Davis, *Risen Indeed: Making Sense of the Resurrection* (SPCK, 1993); Gary R. Habermas et al., *Did Jesus Rise from the Dead?* (Wipf & Stock, 2003); Richard Swinburne, *The Resurrection of God Incarnate* (Clarendon, 2003); N. T. Wright, *The Resurrection of the Son of God* (SPCK, 2003).

29. I should also register my debt to *The Complete Works of Francis A. Schaeffer: A Christian Worldview* (Crossway, 1982). See also: Thomas V. Morris, *Francis Schaeffer's Apologetics: A Critique* (Moody Press, 1978); Scott R. Burson and Jerry L. Walls, *C. S. Lewis & Francis Schaeffer: Lessons for a New Century from the Most Influential Apologists of Our Time* (IVP, 1998).

because I didn't want to make a pressurized decision. I *was* baptized, on December 15, 1991, aged 17. As someone who couldn't put a date on when they had first chosen to trust Jesus, I found this public ritual a useful marker; but I didn't view it as an arrival at spiritual maturity, having long realized that "the way" of Christ is one of daily discipleship.

Studying "Classical Civilization" at college introduced me to the philosophers of classical antiquity,[30] and I ended up reading philosophy as an undergraduate at Cardiff University (including a year also studying English Literature and Music). Here I met Professor Michael Durrant, the first Christian philosopher I knew in the flesh. He was my personal tutor, stretched my mind past its limits with his lectures on Aristotle, and acted as president of the Student Philosophical Society that I ran with some coursemates.

Having been encouraged by the agnostic lecturer who taught me philosophy of religion at Cardiff, I focused on this area as I did my M.A. at Sheffield University (where I joined the Joint Chaplaincy Society), and then my M.Phil. at the University of East Anglia (UEA), where my main supervisor was atheist Nicholas Everitt.

I helped lead the UEA's Christian Union and Anglican Theological Society. The latter was set up by an Anglican chaplain, the Reverend Dr. Garth Barber, who was an astrophysicist and cosmologist. Whilst at UEA I participated in my first debate on God's existence, with philosopher Michael Martin, in the pages of *The Philosopher's Magazine*.[31] I also wrote *The Case for God* (Monarch, 1999). I'm not sure when I had time to write my thesis (on transcendental values and God as the maximally beautiful being), but I did!

After obtaining my M.Phil., I found a job as a "student worker" for a Church of England congregation in Leicester. My employers wanted me to keep writing and learning alongside my pastoral duties, setting aside a day a week for this purpose (I took distance courses in theology). Dur-

---

30. See: John Mark Reynolds, *When Athens Met Jerusalem: An Introduction to Classical Thought* (IVP Academic, 2009).

31. "Is There a Personal God? Head to Head Debate. Atheist Michael Martin and Christian Peter S. Williams Debate the Existence of a Unitary, Personal God," *The Philosopher's Magazine*, no. 8 (Autumn 1999): 19–23.

ing my three years in Leicester I was invited to debate the existence of angels on an atheist website, and frustration with the available research materials resulted in my own book on the subject.[32] It was also during this time that Dr. Stecher first contacted me, having read *The Case for God*. Much correspondence followed, and we met up in London. We developed our correspondence into a book we published with the www.bethinking.org website. Having found Carl a serious and congenial interlocutor, I was delighted when he contacted me about developing this project, and I'd like to take this opportunity to thank all my coauthors.

After Leicester, I moved to Southampton to work alongside a Christian educational charity called The Damaris Trust. I was apprenticed by cofounder Nick Pollard, a former research psychologist turned author and social entrepreneur.[33] Damaris closed after fifteen years, but through it I developed an association with Gimlekollen School of Journalism and Communication in Norway (now part of NLA University College), where I now serve part-time as the Assistant Professor of Communication and Worldviews (although I still live in Southampton).[34]

These "Horizon" chapters debunk any pretense that this book's contributors come to the debate about Jesus' resurrection as disinterested blank slates; but to avoid the *ad hominem* fallacy, we must resist any temptation to focus upon the contents of one another's psychology at the expense of dealing with the content of one another's arguments. So, let us seek truth together, for "Just as iron sharpens iron, friends sharpen the minds of each other" (Proverbs 27:17, CEV).

---

32. See: Peter S. Williams, *The Case for Angels* (Paternoster, 2002). See also: Peter S. Williams, "Do Angels Really Exist?" www.bethinking.org/christian-beliefs/do-angels-really-exist.

33. See: Nick Pollard, *Evangelism Made Slightly Less Difficult*, new ed. (IVP, 2004).

34. For more about me and my work, please visit www.peterswilliams.com.

A Path to Secular Reason

Richard Carrier, Ph.D.

I published my first book, *Sense and Goodness Without God*, in 2005, after having been an atheist activist for nearly fifteen years. It sought to accomplish what I'd found no prior atheist book do: lay out in thorough fashion what we should believe, rather than merely what we don't. It presents a complete worldview, based on science, evidence, and reason, including everything from epistemology and metaphysics to aesthetics and moral philosophy, every element coherently integrated with the others. The story of how I got there, from childhood, through my experiences with religion, my coming to atheism, and settling the ardent pursuit of critical philosophy as my creed, I tell in an early chapter of that very book (pp. 9–19). I haven't space to explore it all here, but I can summarize it, and now go beyond it—as it's been another nearly fifteen years since.

I grew up in Southern California, and my experiences with religion as a child were all good. It wasn't until I became a voting adult that I discovered I had been sheltered from its fundamentalism, for I found that standing against me on every human rights issue, every issue of importance to our future, were fundamentalist Christians. My engagement with them in debate, especially online, enlightened me. I had never believed so many people could be so deeply and fanatically misled, and so impervious to evidence and reason.

I was already by then a devout Taoist. I had had a nominal and very liberal Christian upbringing, but was never a confessing Christian, nor did my family expect me to be. They wanted me to discover for myself what's right and true. My first and only religious faith was in Taoism, which I came to by a powerful and what I considered then a literally miraculous religious experience in my teen years (fully described in *Sense and Goodness*). Continued religious experiences, and the remarkably positive effect the faith had on my character and well-being, confirmed Taoism's truth to me for many years after, and it was my declared faith when I entered the United States Coast Guard in 1990, three years after graduating high school in 1987.

That background surprises many Christians, who expect me to have had some harsh religious childhood that turned me away from the faith. My upbringing was also not as privileged as many Christians I encounter assume. I grew up very safe and happy, but my family was very blue-collar poor. My eventual Ivy League college education would be entirely funded by scholarships, fellowships, and personal debt. Before my military service, I cut firebreaks in the hills and worked park maintenance and construction jobs. Frugality and a lack of means have always been my norm. For much of my childhood I did not even own a bed; for several years my mother was our only parent, and I had to help raise my two younger sisters. We did all sorts of things often unimaginable to the middle class, like regularly shop at a "day old" store, a place most people don't even know exists, usually hidden behind municipal airports or other out-of-the-way places. It was where all the expired products from regular grocery stores were sent, to be sold at discount to those less concerned about stale bread and dodgy canned goods.

My eventual stepfather was an excellent parent and computer programmer who encouraged my learning; my first IBM PC we built together in the late 1980s. And my mother was always keen on cultivating my intelligence and curiosity; she knew how important education was. One of the few luxuries she would budget for was to buy a single volume of an encyclopedia every week or two. I remember a white-bound standard set of some kind with its thick volumes, and also a serialized encyclopedia of animals, and reference books on the solar system. I read each volume cover to cover, always with joy and fascination. This played a big part in how I unexpectedly escaped our poverty to eventually fund my way to that prestigious Ph.D.

But it's my Taoism that is usually the most surprising to Christians, some of whom forget Christianity isn't the only religion people can be miraculously converted to, and who often assume atheists are produced by bad experiences with the Church. I didn't come from a fundamentalist background, so I was never saddled with the anger many atheists have after realizing how abused and lied to they had been their whole lives. Yet my conversion experience is eerily similar to everything Christians relate as convincing them *their* faith was true. How can it have had all the same effects (such as of a great joy and peace), and been caused by all the same experiences and feelings (such as of a supernatural presence of power)? Taoism and Christianity cannot *both* be true. And this gave me an insight most people I encounter lack: I saw first-hand what it is like to be misled into a happy state of belief in a false religion. And it looks exactly like how people come to Christ. In fact, I have yet to discover any discernible difference. Taoism made me a better person, improved my life, and was wonderful. It was also false.

I was in the military, serving a year at sea patrolling the North Pacific on treaty-and-law enforcement and search-and-rescue missions—as a sonar technician, torpedoman, duty gunner's mate, and flight-deck firefighter—when I became an unbeliever. It happened not through any traumatic experience, but simply as a result of continuing in the spirit of questioning and learning I'd acquired from my upbringing. Always studying in my spare time, I discovered the flaws in Taoist teachings, and the science of religious experience and cognitive bias that explains how we trick ourselves into believing experiences we are having are supernatural and uniquely true, rather than constructed by our minds out of material absorbed from our surrounding culture and contacts.

My first thought upon realizing Taoism was made-up—just a useful but flawed repository of human wisdom, atop an array of religious experiences that were subconscious constructs our minds build for us—was to ask, "What, then?" Taoism gave me a comprehensive worldview that explained every aspect of human life and existence. If it wasn't true, what should replace it? What *should* I believe, about morality, beauty, our minds, our world? And why should I believe that as opposed to something else? These questions led me to realize there was only one creed actually worth having faith in: a commitment to critical philosophy, to evidence-based reasoning, and to a continual self-critical analysis of our own beliefs to ensure we are not misleading ourselves. That was around 1992.

Had it not been for my devotion to and study of Taoism, it might not have occurred to me that a religion *is* a comprehensive worldview, and that it therefore controls how we perceive and think about *everything*, and that it cannot simply be abandoned without something inevitably filling its place. We *always* have some idea of what things are and how they work and of how we can even know the answer to questions like that—simply to navigate the world toward any worthwhile goal. So is our idea a good one? How do we know it's not completely wrong? That there isn't a much better idea out there? We need to take those questions seriously, because if we get the answer wrong, we'll be trapped in a lie, yet never able to know it. To avoid this, we have to constantly be questioning and checking and challenging our own beliefs, not least by always exposing ourselves to their best critics. That is the only way we can ever be sure our beliefs are sound, rather than some insulated delusion we've merely ended up with.

I began writing then what would evolve into *Sense and Goodness Without God*, changing and updating it constantly as I devoted myself to studying the relevant science and philosophy behind every chapter. As I understood more about reality, my worldview became better informed, and more coherent and defensible. I also became involved in the atheist movement, joining such organizations as American Atheists and the Freedom From Religion Foundation, and eventually landed an editorship at The Secular Web in the late 1990s—then the leading international hub of atheist literature, thought, and debate online—eventually becoming its editor in chief, before retiring to pursue other things. During the same time, after my honorable discharge, I went to college and eventually completed a B.A. in history with a minor in classical civilizations at U.C. Berkeley, and an M.A., M.Phil., and Ph.D. in history at

Columbia University, specializing in ancient Greco-Roman intellectual history (philosophy, science, historiography, and religion). I then went on to complete fan-funded postdoctoral work on the historicity of Jesus, in effect writing a second peer-reviewed dissertation, *On the Historicity of Jesus* (Sheffield-Phoenix, 2014), which reexamines the circumstances and causes of the entire origination of Christianity as a religion.

In the course of all this, I got married, lived mostly happily as a homemaker and part-time writer for two decades, then amicably divorced, and now live as an openly polyamorous man. This is another unusual fact about me that Christians tend not to understand (and one I've also written a lot about, as one can find on my Web site richardcarrier.info).

My encounter with fundamentalist Christianity in political life left that version of Christianity as something alien and "other" to me, much like how Christians must see Islam or Hindu nationalism. It was never a part of my life, which is why it never damaged me directly. It was my divorce that really opened my eyes to how pernicious the harmful impact of the Christian worldview is on the whole of Western society. One does not have to be Christian to have grown up swimming in Christian assumptions about how we are supposed to live and treat people. I was never told that my views regarding monogamy and sexual autonomy were "Christian." Yet, historically, that's exactly what they are. A great deal of struggle and dissatisfaction in our lives could have been avoided if we'd never heard of these Christianized assumptions about how people should live their lives; if we had been taught instead to explore, contemplate, and build the lives that *actually* fit us and make us happy, and good partners and neighbors. Not what others *assume* will do so. This same lesson follows for how we perceive and treat people who are gay or trans; who are sexually active or into kink, or need to avoid or end a pregnancy; who don't want to conform to Christianized gender roles or norms or share the worst Christian ideas about war or welfare.

But though my personal life informs my goals and worldview (so it's useful for you to know), my academic life is what led to my being a contributor to this volume. Do not allow the one to bias your assessment of the other. My Ph.D. was on ancient science and its reception in the Greco-Roman world, but by then I'd also written on and studied numerous subjects of interest to the atheist debating circuit. By now I've written several peer-reviewed papers and monographs on ancient Christianity, and out of several areas of expertise I developed—including not just history but contemporary moral and naturalist philosophy—it's of most importance to the present volume that I became one of the leading atheist experts on resurrection apologetics.

As far as I know, I am still the only expert on resurrection apologetics with a doctorate specifically in the subject of ancient history. In that capacity I've formally debated such luminaries as Mike Licona and William Lane Craig, and written several works on the subject after *Sense and Goodness*, including extensive scholarly chapters in *The Empty Tomb* (edited by Robert M. Price and Jeff Jay Lowder for Prometheus in 2005) and thorough updated summaries in other volumes (edited by John Loftus, also for Prometheus), *The Christian Delusion* (2010), *The End of Christianity* (2011), and *Christianity Is Not Great* (2014). I also lay out a more colloquial case for why I don't find the resurrection of Jesus any more believable than other ancient myths in my own brief *Why I Am Not a Christian*, and a larger educational case against common misinformation about the ancient world, on which resurrection apologetics often depends, in *Not the Impossible Faith*. My academic monograph *On the Historicity of Jesus*, though not on the resurrection directly, also contains a great deal of material on the context of what actually launched the religion and its mythologies, and on the reliability of its literature. This was supplemented by my treatment of historical methods in application to the Bible and Christianity in *Proving History* (2012) and *Hitler Homer Bible Christ* (2014). And my latest works, on ancient science (for Pitchstone), *Science Education in the Early Roman Empire* (2016) and *The Scientist in the Early Roman Empire* (2017), also critique Christian claims about Christianity's role in inspiring modern science.

My constant engagement in debate on the resurrection and other issues pertaining to religion has become one of my principal passions because I have always seen Christianity as central to causing my fellow citizens, even *non*-Christians, to make bad decisions that harm their neighbors, and sometimes even themselves. It is not the only worldview that does this, but in the Western world it is the most widely embraced worldview that does. Its harm ranges from the emotional and societal damage Christians' unreasonable moral judgmentalism causes in the world, to their inclination to disparage or avoid teaching children or adults sound principles of critical thought and respect for personal autonomy—even, all too often, to abuse, manipulate, or coerce their children and peers into adopting their religion and its varying assumptions, rather than encouraging them to choose their own and giving them the tools actually necessary to make a sound and unbiased choice in that endeavor. The world can never be a better place until we change that. And I continue to find that when we try to make that better world, too many Christians are still standing in our way. Consequently, it's become my goal to focus my knowledge and skill on dismantling the rhetoric, misinformation, and rationalizations that sustain Christian belief, and to replace it with a more critical philosophical humanism.

It's also my passion to study history and debunk misrepresentations of it. Error, both factual and logical, is frustrating when disseminated to an unsuspecting and uninformed public. Wrong history leads to wrong policy, and wrong ideas of who we are and how we got here. I enjoy being a part of the system we need to fight false or distorted history. Indeed, this goal and passion informs all my other endeavors and interests in history. But the other half of my life is dedicated to philosophy, to building the most probable worldview, based on self-correcting and ever-updating knowledge and understanding of the world as it actually is, and not as people's faiths imagine it to be. The resurrection of Jesus does contact both halves of my life: first, of course, in respect to how anyone can claim such an event can be believed true on what I find to be such a poor quality of the evidence we actually have (an error that touches me most especially as a historian and educator); and second, in respect to how "the resurrection" is then used to manipulate people into adopting and enacting an entire array of other beliefs that cause harm to the public, from gender and sexual oppression to apocalypticism, and so many other false beliefs about what laws we should have and how people should be treated or judged. It's no trivial matter, like whether

Atlantis existed or Bigfoot haunts a forest. The resurrection myth is being painted as history for use in molding society and affecting millions of human lives. That's a matter of grave concern to me.

My goal here is informed by my goal in life generally: it is important that human beings examine factual claims with an eye to being critical of even their own judgment. Humanity invented logic and science, and all the methods and techniques of evidence-based reasoning, precisely to help us catch our own errors. So here, the question debated is simply whether there is enough evidence to warrant believing a Jew named Jesus literally rose from the dead two thousand years ago. Are the arguments that there *is* enough evidence for that *logically valid*, or do they depend on fallacies that we know often mislead people into false beliefs in every other domain of our lives? Are those arguments based on claims to fact *that are true*, or claims that are false or unknown, or very different when put back into their original context? Not only is answering these questions of paramount importance for this single issue, but they are also questions we need to learn how to ask and answer in every other question about life and reality. This particular debate can serve as an example, and a training ground—a practice run—for learning how to ask those questions, and finally how to answer them correctly.

PART TWO: THE CASE AGAINST JESUS'
RESURRECTION AS A FACT OF HISTORY

The Historical Evidence Is Insufficient and Contradictory

Carl Stecher, Ph.D.

Although I have been a skeptic for approximately 60 years and cannot now even imagine becoming a Christian, unlike most "new atheists" I am not generally hostile to religious beliefs, Christian or other. I have a beloved sister who is a devout Christian, and although l cannot share her belief I respect it and see the value she finds in it. I listen to grieving parents of the Sandy Hook massacre saying their only consolation is knowing their five-year-old child is now with God, that someday they will be reunited. For me this is a delusion, and in their situation I could find no comfort, but how cruel it would be to attack, to even question their belief.

It cannot be denied that many people find value in religious belief. It can and does inspire empathy, comfort the suffering, motivate acts of charity, staff schools and hospitals, draw people into communities. As a skeptic and secular humanist, I feel my first obligation is to do no harm. Let well enough be. I have no right to impose my conclusions on others, to overwhelm them, if this is possible, with evidence that the God they believe in exists only in their minds. But certain circumstances, I feel, justify the expression of my conclusions, even in some cases to those who might prefer that I remain silent.

One such circumstance is in response to evangelism, to those believers who argue for the *necessity* of belief. Prominent Christian scholars such as William Lane Craig, Gary Habermas, Michael Licona, Craig Blomberg, and N. T. Wright have written massively—literally thousands of pages—and toured the college lecture and debate circuits arguing that the physical resurrection of Jesus is as certain a historical fact as the destruction of the Jerusalem Temple by the Romans in 70 AD, or the Patriots' Super Bowl victory in 2017. For example, N. T. Wright is an Anglican scholar with impeccable academic credentials (Oxford, Cambridge, Harvard, McGill) and exalted status (he was Anglican Bishop of Durham and a member of the House of Lords). Wright, in his massive tome *The Resurrection of the Son of God* (Fortress Press, 2003), concluded that the historical evidence is overwhelming: Jesus was physically resurrected. The implications are clear: *all* other religious beliefs—Islam, Judaism, Hinduism, other interpretations of Christianity, skepticism, atheism—all are necessarily wrong, and anyone who fails to accept the physical resurrection of Jesus as a fact of history is either perverse or ignorant. It's a short step from this to the conclusion, "*That at the name of Jesus every knee should bow, in heaven, and on earth . . . and every tongue confess that Jesus Christ is Lord*" (Philippians 2:10–11).

I would like to emphasize that the topic we are exploring is limited and very specific: *is the physical resurrection of Jesus a fact of history?* We all agree that it is an article of faith, and I would never argue against it so defined. But I will argue that the historical evidence is totally insufficient and that Jesus' resurrection falls far short of historical certainty or even historical probability.

Bedrock facts for this debate: Jesus, an itinerant rabbi with local fame for teaching, healing, and miracle working, was crucified by the Romans during the rule of Pontius Pilate, probably at the instigation of the Jewish Temple authorities; his alleged crime was insurrection—claiming to be the King of the Jews. After his death some of his disciples had experiences that convinced them that Jesus had been miraculously resurrected and was in fact Messiah, the Christ, who would return within their generation to rule over the newly established Kingdom of God. From this Jewish origin a new religion gradually developed in many locations in the Roman Empire, especially among gentiles deeply influenced by Greco-Roman culture and originally attracted to Judaism by its ethic and monotheistic theology.

Central and indispensable in the evidence cited for the physical resurrection of Jesus as a fact of history are the accounts of his appearances to his disciples. For the purposes of history, the only documents of use are the New Testament Letters of Paul and the three Gospels identified in the second century as Matthew, John, and Luke, and also Acts of the Apostles, which was written by the same author as the Gospel according to Luke. These New Testament documents are the only first-century sources to give any account of the resurrection appearances. This is remarkably little evidence, which, fortunately for our purpose, allows us to analyze it all in detail—a task that the proponents of historicity, despite the thousands of pages they have written, have sadly neglected.

The scholarly consensus is that the following, from 1 Corinthians 15:3–8, was written by Paul in the early 50s, some twenty years after Jesus' execution:

> First and foremost, I handed on to you the tradition I had received: that Christ died for our sins . . . that he was buried; that he was raised to life on the third day . . . and that he appeared to Cephas [Peter], and afterwards to the twelve. Then he appeared to over five hundred of our brothers at once, most of whom are still alive, though some have died. Then he appeared to James, and afterwards to all the apostles. Last of all he appeared to me too.

In Paul's voluminous writings recorded in the New Testament (Romans, Ephesians, 1 & 2 Corinthians, 1 Thessalonians, Galatians, Philippians—approximately 24,000 words), this is the only passage—about 80 words—in which he cites the appearances of the risen Jesus. Because Paul is citing a tradition that he encountered as little as two years after Jesus' crucifixion, conservative Christian apologists hold that these words have strong historical reliability.

Let's look at Paul's testimony from a different perspective. Suppose today the editor of a modern reputable news source—such as the *New York Times, Wall Street Journal,* or *PBS NewsHour*—received from a reporter a story that sometime around 1999 a famous Jewish rabbi had been seen alive, several times by named individuals, twice by groups, and once by another very large group, after he had been certified dead by a reputable physician and had been buried for three days. The story contains the names of the two individual witnesses, but unfortunately they are not available for confirmation. The story contains no other information about its source or sources, what the witnesses saw or heard, how they identified the resurrected rabbi, whether the rabbi said or did anything, nor does it indicate just when and where these experiences occurred. Galilee? Jerusalem? Bethany? Sheboygan? Paul, the author of this report, stated that he too saw the resurrected Jewish rabbi, but Paul is dead and is not available to provide additional information.

When I was a ninth grader at South Side Junior High School, our English class had the responsibility of producing the *Monthly Junior High School News*. We were instructed that every news story had to answer the following questions: Who? What? Where? When? But Paul's report provides no information about any of these concerns except "who." It's just a list of alleged "appearances," indicating nothing about their nature or circumstances. Would any editor think this report, so lacking essential information, credible and worthy of publication? No. So why should any historian give credence to Paul's report, now almost two thousand years old?

Paul is, however, elsewhere more specific about the appearance that he experienced himself. "Luke" reports Paul's first-person account:

> What happened to me on my journey was this: when I was nearing Damascus, about midday, a great light suddenly flashed from the sky all around me. I fell to the ground, and heard a voice saying: 'Saul, Saul, why do you persecute me? I answered, 'tell me, Lord, who you are.' 'I am Jesus of Nazareth, whom you are persecuting,' he said. My companions saw the light, but did not hear the voice that spoke to me. (Acts 22:6–11)

Paul reports that it was some time before he regained his sight.

Paul's narrative, assuming its authenticity, is relevant to understanding how loosely he uses the term "appearance" in the 1 Corinthians passage. An "appearance" may be nothing beyond a blinding light and a voice from the sky that only one person can hear. All this suggests a hallucination; there has been considerable discussion that Paul was epileptic, making him especially vulnerable to hallucinations. And according to Princeton University professor Ronald J. Corner in his text *Fundamentals of Abnormal Psychology* (Worth Publishers, 7th edition, 2010), hallucinations are also a common symptom of schizophrenia, auditory hallucinations by far the most common. My colleague Richard Carrier makes a fully plausible case that Paul's discipleship conforms to a "benevolent mental disorder" labeled the "happy schizotype."[1]

Given Paul's account of his own encounter, any modern news source would find even more reason to reject Paul's account of the resurrection appearances to the disciples. No experienced reporter would even submit Paul's story. This should be emphasized: the only "eyewitness" to the resurrected Jesus saw only a blinding light and heard a voice no one else could hear.

Let's turn to the Gospel accounts. Only Matthew, Luke, and John report appearances of the risen Jesus.[2] These three Gospels were written in Greek, not the Aramaic of Jesus and his disciples, 40 to 65 years after Jesus' death, at locations outside of Palestine by anonymous authors who were not eyewitnesses and did not know Jesus in life.[3] The titles "According to Matthew . . ." were assigned in the second century. The sources the three Gospel writers used for their accounts of the resurrection appearances are not identified. And further, there is no way of knowing how many tellings and retellings of resurrection stories trans-

---

1. In Robert M. Price and Jeffery Jay Lowder, eds., *The Empty Tomb: Jesus Beyond the Grave* (Prometheus Books, 2005), 187. For a detailed survey of the evidence and underlying science: Richard Carrier, *On the Historicity of Jesus* (Sheffield Phoenix, 2014), 124–37.

2. Mark's text ends at 16:8 with the discovery of the empty tomb; the rest of Mark, 16:9–20, virtually all scholars identify as inauthentic, a later addition by another unknown author. See Richard Carrier, *Hitler Homer Bible Christ* (Philosophy Press, 2014), 231–312.

3. See *The Oxford Companion to the Bible* (Oxford University Press, 1993), 259.

pired before these stories were written down by the anonymous authors of these Gospels. As the stories come to us they are hearsay upon hearsay upon hearsay practically *ad infinitum* for all we know.

Paul in Galatians 2:6 states that he consulted with Peter, James, and John in Jerusalem approximately twenty years after Jesus' death to make sure he was preaching the true gospel. He writes, "these men of repute . . . imparted nothing further to me." So they didn't tell him about Jesus' last words or the ascension, as reported 15–25 years later still (but only by Luke). They didn't tell him about the earthquake and the raised saints reported only by Matthew 15–25, also many years later. They didn't tell him about "doubting" Thomas as reported over another 40 years later, and only by John. And they didn't tell him about Joseph of Arimathea and the empty tomb, as reported decades later by all four Gospels. Pretty good evidence that all these stories originated in the decades *after* Paul's ministry. But given the absence of even basic information in Paul's account, these Gospel accounts are the *only* substantive evidence about the resurrection appearances; the question of historicity depends upon their reliability.

Consider Matthew's account of the moment of Jesus' death: "the earth shook, rocks split, and graves opened; many of God's saints were raised from sleep, and coming out of their graves after [Jesus'] resurrection entered the Holy City, where many saw them" (Matt 27: 51–53). Yet not a hint of these astonishing events is recorded in the other Gospel accounts or any Roman or Jewish document. As Thomas Paine noted in *The Age of Reason,* "The things, supposing them to have been facts, were of too much notoriety not to have been known, and of too much importance not to have been told." This is clearly a legendary embellishment, not history; it is one of many legendary passages that undermine Matthew's credibility.

There is even stronger reason to reject Luke's historical reliability. Historians agree that "Luke," whatever his actual identity, was the author of both the Gospel given his name and Acts of the Apostles, an account of the early Christian church. Acts 1:4–11 reads:

While [the resurrected Jesus] was in [his disciples'] company, he directed them not to leave Jerusalem ... When they were all together ... he was lifted up before their very eyes, and a cloud took him from their sight. They were gazing intently into the sky as he went, and all at once there stood beside them two men robed in white, who said, 'Men of Galilee, why stand there looking up into the sky? This Jesus who has been taken from you up to heaven will come in the same way as you have seen him go.'

Note that according to "Luke" Jesus speaks his final words on earth and makes this spectacular departure in front of all his disciples. Imagine yourself a disciple witnessing this astonishing event. Or imagine yourself Paul, or the author of Mark, Matthew, or John, each an evangelist preaching the gospel of the resurrected Son of God. But not one of you reports this earth-shaking occurrence? This situation, when one source reports an event of transcendent importance but other sources, which should know of the event but make no mention of it, is usually called an "argument from silence." I prefer to call it *disconfirmation by silence*. It is compelling only when, as here, the reason to confirm the information is far more compelling than any reason to *not* confirm it. I challenge proponents of historicity to explain why these four sources all fail to confirm Luke's ascension story.

This narrative with Jesus' supposed final words and physical ascension into the sky is hardly the only legendary element in the Gospels. Raymond Brown, perhaps the most distinguished Roman Catholic scholar in recent memory, in his exhaustive study of the birth narratives in Luke and Matthew, identifies at least a dozen contradictions in their accounts, clearly indicating that they are legends, not history.[4] About Matthew's story of guards at Jesus' tomb, Brown concludes, "there is neither internal nor external evidence to cause us to affirm historicity."[5] It can be said without exaggeration that these two Gospels are infected

---

4. Raymond E. Brown, *The Birth of the Messiah*, updated ed. (Doubleday, 1993), 33–37.

5. Raymond E. Brown, *The Death of the Messiah*, vol. II (Doubleday, 1994), 1312.

by legendary elements from beginning to end. What is much less clear is what in the Gospel narratives is history, and what is legend. How do we determine where history ends and legends begin?

Again, let's look at this from a different perspective. Let's suppose that we have independent reports from four different sources of a recent major league baseball game: the *Chicago Tribune, Boston Globe, New York Times*, and *Wall Street Journal* all have reporters on the scene. All the reporters, by chance, are evangelical Christians; remarkably, their first names are Matthew, Mark, Luke, and John. Luke, writing for the *Boston Globe*, reports that at the seventh-inning stretch, the singing of "Take Me Out to the Ballgame" was interrupted by a great blast of trumpets, then out of the clouds a host of angels descended, singing "Hosanna! Hosanna!" and David Ortiz was visibly lifted up to baseball heaven. But the other reporters make no mention of this extraordinary and earthshaking event, only noting that the winning Red Sox scored three runs in the bottom of the seventh. Would not their silence discon-firm the extraordinary event reported by Luke, the *Boston Globe* report-er? In the absence of any supporting evidence, would the *Boston Globe* even publish the report? And if it did, would anyone believe it? So too, if the ascension as reported by Luke had actually happened, surely Paul, Mark, Matthew, and John would have also reported the event.

The same credibility problem bedevils the Gospel of John, not writ-ten until at least 60 years after Jesus' crucifixion. John in Chapter 11 portrays the raising of Lazarus from the dead. This story is told in con-siderable detail, over 46 verses. Jesus himself gives it great theological significance, saying to Lazarus' sisters Martha and Mary, "I am the res-urrection and the life. Whoever has faith in me shall live, even though he dies" (11:25). Lazarus has been dead four days and his corpse is already stinking. "Then Jesus raised his voice in a great cry: 'Lazarus, come out.' The dead man came out, his hands and feet bound with linen bandages, his face wrapped in a cloth . . ." (11:41–43).

It's a terrific story! What Christian doesn't know it? Like Luke's as-cension story, Jesus' disciples witness the raising of Lazarus—several are mentioned by name. It is so widely witnessed that, according to John, the Pharisees and the chief priests hear of it and convene a meeting of the Council. "They said 'if we let him go on like this the whole populace will believe in him'. . ." (John 11:48).

So, the historian should ask, why is there no hint of Lazarus in Paul or the Gospels of Mark, Matthew, and Luke, written decades before John? If this raising of the dead actually happened, why for 60 years did not any of them tell the story so that "the whole populace will believe in him"?

There is other evidence that John deviates into fiction. Consider the story of "doubting" Thomas, who does not believe in Jesus' resurrection until, in the Upper Room in Jerusalem, at Jesus' invitation he puts his hand into Jesus' wound, and Jesus says, ". . . be unbelieving no longer," with Thomas responding, "My Lord and my God!" (20:24–28). It's a wonderful story. But we must ask again why none of the other Gospels, all written long before John, record this story of "doubting" Thomas. According to John, all the other 11 disciples witnessed this event. But there isn't even a hint in the other Gospels of "doubting" Thomas. Nor from Paul.

It's still a wonderful story. But it's not history.

Aside from the clearly legendary elements in the Gospel accounts, their historical value is also undermined by clearly fictional elements. Let me explain this by comparing these to the fictional elements in a very good movie I saw several years ago titled *Philomena*. It was one of those movies "based upon a true story," but parts of it were clearly fictionalized. The movie tells the story of an Irish adolescent girl, Philomena, who got pregnant and was abandoned by her family and taken in by a convent, where she was subjected to essentially slave labor in return for room and board and care of her infant son. At the end of two years she was forced to give up all contact with her son, who had been adopted by a wealthy American family, the convent making a significant profit on this enterprise. Years later, with the help of a journalist interested in the story, Philomena makes a determined effort to learn what became of her son and to reestablish her relationship with him.

Having seen the movie and interested in knowing more, I was happy to discover the book the movie was based upon. In the preface, the author, Martin Sixsmith, who describes himself as an "investigative reporter," wrote about the extensive research he had done, including many interviews. The book included intimate verbatim conversations between Philomena's son (who had died of AIDS before Sixsmith came upon the story) and a trusted Catholic priest, and between the same son and his psychotherapist concerning the boy's concerns about his homosexuality. Wait a minute, I thought, there's no way that Sixsmith had access to these exchanges; he's making this up.

I went online and my suspicions were confirmed: somebody who Sixsmith had interviewed wrote that Sixsmith grossly misrepresented what he had said and fictionalized the story. If you read the Gospels closely, and especially John, you are likely to come to the same conclusion: episodes and conversations are related for which there could have been no actual source. Like Martin Sixsmith, the Gospel authors made stuff up.

Take, for example, Matthew 27: 3–8:

> When Judas the traitor saw that Jesus had been condemned, he was seized with remorse . . . 'I have sinned . . . I have brought an innocent man to his death.' But the priests said, 'What is that to us? It is your concern.' So he threw the money down in the temple and went away and hanged himself. The chief priests took up the money, but they said, 'This cannot be put into the temple fund; it is blood-money.'

So who was the witness who reported these words to the author of Matthew? Not Judas; he's hanged himself. And can you imagine one of the priests saying to the author of Matthew, or anyone Matthew consulted, "We thought you'd like to know what passed between us and Judas." Clearly, there was no witness to report these words to the author of Matthew. It's a good story, but it should not be mistaken for history.

Similarly, Matthew and Matthew alone tells the story of the temple priests and Pharisees convincing Pilate to put a guard on Jesus' tomb, lest his disciples steal Jesus' body and then claim that he was raised from the dead. When Jesus is nevertheless resurrected, the chief priests suborn the guards to commit perjury, giving them a substantial bribe. They supposedly told the guards, "if this should reach the governor's ears, we will put matters right with him and see that you do not suffer" (28:15). As in some of the interviews portrayed in Philomena, there is no plausible witness to this exchange. Matthew has again fictionalized his story but also undermined its historical credibility.

The Gospels have many such fictionalized stories, especially in John, which has the most detailed account of the trial of Jesus and its aftermath. Prior to this, Jesus has an extended conversation with a Samaritan woman that extends over 19 verses of "he said . . . she said"; John makes it clear that there were no witnesses to record this exchange (4:8–27). Similarly, John portrays a private encounter between Pilate and Jesus with Pilate questioning Jesus, and Jesus' responses, all of which is *not* witnessed by Jesus' foes: "the Jews themselves stayed outside the headquarters to avoid defilement, so that they could eat the Passover meal" (18:28). So what was John's source for this exchange? Again, this has all the earmarks of something "based upon a true story"; it is not reliable information for the historian.

What clearly happened is that the authors of Matthew, Luke, and John are writing at different times and in different Christian communities, each with its own traditions and different tales about the risen Lord. The Gospels contain information that is probably historical—Jesus' execution by the Romans, for example—but also passages that are legendary embellishment and others that are fictionalizations. What is lacking is any method for differentiating the historical from the legendary and fictional elements. Added to this, it's often the stories they *don't* tell that undermine the historical credibility of the stories that each one of them *does* tell.

Another factor that undermines any historical credibility the resurrection appearance stories have is that they contradict each other in almost every way. Defenders of the historicity of the resurrection claim that the contradictions are insignificant, only involving minor details. And this is true of most of the contradictions. But some, in fact, go to the very core of the stories. For example, consider the conflicts between Luke and Matthew as to what Jesus' female disciples experienced at the tomb and where the appearances occurred.

In Matthew 28:7 the angel at the tomb tells the women, "He has been raised from the dead and is going ahead of you into Galilee; there you will see him." The women then encounter Jesus and he repeats the same message, "Go and take word to my brothers that they are to leave for Galilee. They will see me there." The women clearly convey this message, because in the very next passage "the eleven disciples made their way to Galilee, to the mountain where Jesus had told them to meet him." In Matthew this is the only postmortem meeting between Jesus and his disciples. It is there that he instructs them to make disciples in all nations and departs from them (28:20). There is no hint in Matthew's account of any other appearances.

But in Luke's account, in which, quote, "the women reported *everything* to the eleven and all the others" (24:9), the angel who speaks to the women at the tomb makes no mention of Galilee, which is at least 90 miles away, an arduous three-day journey by foot or mule. A round-trip journey from Jerusalem to Galilee in the first century would be at least as difficult and taxing as a round trip now from Philadelphia to Timbuktu (tourist class). Contrary to Matthew's account, the women do not encounter Jesus, so of course he can't tell them to go to Galilee to see him again. This difference is itself of fundamental importance. An empty tomb is just an empty tomb, but if the women had encountered and conversed with Jesus, three days dead, surely they would have reported this to the disciples!

All the appearances recorded by Luke in his gospel are in Jerusalem on the same day the women discover the empty tomb. Within 24 hours Jesus appears to two disciples on the nearby road to Emmaus, then to the eleven and others in Jerusalem, sharing a fish lunch, then ascends into heaven *after instructing them to stay in Jerusalem*. Nowhere is there even a hint that they are to go to Galilee to see him, as Matthew insisted (Luke 24).

The historicity of Luke's account is even further undermined when the author of Luke writes his sequel, Acts of the Apostles; here he portrays Jesus' postmortem appearances as happening not in a single day, but extending over 40 days. In doing so he contradicts not only himself (Luke 24:36–53), but also again Matthew's account of the appearances in Galilee. "After his suffering he presented himself alive to them during forty days . . . while staying with them, *he ordered them not to leave Jerusalem, but to wait there for the promise of the Father*" (Acts 1:4).

The author of Luke does make clear how extraordinarily limited were the appearances: "God raised him to life on the third day, and allowed him to be clearly seen, not by the whole people, but by witnesses whom God had chosen in advance—by us, who ate and drank with him after he rose from the dead" (Acts 10:40–41).

Again, all scholars agree that the only significant information we have of the appearances to his disciples is found in the testimony of Paul and the three Gospel writers. But careful analysis reveals Paul's testimony so lacking in essential information that it is useless for historical purposes, and Matthew, Luke, and John's Gospels contradict each other about the most essential information; all that the historian can conclude is that at least some of the information must be wrong, but there's no way of determining what if any of it is actually historical. All are infected by legendary elements and fictional passages about even the most essential facts. In the thousands of pages proponents of historicity have written, these problems receive very little attention.

How Might Resurrection Stories Have Begun?

N. T. Wright argues that the physical resurrection of Jesus is a historical certainty because only if the resurrected Jesus actually appeared to his disciples can we account for the beginning of the Christian faith. "All the efforts to find alternative explanations fail, and they were bound to do so."[6]

But I don't think that's true. The proponents of Jesus' resurrection as a fact of history, in the thousands of pages that they have generated to support their position, have neglected to consider many possible natural explanations for the disciples' belief that Jesus was physically resurrected, explanations that involve commonplace human behavior noted in many cultures, including our own, and which have been evi-

---

6. N. T. Wright, *The Resurrection of the Son of God* (Fortress Press, 2003), 717.

denced by many university studies and experiments.

First, we have to look at the very concept of appearances. We all know that appearance and reality aren't necessarily the same. If they were, I've seen a man in a cape saw a woman in half. When we consider the appearances of the risen Jesus, we must remember that an appearance of an appearance is not necessarily the reality of an appearance.

Let's begin with grief hallucinations, the one natural explanation that has received some consideration from conservative Christian scholars. According to an article by Vaughan Bell in *Scientific American* on December 2, 2008:

> The dead stay with us, that much is clear. They remain in our hearts and minds, of course, but for many people they also linger in our senses—as sights, sounds, smells, touches or presences. Grief hallucinations are a normal reaction to bereavement. We now know that hallucinations are common in sober healthy people and that they are more likely during times of stress. As a marker of how vivid such visions can seem, almost a third of the people reported that they spoke in response to their experiences.

It would not be at all surprising if one or more of the disciples had a grief hallucination of Jesus.

But what about appearances to a group? A common argument of proponents of the historicity of Jesus' resurrection is that the accounts of the experiences of "groups" of disciples cannot be dismissed as hallucinations. In *The Case for the Resurrection of Jesus*, for example, Gary Habermas and Michael Licona write, "today we know that hallucinations are private occurrences, which occur in the mind of an individual. They are not collective experiences."[7] Thus, the argument goes, the appearances of Jesus to groups of disciples must have been actual encounters with the resurrected Son of God.

This, however, is contradicted by numerous accounts of the Virgin Mary appearing to groups. The Web site Catholic Online once reported:

---

7. Gary Habermas and Michael Licona, *The Case for the Resurrection of Jesus* (Kregel Publications, 2004), 106.

Other apparitions continue to be approved at the local level, e.g. the December, 2010 local approval of the 19th-century apparitions of Our Lady of Good Help, the first recognized apparition in the United States. An authentic apparition is believed not to be a subjective experience, but a real and objective intervention of divine power.[8]

And the Salem Witch Trials have full court records of mass delusions.[9]

In this regard consider also the transfiguration of Jesus:

> Six days later Jesus took Peter, James and John with him and led them up a high mountain by themselves. And in their presence he was transfigured: his clothes became dazzling white, with a whiteness no bleacher on earth could equal. They saw Elijah appear and Moses with him, talking with Jesus. Then Peter spoke: 'Rabbi,' he said, 'it is good that we are here! Shall we make three shelters, one for you, one for Moses, and one for Elijah? For he did not know what to say, they were so terrified. Then a cloud appeared, casting its shadow over them, and out of the cloud came a voice: 'This is my beloved Son: listen to him.' And suddenly, when they looked around, only Jesus was with them: there was no longer anyone else to be seen. (Mark 9:2–7)

This remarkable transfiguration passage, repeated in both Matthew and Luke, reports a group experience shared by three disciples of seeing Elijah and Moses returned from the dead to converse with the transfigured Jesus. This was clearly the disciples' understanding, since there would be no sense in making shelters for ghosts or for something understood as a vision. But then Elijah and Moses suddenly disappear, spooklike, just as the resurrected Jesus disappears from the two disciples after a meal on the road to Emmaus in Luke 24:31.

---

8. See: www.catholic.org/mary/appear.php.

9. Surveyed by Matt McCormick, "The Salem Witch Trials and the Evidence for the Resurrection," in *The End of Christianity*, ed. John W. Loftus (Prometheus, 2011), 194–217.

But are we really to take this transfiguration episode as historical fact? If so, we must wonder how the disciples were able to recognize Elijah and Moses. Presumably they were not previously acquainted, and Jewish law prohibited portraiture. Perhaps Moses was still holding the Ten Commandments? And when was the last time we have a reliable source—the *New York Times*, say—reporting the voice of God coming out of the sky? At the very least, these passages in the Synoptic Gospels call into question the disciples' ability to understand what they were actually witnessing. If that were true here, would it not also be true in their reports of the risen Jesus? If these transfiguration passages were to appear anywhere but in the Bible—in the Koran, for example, or the Book of Mormon—is there any chance that Christian scholars would interpret this as an event in history? Indeed, no informed reader outside of the Christian faith is likely to come to this interpretation. This in turn further undermines the credibility of the resurrection accounts.

Consider the possibility of a dream experience being mistaken for an actual experience. As related by Paul King, a computational neuroscientist at the Redwood Center for Theoretical Neuroscience,

> [Dreams] have an experiential component as well, and lead to the formation of memories in the brain's neural networks. In fact, one of the proposed models of sleep is that sleep supports a memory consolidation process in which memories from the day are reorganized into a more efficient form and transferred from one brain region (the hippocampus) to another (the cerebral cortex). There is evidence that this process correlates with dreaming. In extreme cases, such as delusional episodes, imagined experiences occurring during the awake state are remembered as actual events.[10]

Given that episodic memories are highly malleable and subject to interference, and that dreams create episodic memories, it is not surprising that awake and dream memories might get confused some-

---

10. Paul King, "Why Do I Sometimes Confuse Memories of Dreams with Memories of Reality?" *Quora 2* (January 2014), www.quora.com/Why-do-I-sometimes-confuse-memories-of-dreams-with-memories-of-reality/answer/Paul-King-2.

times, or that record-keeping details, like whether an event occurred during sleep or not, could get misattributed.

There are studies that support this. As explained by Professor Elizabeth Loftus, of the University of Washington Psychology Department,

> If therapists discuss a topic during a waking session, material about this topic may, as a consequence, get into the patient's dreams at night. When the dreams are discussed at the next waking session . . . the patient may come to falsely believe and misremember a past that never happened, except in the patient's dream. Subjects studied a list of items on Day l. On Day 2, they received a false suggestion that some items from their previously reported dreams had been presented on the list. On Day 3, they tried to recall only what had occurred on the initial list. Subjects falsely recognized their dream items at a very high rate—sometimes as often as they accurately recognized true items. They reported that they genuinely "remembered" the dream items, as opposed to simply "knowing" that they had been previously presented. These findings . . . suggest that dreams can sometimes be mistaken for reality.[11]

Let me illustrate from personal experience. I was teaching freshman composition. In response to an assignment to write a personal experience paper, a student, a married woman in her 30s, wrote of a memory from her childhood: she had had a terrifying encounter with a would-be child molester, barely beating him to the safety of her own home. But she related that she had been unable to convince her parents of the danger she had been in; they simply ignored her tears and words, providing neither reassurance nor comfort. In conference she told me that she had never confided this story to anyone, not even her husband, but it had haunted her for years. I cautiously suggested to her the possibility that this was a memory of a dream, not of an actual experience. This had never occurred to her. I saw her again the next day and she said, "I think it was a dream."

Suppose one disciple said to the others: "I couldn't sleep last night.

---

11. Elizabeth Loftus, "Memory Distortion and False Memory Creation," *Bulletin of the American Academy of Psychiatry and the Law* 24, no. 3 (1996): 281–95, cogprints.org/599/1/199802009.html.

And then suddenly I was in a room somewhere, and Jesus was standing right in front of me. And you were there, Peter, and you, James, and Andrew, you were all there. And Jesus spoke to us, and ate some broiled fish, and then he was gone." A dream experience, which after many retellings is remembered as an actual group encounter with the risen Jesus. Or possibly misheard—hearing aids were not invented until centuries later.

The possibility that something simply misheard could become the source of a mistaken belief has potentially comic consequences. In Monty Python's *Life of Brian*, John Cleese, struggling to hear a very distant Jesus, tries to explain why cheese makers should be blessed, deciding that all manufactures of dairy products are probably equally blessed. My wife (long before we were married) walked past the classroom in which my English class was studying *Macbeth*; later that day she asked me what in the world we were talking about having heard my teacher say, "Out, out, beef cattle!"

Proponents of the historicity of the resurrection often claim that we have multiple attestation in the encounters listed by Paul to groups of disciples. But looking carefully at the Gospel accounts, we do not have a single case of a group encounter attested by more than one member of the group. In fact, we don 't even have a single case of a group encounter attested by *any* member of the group. All we have is stories about group encounters made by nonparticipants—Paul and the anonymous authors of the Gospels—using unidentified sources.

This is equivalent to my telling you that 12 of my friends have told me they saw Craig Blomberg walking on water. I might be shouting, "It's a miracle!" But you might want more information. Am I, your only source for this story, a source you can rely on? Do I have a history of hallucinations or drug use? Who are the friends who are my source for this story? Can we be sure this isn't a practical joke? If Craig did actually walk on water, when did his happen? In January? Is it possible the water was frozen?

Still another possible natural cause for the disciples' belief that Jesus had returned from death: mistaken identity. After Jesus' execution, a disciple in great excitement tells the other disciples, "I was in the market this morning, and I saw Jesus! I called to him, but the Roman legionnaires marched between us, and when they were gone he was no longer there." Remember, eyeglasses, like hearing aids, were not invented until centuries later. Nearsighted people had no help. And in several of the appearances reported in the Gospels, notably the one on the road to Emmaus and Mary Magdalene's encounter with Jesus, there were problems recognizing him (Luke 24:16; John 20:14; note even Matthew 28:17). Such misidentifications of the dead are common to this day. Following Elvis' death and burial many people believed that he was still alive; they had seen him at the local CVS or driving in a convertible. When Michael Jackson died, the same phenomenon occurred. In both cases there are thousands of well-documented "sightings" by eyewitnesses who can and have been interviewed and cross-examined.

Please understand I mean no disrespect in comparing the reports of Jesus' surviving his own death to that of Elvis Presley and Michael Jackson. But the parallels are striking. All three died relatively young and unexpectedly. After their reported deaths their devoted followers reported seeing them alive. In Jesus' case his disciples concluded that God had resurrected him. In the case of Presley and Jackson, devoted fans concluded that the performers, weary of the burdens of celebrity, had faked their own deaths, seeking peace and seclusion. The biggest difference is that the evidence for the Presley and Jackson sightings is far, far stronger than for the Jesus appearances. Google these and see for yourself.

Another source of the appearance stories might well be that "we are . . . prone to completely co-opt memories of events as if they had happened to us when in fact someone else experienced the events and told us about them."[12] This phenomenon has been verified recently by university psychological experiments. I have witnessed it myself. Some years ago I read an anecdote in *Reader's Digest* about a woman from the Midwest shopping for jewelry in a Boston department store. This woman was confused when a clerk asked her, "Do you have P-S-D-S?" She eventually worked out that this was the Boston way of asking, "Do

---

12. Matt McCormick, *Atheism and the Case Against Christ* (Prometheus Books, 2012), 88.

you have pierced ears?" I related this story to my wife, who was very amused. Several years later, I heard my wife tell the story to friends. But in my wife's version, this had happened while she was shopping in Boston with her mother—my wife and her mother both having been born in Wisconsin. I told her that the story had actually originated in *Reader's Digest*, but my wife still believes that it happened as she remembers.

Still another possibility. It's been widely noted that there was rivalry between Jesus' disciples. "An argument started among the disciples as to which of them would be the greatest" (Luke 9:46). Peter boasts that though the other disciples may fall away, he never will (Matthew 26:33). The brothers Jesus nicknamed "the sons of thunder" seek to be granted the right to sit at Jesus' right and left hand in the kingdom (Mark 10:35–38). (What chutzpah!) This too could have been a source of appearance stories. Andrew reports a vivid dream in which he was sure Jesus was speaking to him. Not to be outdone, Peter claims that Jesus appeared to him too. A very human reaction. Years later, because of memory distortion, Peter fully believes that Jesus appeared to him. And that it wasn't a dream.

An eighth plausible cause for the resurrection belief is the disciples' psychological motivation to reduce their cognitive dissonance. As characterized by author Kris Komarnitsky,

> [H]uman beings have a tendency . . . to look for and arrive at conclusions that confirm what we already believe . . . This sometimes leads to extraordinary displays of rationalization when strongly held beliefs are inescapably disconfirmed by reality.[13]

The study of this phenomenon was pioneered in the 1950s by social psychologist Dr. Leon Festinger; in 1999 the American Psychological Association's Scientific Conference characterized Festinger's theory as "one of the most influential theories in social psychology."[14]

Komarnitsky cites several relevant examples of cognitive-disso-

---

13. Kris D. Komarnitsky, *Doubting Jesus' Resurrection: What Happened in the Black Box?* (Stone Arrow Books, 2014), 45.

14. Ibid., 46.

nance reduction: one of the most instructive is the Millerites, the Christian sect founded in 1818 by William Miller, who convinced thousands of American Christians that Jesus would return between March 21, 1843 and March 21, 1844. When this prediction failed, instead of the movement collapsing, a recalculation predicted that the Second Coming would occur October 22, 1844. "Based on this new date, things reached an incredible pitch of fervor, zeal and conviction."[15] When this prediction also failed, the Millerites were informed that the date had been correct, but the Second Coming had occurred in heaven, not on earth; Jesus was making an "investigative judgment of the world," which, when finished, would be climaxed by his (actual) Second Coming. Through the process of cognitive-dissonance reduction, the faith survived and the movement flourished as the Church of Seventh-day Adventists, with millions of members worldwide.

Another more recent case cited by Komarnitsky was that of New York–based Rebbi Schneerson, an Orthodox Jewish rabbi so revered by his thousands of followers—Komarnitsky estimates 200,000 worldwide—that many thought him to be the long-awaited Messiah. When he suffered a stroke that left him unable to speak, many adjusted their expectations, referring to Isaiah 53, that he was "a man of sorrows and familiar with suffering," and that as Messiah he had taken on the sins of the world. When he died in 1994, "incredibly, this still failed to extinguish the belief among his followers that he could be the Messiah; many believed that he would be resurrected."[16]

True, cognitive-dissonance reduction might not by itself explain the disciples' belief. But in combination with other natural explanations, this factor has strong credibility. I have already explored the many other plausible natural explanations for the genesis of this belief—grief hallucinations, mistaken identity, dreams mistaken for reality, misheard or misinterpreted testimony, unconscious appropriation of another's experience, memory distortion, disciple rivalry. No one of these would likely be sufficient for the sincere belief of some of the disciples that

15. Ibid., 51.

16. Ibid., 56.

Jesus had been resurrected. But all of these have been the subject of university research, and all of them are common occurrences observed in many cultures. Given the extraordinarily limited quality and quantity of the evidence available in Paul's Epistles and the Gospel accounts, these natural explanations appear fully plausible. These quite natural, understandable beginnings could have easily led to a belief that Jesus had been miraculously resurrected, and to all the Gospel stories, with their fundamental contradictions and fictional and legendary embellishments. No miraculous resurrection required.

Is there any evidence that one or several of these causes for the resurrection belief actually happened? The only evidence is that the disciples—at least some of them—came to believe that Jesus was raised from the dead. By the very nature of things, there could be no other evidence 2,000 years later. And apparently the vast majority of Jews living in Jerusalem in the first century, those who were in the best position to judge, were unconvinced that Jesus had been resurrected. When the Romans destroyed Jerusalem in the seventh decade, they destroyed a Jewish city and temple; there is no evidence that any first-century Jewish or Roman document even noticed the small sect of Jews who were Jesus' disciples.

These natural explanations have several advantages over the claimed historical proofs of Jesus' physical resurrection. First, they do not require a belief in an extraordinary contrary-to-nature event on the basis of evidence that has little to no historical credibility. Second, all the possible natural explanations reflect common human behavior and are well documented in many societies, ancient and modern. Third, they avoid the problems presented by the major contradictions in the Gospel accounts, including the disconfirmations by silence. Such contradictions would be expected if the stories developed as I have suggested. Fourth, this account does not require the existence of God, a specifically Christian God, to work the miracle of resurrection.

And this in turn precludes the need to establish this God's supposed attributes of omnipotence, omniscience, and omnibenevolence, despite the fact of pervasive evil in the world this God supposedly created. And despite the question of why this God, supposedly the loving father of all mankind, has revealed himself only to Christians, leaving billions of humans with no hope of salvation, no comfort for suffering. In Jesus' words, "Whoever puts his faith in the son has eternal life . . . no one comes to the Father except by me" (John 3:36; 14:6). The case for the resurrection as an historic fact, besides the weakness of the biblical evidence, opens up myriad other problems suitable for other debates, none of which exist in the much simpler and more plausible natural explanations.

The Claim of an Empty Tomb

N. T. Wright holds that the "empty tomb," together with the appearances to the disciples, is essential to the historicity of the resurrection. According to many proponents, the vast majority of New Testament scholars accept the empty tomb as established fact.

The first question to be asked about this appeal to the authority of "the vast majority of New Testament scholars" is what proportion of these scholars are precommitted to biblical inerrancy and thus would have a confirmation bias in favor of anything that would bolster their argument for historicity. The external pressure to reach the approved conclusion should not be underestimated. Michael Licona authored a highly praised scholarly study of the resurrection of Jesus in which he suggested just the possibility that the raising of the saints in Matthew's account of Jesus' death might be understood in a nonliteral sense.[17] For this heresy he found it necessary to resign from his seminary teaching post and he was blacklisted by many conservative Christian colleges and seminaries. Craig Blomberg courageously came to Licona's defense; as a result, Craig himself has been bitterly attacked for his supposed abandonment of biblical inerrancy by Norman Geisler, a prominent New Testament scholar and the knight errant of biblical inerrancy. On this issue I think Craig to be on the side of the angels, metaphorically speaking.[18]

---

17. Michael R. Licona, *The Resurrection of Jesus: A New Historiographical Approach* (IVP, 2010), 548.

18. See: "A Roundtable Discussion with Michael Licona on the Resurrection of Jesus," *Southeastern Theological Review* 3, no. 1 (Summer, 2012): 71–98, www.risenjesus.com/wp-content/uploads/a-roundtable-discussion-with-

It should also be asked how many Jewish, Muslim, Hindu, and atheist scholars have written studies on the resurrection of Jesus? How many of them concluded that the empty tomb was a fact of history?

The common fate of those crucified by the Romans for insurrection, as thousands were, was for the body to be left hanging on the cross, eventually to be dumped in a shallow grave for felons, there to be consumed by dogs. The whole point of crucifixion was to set an example: this is what happens to those who challenge the authority of Rome, a painful and shameful public execution followed by the desecration of the body. But the Gospels give us a completely different story about the burial of Jesus, introducing an otherwise unknown Joseph from an otherwise unknown Arimathea. According to various Gospels, this Joseph was a member of the Council or even a secret disciple of Jesus. He asked Pilate for Jesus' body to give Jesus a lavish burial. And according to all the Gospels, Pilate was a rather nice fellow, finding no fault in Jesus, washing his hands of the whole matter, having given Jesus up for crucifixion only to satisfy a howling mob of Jews. But Philo of Alexandria, and Josephus, author of a massive first-century history of the Jews, both portray Pilate as so brutal that he had to be removed from office because of his violent excesses.

Consider the situation Pilate faced according to the Gospels' accounts. Jesus' own compatriots had hauled him before Pilate as an insurrectionist. He had been hailed in the street as the Messiah who was to free the Jews from Roman domination and establish the Kingdom of God. He had created a disturbance at the temple during the Passover celebration, when Jerusalem, a tinderbox of unrest, was mobbed by pilgrims and the Roman garrison was reinforced in anticipation of trouble. Jesus when arrested had refused to defend himself, even accepting the title "King of the Jews" (Luke 23:3). And Pilate wished to release him? He executed him only because he was intimidated by the rabble he was supposed to govern? This would be a dereliction of duty and is at complete variance with what we know of Pilate's character from other sources. Not a likely story.

And how plausible is the story of Joseph of Arimathea? An insurrectionist has just been crucified—are we really to believe that Joseph revealed himself to the brutal Pilate as a sympathizer and asked permission to give the confessed insurrectionist a costly burial? He would be practically begging to share Jesus' fate. According to the Gospels, Jesus' disciples had more good sense. When Jesus was arrested they scattered and hid themselves. Only Peter had the courage to lurk around a bit to learn his master's fate, and even he three times denied knowing Jesus. So the story of Pilate and Joseph of Arimathea and the empty tomb is wildly implausible.

There is further evidence against the empty tomb story. Consider William Lane Craig's defense of the story: Craig points to a passage found only in Matthew 27 that the chief priests and the Pharisees requested to Pilate that a guard be placed at the tomb because of the story that Jesus was to be raised in three days; they feared that the disciples would steal the body and then claim that Jesus was raised. When Jesus was indeed raised, they suborn the guards to commit perjury to cover up the truth—specifically, the Roman guards are told in Matthew 28 to claim that Jesus disappeared while they were asleep. But sleeping on duty would have been a capital offense! And after the experience of the Holocaust, do we really want to go back thinking that the priests and Pharisees were perfidious liars, rejecting clear proof that Jesus was indeed the Son of God, and thus bringing the curse of God upon Jews? (The Pharisees, it should be remembered, were the group that survived the destruction of the temple and the sack of Jerusalem by the Romans to found the post-temple Rabbinic Jewish faith, a faith that has been tragically victimized across the centuries, first in Christian pogroms and later in the Holocaust.) Unfortunately, anti-Semitism is once again robust and as lethal as ever. Reading William Lane Craig, with his frequent mention of "the Jews" as Jesus' enemies, I get a sick feeling that history might be ready to repeat itself. Again.

But what William Lane Craig fails to note is that what he calls a "polemic" is not a Jewish polemic, but a *Christian* account of a *supposed* Jewish polemic. We never get the authentic Jewish side of the story. And the Gospel account involves glaring implausibilities. For example, how did the priests know that Jesus' disciples would claim that Jesus would be resurrected? Our own Craig Blomberg has written, "although it may be true that the disciples ought to have been expecting Christ's resurrection, the gospels tell us that in fact they were not."[19] N. T. Wright, defending the historicity of the resurrection, writes that at no point did his disciples show any sign of understanding Jesus' statement to them that he would be raised from the dead on the third day.[20] So how did the "enemies of Christianity" (to use William Lane Craig's words) hear about Jesus' prediction of his resurrection and come to understand his words when his disciples could not? If only we had a contemporary Jewish version of the story. But we don't.

There is also no empty tomb in Paul's letters; all Paul says is that Jesus was buried—no tomb, no Joseph of Arimathea, no discovery of an empty tomb on Easter. Modern proponents place critical importance on the empty tomb in establishing the resurrection as a historical fact. For Paul, the resurrection was everything, the center of his faith. If you were Paul, would you not cite the evidence of the empty tomb? But the first time the empty tomb story appears is in Mark, decades later and long after any evidence would have disappeared.

Another blow against the empty tomb claim: N. T. Wright, William Lane Craig, and Craig Blomberg himself all agree that there is no evidence that the first-century disciples ever venerated the alleged empty tomb; even the location of the tomb was lost, only to be refound, miraculously, centuries later. In Blomberg's words, "The empty tomb seems almost certainly to be a historical fact, since . . . no gravesite was ever venerated in early Christianity." But does this make any sense? Craig and other proponents of historicity argue that the tradition of the Jews was to venerate tombs of saints that contained their bones, but Jesus' bones were not in the tomb, so there was no impulse to venerate it. But is it really possible that the site of the resurrection, the foundational belief of the Christian faith, would not be venerated? Wouldn't

---

19. Craig Blomberg, *The Historical Reliability of the Gospels*, 2nd ed. (IVP Academic, 2007), 104.

20. Wright, *Resurrection*, 410.

there have been an overwhelming impulse to visit this most holy site and say, ". . . and here is the great stone that was rolled away, and here is the table upon which the dead body of our Lord was laid before his resurrection"? And this is where his disciples would have taken the Jewish skeptics to show them the empty tomb. If there had ever been a tomb. Much more likely, the empty tomb story was invented by Mark or by his anonymous sources three decades after the event.

I am going to ask you to use your imagination. Every day thousands of people go to the gravesite of John F. Kennedy in Arlington National Cemetery. Imagine that a story started circulating that Kennedy's body was no longer in the grave, that God had physically resurrected him, and that Kennedy had been seen by dozens or even hundreds ascending to heaven.

Then try to imagine, a year or so later, a life-long Democrat planning a vacation trip to Washington, D.C. Can you imagine such a person saying, "Louisa, I don't see any point in visiting Kennedy's gravesite. After all, his body isn't there anymore. Let's go to the zoo instead to see the pandas." And within a decade or so Kennedy's gravesite has been so neglected that nobody can remember where it was. Can you imagine that? I can't. I confess that I am bewildered that proponents of the physical resurrection can view the fact that Jesus' first-century disciples' failure to venerate Jesus' tomb, or even keep track of its location, as evidence that the tomb was discovered to be empty.

Even if, implausible as it seems, there was an empty tomb, would this have provided significant evidence for Jesus' resurrection? Might the tomb, if it did exist, have been discovered empty without a miraculous resurrection and without long-discredited stories about the disciples stealing the body or the women going to the wrong tomb? It's possible that a few of those who knew and loved Jesus, conceivably even Joseph from the Council, if he existed, had more courage than the others and decided to rescue Jesus' body from the disgrace of the criminal's common grave. If they had any sense, they would have bribed the Roman soldiers at the execution scene rather than approaching the brutal Pilate. Friday night, for the Roman equivalent of 50 bucks, they get the Roman soldiers to take down the body of Jesus. They find an empty tomb and bury Jesus there, perhaps observed by the women who have witnessed the execution and by some of the soldiers. Saturday night the soldiers return to the tomb to destroy the evidence of their own corruption, and dump the body in the common grave. No evidence would have survived. No one would have wanted to risk death by confessing involvement. And so the women come to the tomb Sunday morning and find it empty. And since the empty tomb story originated with Mark (or his unidentified source) and is clearly the source for the other three Gospel accounts, they might also have adopted (and added to) Mark's story of Joseph of Arimathea. Sort of a package deal.

Is there any evidence that this is what happened? No. Almost two thousand years later we have insufficient evidence to determine what actually happened. Is it a *plausible* explanation for an empty tomb, if there was such a tomb? Why not? It is more plausible than the Gospel story because it doesn't require a suicidal Joseph of Arimathea, a Pilate behaving totally out of character and contrary to his duty, and a specifically Christian God to provide a miracle. And it could easily be the source, after many tellings and retellings, of the story of the empty tomb that is recorded years later in the Gospels. Hence the alleged empty tomb, when carefully analyzed, does not provide any evidence to establish the resurrection as a fact of history.

Conclusion

The insufficiencies in the evidence for the resurrection as a fact of history are legion. Mark relates no resurrection appearances. Matthew tells a tale of a huge earthquake, graves opening, and resurrected saints wandering the streets of Jerusalem. The other Gospels mention no such astonishing events, nor does any Jewish or Roman source. Luke tells the story of Jesus' final words to all his disciples and his exit from this world by ascending into a cloud, the dramatic climax of the resurrection story. But Paul, Mark, Matthew, and John say nothing of this. John tells of the raising of Lazarus, a story so powerful that if it became known, everyone would believe in Jesus. The other Gospels, written decades before John, tell no such story. John tells the story of "doubting" Thomas—you all know it. John specifies that all the disciples witnessed this. But none of the other Gospels make any mention of it.

Other weaknesses in the evidence abound—the insufficient information in Paul's account, not even indicating where and when the alleged appearances occurred and what the disciples heard and saw; the fact that Paul, the only eyewitness, was blinded and heard a voice nobody else could hear, strongly suggesting a vision or a hallucination; the inherent weaknesses of the Gospel accounts—anonymous authors writing in distant communities using unidentified sources decades after the events described, to name a few; the disconfirmations by silence, of events far too important to go unreported by all but one Gospel source; and the outright fundamental contradictions in the accounts, notably, the disagreement about whether Jesus appeared to and spoke with his female disciples, and the conflict about where all the appearances occurred. Also consider the availability of natural explanations for the appearances—grief hallucinations, dream experiences, misheard or misinterpreted testimony, unconscious appropriation of another's experience, mistaken identification, memory distortion, disciple rivalry, cognitive-dissonance reduction—very few of these are considered in the thousands of pages written by Christian apologists claiming the resurrection to be a fact of history. All this leaves the case for the historicity of the resurrection in tatters.

Does this mean that we can be certain that Jesus was *not* raised from the dead? I do not claim this. Two thousand years after Jesus' crucifixion we can't know for certain why some of Jesus' disciples thought they saw Jesus raised from the dead, nor how the empty tomb story began. What can be established is that the historical evidence for Jesus' physical resurrection is not nearly sufficient. Purely natural explanations can't be ruled out, and seem much more probable. But improbable things happen every day—somebody wins Megabucks; a person on his deathbed unexpectedly returns to good health. Perhaps genuine miracles do happen. Those who believe in Jesus' resurrection are free to believe, despite its improbability and the lack of historical verification. And those who do not believe can find powerful justification for their skepticism.

A Reply to Carl

Craig Blomberg, Ph.D.

The greatest strength of Carl Stecher's arguments is that none of them requires any significant time lapse between Jesus' death, most likely in 30 C.E., and the beginning of resurrection faith on the part of his closest followers. Following on the heels of atheist historian Gerd Lüdemann (as I'll discuss in my case for the resurrection later in this volume), any historically plausible hypothesis of Christian origins has to account for the unbroken record, decade-by-decade of testimony to the resurrection starting from the early 30s at the latest. One may not believe that resurrections are possible, or one may believe that the evidence is insufficient to make the resurrection of Jesus probable. But it defies credibility to reconstruct Christian origins and claim that *belief* in Jesus' bodily resurrection was not present from the earliest stages of the Jesus movement. Carl cannot be accused of defying credibility; he has made not one but several suggestions that all potentially account for resurrection faith beginning soon after Jesus' death. Because I still do not find his alternatives persuasive and will need to spend much of this response explaining why, I do not want to let this significant agreement pass by without underlining it. Lest it appear that I am rejecting everything about Carl's proposals, I want to begin by expressing appreciation for his unwillingness to ascribe resurrection faith to some late, slowly evolving legend.

One of Carl's suggestions for the rise of resurrection faith without an actual bodily resurrection of Jesus is the possibility of dreams being mistaken for real experiences. There is no doubt that this has happened repeatedly in human experience. Part of the appeal of the 2010 movie *Inception* is doubtless related to this phenomenon. It is difficult at times to remember if something one has had a very vivid dream about actually happened or not. If one has a recurring dream, it may become even more challenging to distinguish between dreams and reality. Shared dreams are another matter but I don't doubt that they occasionally occur. I once reported a dream I had to a friend who had spent the previous day with me only to learn that he had had a similar dream the previous night. Shared experiences can lead the subconscious to produce similar later nighttime musings. But among how many people at the same time? I am not aware if there is any research documenting the greatest number of people who have experienced not just shared but identical dreams. But I would be very surprised if there were accounts of anywhere close to five hundred people independently having identical (and not just similar) dreams at the same time, and Carl has not adduced any evidence that such accounts exist. Yet that is the number that Paul says saw Jesus at once (1 Corinthians 15:6).

Be that as it may, it seems unlikely that the original disciples of Jesus would all have accepted the testimony of just one or even a few of them saying they had seen Jesus if the others hadn't, especially when we see how unwilling Thomas was to believe the collective report of all the other ten without his own personal eyewitness experience (John 20:25).[1] Even if one rejects the Thomas story itself as a legend, it would still represent how one of the disciples would have been expected to act upon hearing an account of Jesus' resurrection if he had not personally seen the Risen Jesus himself. One or two disciples mistaking a dream for reality would not readily have convinced the remaining ones of the

---

1. "Although this statement of Thomas may seem to be quite obstinate, there is a sense in which contemporary believers ought to thank God that someone like Thomas was there to do the reality check for us." Gerald L. Borchert, *John 12–21* (Broadman & Holman, 2002), 212–13.

truth of something as spectacular as Jesus' resurrection if they had no similar experiences.

That is where another cluster of options comes in. Alone, or with the dream theory, are mishearing, misinterpretation, or misappropriation. What began as a comment about a dream was later remembered as a real experience, perhaps because the tradition was misheard. One could add related possibilities: perhaps the reference to the dream dropped out and people who didn't know the original story assumed it was recounting a real event. Or maybe they just didn't hear that part of the story and so began passing it off as if it were real. But again the same objections obtain. "Gossip" alone doesn't convince people of something as counterintuitive as a resurrection, and certainly not if it is going to be something that reshapes a person's entire worldview, commitments, how they spend the rest of their lives, and how, in some instances as with some of the original apostles, they are willing to die for their faith.[2]

The idea of mishearing a few key words is even less likely as the stimulus for resurrection faith. It is one thing if several people are genuinely telling others that Jesus is risen, based on what they think is reliable testimony, however faulty. It is something altogether different, if the original tradent is misheard. To begin with, the theory would be convincing only if words could be identified, either in Greek, Hebrew, or, most likely, Aramaic, that someone could easily have spoken, which sounded very similar to the words for a statement about Jesus having been raised from the dead. One can understand and laugh at "blessed are the peacemakers" becoming "blessed are the cheese makers" in an English comedy skit. But unless some word or words in one of the relevant ancient languages for a statement about Jesus' resurrection or its semantic equivalent closely resembled another word

---

2. I do not want to place as much emphasis as some scholars do on the traditions that all of the apostles except John (and of course Judas) died a martyr's death for their faith, because some of the sources in which this material occurs is very legendary in nature. Others are more securely established, however, so the wording "as with some of the original apostles" is fair enough. See further Thomas E. Schmidt, *The Apostles after Acts: A Sequel* (Cascade, 2013).

or expression that could also have been plausibly spoken, the analogy doesn't get us anywhere. Carl must propose a relevant play on words or paronomasia. I am not suggesting that there are no such options, particularly in the Aramaic that the first Jewish disciples in Israel are likely to have spoken,[3] just that unless one came up with a plausible one, it is impossible to evaluate the likelihood of such a mishearing. The Aramaic for "he is risen" is the single-syllable word *qam*. "Jesus is risen" would be *Yeshua qam* and "Messiah is risen" would be *Meshiach qam*. So if one were looking for something that could be misunderstood for these statements one would need to find similar Aramaic word combinations that meant something different. Then one would need to explain how the misunderstanding occurred often enough that enough authoritative individual witnesses believed it, without any additional evidence, and began to proclaim it to others who believed it without any actual eyewitness sightings to back their story up. Here is where the improbability of the explanation begins to enter in.

Imagine, for example, what would be needed to convince Carl that a respected naturalist authority who was also one of his friends had declared "atheism should be faulted," when he really had said "racism should be halted." Carl would probably require considerably more than just a few reports from people who claimed they had heard the former to be convinced of the latter. If he couldn't ask his friend directly, he would ask each reporter where they got their information from and trace it back to its source. Sooner or later the misunderstanding would be disclosed, and Carl would retain his atheist convictions without misgivings! Everything we know of about the apostles' attitude after the death of Jesus suggests that they were no more looking for Jesus to be raised from the dead, despite his predictions, than Carl would be looking for an atheist friend to be blaming his own worldview for something.

---

3. In several publications, Stanley E. Porter has persuasively argued that Jesus and his first followers likely knew a little Greek and Hebrew in addition to Aramaic, but Aramaic would still have been their first spoken language and idiom of choice when speaking with each other. See esp. his "Did Jesus Ever Teach in Greek?" *Tyndale Bulletin* 44 (1993): 199–235.

Another option Carl offers is the case of mistaken identity. At first glance, this seems more promising than the previous two and could well be harder to disprove. He could have even strengthened this suggestion by pointing out that a standard explanation for why Judas had to identify Jesus in the group of a dozen Jewish men gathered in the garden of Gethsemane was that he must have looked more or less like several of the others, especially in the dark. Most first-century Jewish men wore beards, moustaches, and forelocks. Most had dark hair and dark skin If Jesus were of average height and weight and if he and his disciples all wore simple, ground-length robes, it could well have been easy to confuse one of the others for Jesus.[4] And if that was true of his disciples, it would surely have been true for other late twenty- or early thirty-something Jewish males, even in broad daylight, especially in a crowded place where people were constantly moving, squeezing in and around others, so that their faces weren't consistently visible.

But, again, there are questions that remain unresolved. If Jesus' *Doppelgänger* were seen frequently in Jerusalem, so that several of the disciples became convinced they had seen him at different times, wouldn't they have moved heaven and earth, so to speak, to try to find him? If this person were unaware that others were mistaking him for Jesus, he would have had no reason to hide, so almost certainly he eventually would have been discovered. People who went to the marketplace or the small shops or even to the temple did so very routinely and predictably in the ancient world, and local residents were privy to the very public lives of most individuals, given that they lived more or less out of doors, using their small homes largely only to sleep in or when they needed to avoid bad weather.[5] Even Jerusalem may have had as few as 25,000–

---

4. Raymond E. Brown (*The Death of the Messiah*, vol. 1: *From Gethsemane to the Grave* [Doubleday, 1994], 252) observes, "this is the first mention in Mark of the crowd hostile to Jesus, so there would be no reason for the readers to think this crowd knows him. The readers also know that it is night and Jesus is surrounded by his disciples."

5. Indoor space was limited and windows small so even cooking was typically done in a courtyard. See further Philip J. King and Lawrence E. Stager, *Life in Biblical Israel* (Westminster John Knox, 2001), 28–35.

30,000 people when festivals were not in progress,[6] and people tended to stay largely within their own parts of their towns and take the same routes to public places. After the Passover pilgrims had gone home, the Judean followers of Jesus would have done everything possible to try to find this Jesus who was said to be risen. In the tightly knit communities and neighborhoods of the day, these disciples would undoubtedly have asked everyone they could, "have you seen Jesus?" or "have you seen somebody who looks almost exactly like him?" Sooner or later these disciples would have had to find out that it wasn't Jesus they had seen after all.

Yet another option Carl proposes involves disciple rivalry. A resurrection appearance would certainly win any theological one-upsmanship competition! Reading John 20:3–10 about the race between Peter and the beloved disciple to the tomb, who gets there first, who goes inside, and who believes, all in varying sequences, has certainly led other scholars to suspect that the account is more about a late first-century rivalry between Peter's and John's followers than a historical account of an event in 30 C.E.[7] But if that is the case then it cannot explain the rise of resurrection faith two generations earlier. But suppose that it also reflected a real rivalry between Peter and John during Jesus' lifetime. Synoptic sayings certainly allude to such competition among various disciples, including James and John versus all the rest (Mark 10:35–41)! In this case, Carl doesn't advance any new possibilities here, but just falls back on the vivid dream and memory distortion ideas. So disciple rivalry really isn't a separate option after all, just a possible motive for any combination of the other options. And there are other explanations for the behavior of Peter and the beloved disciple besides rivalry or competition, some of which may actually be preferable. In Acts, Peter and John are found together on more than one occasion as partners in ministry (3:1–11; 4:1–23; 8:14–17), so it seems more likely that their

---

6. Joachim Jeremias, *Jerusalem in the Time of Jesus* (Fortress, 1969), 84.

7. For a brief survey of different forms of this hypothesis, see Andreas Köstenberger, *John*, 563, n. 17, who argues that it is more likely that "both the beloved disciple and Peter are presented here as a duo of eyewitnesses to the resurrection."

behavior in John 20 has more to do with their varying impetuousness and varying willingness to believe in a resurrected Jesus.[8]

One of the more important of Carl's options is what he calls "grief hallucinations," which is actually a view that has often been suggested, with a variety of permutations. As a result, Gary Habermas has meticulously canvassed the studies of mass hallucinations that scholars have published. He notes the remarkable diversity of the nature of the hallucinations, the numbers of people involved, the kinds of reports passed on, and the like. But the one very consistent feature throughout all the otherwise diverse reports is that there is some location, some physical object, often a statue of a revered person, in other words something tangible that can be identified as the place where these visions, appearances, or hallucinations occur.[9] The Virgin Mary appears to weep, there are appearances of a certain saint or maybe of Jesus himself, and so on. That is why such shrines often spawn pilgrimages of the faithful who come to those locations in hopes of a similar experience.

A fixed location where people have visions of Jesus is the one feature that is strikingly absent from the New Testament accounts. Jesus appears to Mary Magdalene very near the empty tomb (John 20:14–17), to the other women who had been with her as they headed away from the tomb (Matthew 28:9–11), to Cleopas and an unnamed companion on the road from Jerusalem to Emmaus (Luke 24:13–18), to disciples twice in the upper room in Jerusalem behind locked doors (Luke 24:36-43/ John 20:19–23; John 20:26–29), in Galilee possibly on the same hillside where he delivered the Sermon on the Mount (Matthew 28:16–20), by the shore of the Sea of Galilee (John 21:1–23), and near Bethany on the Mount of Olives across the Kidron Ravine from the temple mount

---

8. Even the very skeptical Rudolf Bultmann (*The Gospel of John* [Blackwell, 1971], 684) agrees that the two are being presented as joint witnesses to the resurrection and not as any kind of rivals.

9. Gary R. Habermas, "The Late Twentieth-Century Resurgence of Naturalistic Responses to Jesus' Resurrection," *Trinity Journal* 22 (2001): 179–96; cf. also his "Explaining Away Jesus' Resurrection: The Recent Revival of Hallucination Theories," *Christian Research Journal* 23.4 (2001): 26–31, 47–49.

(Luke 24:50/Acts 1:9–12). In the cases of the appearances to Peter and James individually, and to the five hundred altogether, we are not even given a location (1 Corinthians 15:5–7). There were no consistent factors in the circumstances either, other than that people were clearly *not* expecting or looking for him to appear! The disciples were cowering behind locked doors, understandably fearful for their own lives after Jesus' crucifixion. The disciples on the road to Emmaus have had their faith shattered. James, the brother of Jesus, is not even a believer yet. Peter is shattered because of his threefold denial of Jesus. Mary thinks Jesus is the gardener when she first encounters him, and the other women believe someone has stolen the corpse from the tomb and laid it elsewhere. The disciples as a group, even in Galilee, think they have seen a ghost on one occasion, and at least some doubt on another occasion. Not one of the resurrection appearances is narrated in such a fashion as to suggest the disciples were in any frame of mind to experience visions and assume that they had seen Jesus alive.

Thus, although Carl has commendably tried to flesh out the "subjective vision" hypothesis in a variety of ways, I cannot at this point judge any of them to be successful. In addition, he would need to explain in detail how matters would have unfolded in order to have completely fooled so many people without the truth having ever been discovered.

But what of Carl's objections to the resurrection accounts as we have them? Although we cannot address all of them in detail, we may make the following observations.

First, while it is true there is "remarkably little evidence," as Carl says, from first-century sources, there are in fact remarkably few first-century sources that address topics that have anything to do with first-century prophetic or rabbinic figures in Israel to begin with. Those that do are largely in the New Testament or the writings of Josephus, which *do* refer to Jesus' resurrection. So this line of inquiry actually works in favor of the resurrection, not against it.

Second, Carl likens Paul's testimony to a modern account of a Jewish rabbi from thirty years ago, with the names of two witnesses no longer available for consultation, presumably meaning Peter and James. But both these men were still alive when Paul wrote Corinth in about

55, not dying until the 60s—James in Jerusalem in 62 and Peter in Rome in the mid- to late 60s. So the point of mentioning them along with the five hundred and stressing that most of them were still alive as well, was precisely to imply that they too could be consulted.[10] If someone in Corinth didn't believe Paul's word about seeing the Risen Lord, they could ask him where to find James, Peter, or any of the five hundred who were still alive. We know that Peter himself most probably had been in Corinth (1 Corinthians 1:12), because that is the likely reason for why some there claimed to belong to a faction or party that followed him.[11] He would not settle down in Rome until 60, since he appears to have been evangelizing the western and central parts of what is Turkey today (based on the provinces greeted in 1 Peter). So there was a good chance he would have been in Corinth again in the late 50s for people to question.[12]

In addition, Paul interviewed both Peter and James directly within three years of his own conversion (Galatians 1:18–24), in about 35,[13] so from that time on he was no longer relying just on his Damascus Road experience for supporting his belief in the resurrected Christ. He could have passed on Peter's and James' perspectives firsthand. While some people object to this conclusion, because Galatians 1:11–12 narrates Paul insisting that he did not get his gospel from any human source, that in no way precludes him having learned many supporting details from the other apostles. Experiencing the Risen Christ on the Damascus road showed him that Jesus was alive but it did not teach

---

10. Richard B. Hays, *First Corinthians* (Westminster John Knox, 1997), 257.

11. Although he exaggerates the differences between Peter and Paul, this point is nevertheless well established in Michael D. Goulder, *Saint Paul versus Saint Peter: A Tale of Two Missions* (SCM, 1994; Louisville: Westminster John Knox, 1995), esp. 16–46.

12. Cf. Martin Hengel, *Saint Peter: The Underestimated Apostle* (Eerdmans, 2010), 66–79.

13. For this and other chronological references to the life of Paul, see Rainer Riesner, *Paul's Early Period: Chronology, Mission Strategy, Theology* (Eerdmans, 1997).

him who else had also seen the resurrected Jesus.[14] That information he would have learned when he talked to them directly. And despite Paul's stressing his independence from the apostles in Galatians because of Judaizers coming from Jerusalem preaching a law-keeping gospel that was anathema to Paul, he still acknowledges that he did consult with the apostles on two key occasions (Galatians 1:18, 2:1). In fact, the very verb that Paul uses to describe his getting "acquainted" with Peter in 1:18 can also mean that he "interviewed" him.[15] As C. H. Dodd so famously remarked, if they spent two weeks together they would have talked about more than the weather! The resurrection of Jesus would have surely been central.[16]

Carl does put his finger, though, on a key point here. He recognizes that there is a relationship between Paul's account of his experience with the Risen Christ and the disciples' experiences narrated at the end of the Gospels. Like many others before him, he interprets the Gospel accounts in light of Paul's admittedly subjective experience—his companions heard noise and saw a light but only Paul deciphered words and the person who was speaking (Acts 9:7).[17] But this is the wrong way of drawing the causal lines. The Gospel writers were not patterning their resurrection accounts after Paul's autobiographical testimony. Just because Paul says he had a vision doesn't mean that the appearances during the forty days between the empty tomb and the ascension were also visions, much less subjective ones. It is precisely the reverse. Paul has already learned about the other disciples' experiences (Galatians 1:18–24) *and realizes that his was exceptional and not entirely the same.*

---

14. For an excellent treatment of just how much of Paul's message could have been inferred from his encounter with the heavenly vision of Jesus, and of what could not have, see Seyoon Kim, *The Origin of Paul's Gospel* (J.C.B. Mohr, 1991).

15. James D. G. Dunn, *Jesus, Paul and the Law: Studies in Mark and Galatians* (Westminster John Knox, 1990), 127–28.

16. C. H. Dodd, *The Apostolic Preaching and Its Developments* (Harper & Bros., 1936), 16.

17. Popularized particularly by Hans Grass, *Ostergeschehen und Osterberichte* (Vandenhoeck und Ruprecht, 1961).

He is like one "abnormally born" (1 Corinthians 15:8), who *didn't* get to have the kind of experience the Eleven had when Jesus was still appearing on earth. Then he appeared in bodily form, walked on the ground, could be touched, ate food, and so on. To Paul, he appeared in a heavenly vision. Paul was profoundly grateful for that experience, but it was most decidedly *not* the pattern for the Gospel accounts.[18] Those appearances had already occurred.

Third, Carl raises questions about the ascension, which completes the story of Jesus' resurrection. He finds the story impossible to believe and adds that, if something so spectacular actually occurred it would certainly have been narrated by more than one Gospel writer. But the ascension does not actually appear in any Gospel. Luke narrates it in the Acts of the Apostles (1:9-11). He understands it as the prelude to the sending of the Spirit at Pentecost (2:1–41). But there are no other canonical Acts, and the apocryphal Acts largely trace the supposed journeys of individual apostles at a later date. The reason the ascension doesn't appear in multiple writers may be as simple as observing that only one of the New Testament Gospel writers wrote a sequel. The four Gospels all end with the resurrection or with an announcement of it. The ascension came later. Had there been any true parallels to the Acts of the Apostles, there probably would have been multiple accounts of the ascension.

Fourth, Carl asks why the reawakening of Lazarus is found only in John 11, since it is a precursor to Jesus' resurrection. Here the answer most likely lies in the Gospels' outlines. Mark, the earliest of the four Gospels, decided to recount events that occurred in Galilee or Gentile territory to the north for all but the end of Jesus' ministry. Matthew and Luke followed suit, even while they added substantially more material of their own. In other words, it is only John who narrates that Jesus regularly headed up to Jerusalem from Galilee at the time of the major annual festivals, as Jewish men in good standing with their religious

---

18. For a thorough discussion of the possible implications of *ektrōma* ("one abnormally born"), see David E. Garland, *1 Corinthians* (Baker, 2003), 690–93. To the extent that Paul stresses any equivalence between the other apostles' experiences and his, it is in their reality (p. 691).

authorities were expected to do, and not just at the final fateful Passover when he lost his life. But the resurrection of Lazarus occurs on Jesus' *second-to-last* trip to Jerusalem, so it simply does not fit in the already chosen outlines of the Synoptic Gospel writers. [19] Moreover, all four Gospels do record that Jesus brought other individuals back to life. Mark and Matthew both narrate the resurrection of Jairus' daughter (Mark 5:21–24, 35–43; Matthew 9:18–26), while Luke adds the resurrection of the son of the widow in Nain (Luke 7:11–17). Lazarus may have been dead longer, but the miracle is only quantitatively, not qualitatively, greater, and the point each Gospel writer wants to stress is that Jesus did bring people back to life.

Fifth, why is "doubting" Thomas mentioned only in John? As in responding to the question of the resurrection of Lazarus, we have to realize how John is composing his Gospel. He is writing perhaps thirty years later and most likely knows the contents of the three Synoptics. About 80 percent of his contents are unique to his Gospel. So the main reason that *anything* found only in John appears there is because it is precisely John's purpose to include key events from the life of Jesus that the other three did not utilize. As he explains with some hyperbole at the end of his Gospel, much more could have been included (John 21:25). John 20:30–31 says that the Fourth Gospel was written so that people might believe that Jesus was the Christ and the Son of God. John seems to have had the most evangelistic purposes of any of the four Gospels.[20] If early church tradition may be believed, the other three Gospels were written to communities of those who were already believers. They didn't need this refutation of skepticism to the degree that outsiders might have. But even then, it's important to see what John emphasizes. Jesus replies to Thomas' confession of faith by asking rhetorically, "because you have seen me you have believed?" He is doubtless pleased that Thomas has come to faith, even though he failed to do so on the basis of his fellow disciples' earlier testimony. But Jesus immediately adds,

19. See further Craig L. Blomberg, *The Historical Reliability of John's Gospel: Issues and Commentary* (IVP, 2001), 55.

20. D. A. Carson, "The Purpose of the Fourth Gospel: John 20:31 Reconsidered," *Journal of Biblical Literature* 106 (1987): 639–51.

"blessed are those who have not seen and yet have believed" (John 20:29). In other words, as much as Thomas' account may help the skeptic come to faith, people shouldn't have to experience miracles for themselves.[21] If trustworthy witnesses testify to their experience with miracles, that should be sufficient. In other words, Thomas is not a uniformly exemplary model of faith after all. That could also be a reason for the Synoptics having previously omitted the account about him.

Sixth, how could the first Christians have learned about those narrated events that led up to Jesus' death and resurrection and that occurred between Jesus and Jewish or Roman authorities with none of his followers present? How, for example, do we know what Jesus and Pilate said (or didn't say) to each other when they were alone together? First of all, it is highly unlikely that any Roman governor would ever be left alone with an accused criminal; other guards would have been present. We know that John had "friends in high places" sufficient to gain entry to the high priest's courtyard (John 18:16);[22] who knows what other acquaintances he might have had among the Roman guard? Craig Keener sees evidence here for actual legal proceedings, in which case at least one Roman official would have been assigned to Jesus as counsel. Records of proceedings would have been kept and could have been consulted.[23] Moreover, the plausibility of the disciples hearing about this kind of conversation may be bound up with the plausibility of the resurrection itself. If Jesus did spend considerable time with his disciples over a forty-day period after the resurrection teaching them (Acts 1:3), then he would have had plenty of time to tell them all the details of every part of his Passion narrative that they were not personally present for.

As for the exchange between Judas and the priests not involving Jesus at all (Matthew 27:3–10), here Acts 6:7 gives us an important clue.

---

21. Robert Kysar, *John, the Maverick Gospel*, 3rd ed. (Westminster John Knox, 2007), 95–102.

22. On the assumption that John is "the other disciple," akin to "the beloved disciple" and again here paired with Peter.

23. Craig S. Keener, *The Gospel of John: A Commentary*, vol. 2 (Hendrickson, 2003), 1116.

We read that "a large number of priests became obedient to the faith." If even just one of them had been among those who met with Judas, or had heard from their priestly friends about what transpired, they could easily have passed the word along to other Christians.[24] Even if they didn't take the initiative, curious believers would most certainly have approached them to find out what they knew.

Seventh, Carl's claim that there is no "method for differentiating the historical from the legendary and fictional elements" in the resurrections accounts is simply false. Criteria of authenticity, as we have already seen, have been discussed, refined, and honed over the past century.[25] The Institute of Biblical Research's historical Jesus study group, for example, spent an entire decade investigating twelve key events from the Synoptic Gospels and applying the most currently accepted criteria, concluding that in each instance a strong case can be made for historicity.[26] And one of those twelve events is the cluster of resurrection appearances. Grant Osborne elaborates nine reasons for his conclusions: (1) the transformation of Paul; (2) the transformation of the Eleven who had followed Jesus; (3) the sacrificial lives those followers subsequently lived; (4) the embarrassment of having women as the first witnesses; (5) the early and creedal nature of the attestation; (6) the application of the criteria of dissimilarity from traditional Judaism and subsequent Christianity to many of the details; (7) the plausibility of the individual details; (8) the probability of the empty tomb; and (9) multiple attestation in multiple forms.[27]

---

24. I. Howard Marshall (*The Acts of the Apostles: An Introduction and Commentary* [IVP, 1980], 127–28) notes that the priests "were presumably those attached to the temple in Jerusalem, of whom there was a great number," making both Luke's account and our surmises here probable.

25. For a full survey, see Stanley E. Porter, *The Criteria for Authenticity in Historical-Jesus Research* (Sheffield Academic Press, 2000).

26. Darrell L. Bock and Robert L. Webb, eds., *Key Aspects in the Life of the Historical Jesus: A Collaborative Exploration in Context and Coherence* (Mohr Siebeck, 2009).

27. Grant R. Osborne, "Jesus' Empty Tomb and His Appearance in Jerusalem," in ibid., 775–823.

Eighth, studies have already shown that there is no inherent contradiction among the four Gospel accounts about which women went to the tomb. Various scholars have painstakingly worked through the parallels for the entire resurrection narrative and offered plausible solutions that explain the various seemingly divergent features. John Wenham's entire little book, *Easter Enigma*, shows one plausible way that all the information can fit together into a sensible sequence.[28] The problem, in fact, is not that there are no credible ways of harmonizing the data but that there are multiple possible ways at some junctures, and we do not always know which is the most likely.

This much, however, seems clear. A group of women went to the tomb while it was still dark, arriving roughly at dawn. They discovered two angels, appearing (as they always do in Scripture) like men. One was the spokesman, so Mark and Matthew refer only to him. They announced that Jesus was risen; the women could see for themselves that he was no longer in the tomb. They told them to tell his male disciples to go ahead to Galilee and there they would see him. The women left trembling, afraid, and silent. But joy eventually overcame their fear and they reported what they had seen to the disciples. En route, Jesus appeared to some of them as well. Peter and John rush to the tomb, find the grave empty, and leave again. Mary Magdalene returns with them, lingers, and has an encounter with Jesus in the garden. All this occurs on "Easter" Sunday morning. That afternoon Jesus appears to Peter alone at an unspecified place. In the evening with the Ten (minus Judas who has hanged himself and Thomas who is simply absent), Jesus appears to them behind locked doors. A week later when they are gathered together in (perhaps) the same upper room, this time with Thomas present, he appears again.

Finally, the disciples return to Galilee. Not really knowing what to do or where to go, they resume fishing, as a number of them originally had been fishermen by trade. Jesus then appears to them on the shore, having started a charcoal fire to prepare some breakfast. They have toiled all night without catching fish but at Jesus' command let down

---

28. John Wenham, *Easter Enigma: Are the Resurrection Accounts in Conflict?* (Zondervan, 1984).

their nets and retrieve 153 fish, a figure that has defied the greatest allegorists to arrive at any consensus, probably implying that they were astounded at the quantity and simply counted how many they had![29] Some unspecified number of other appearances occurred over the next forty days, during which time Jesus taught them something akin to the world's greatest Old Testament survey class in history. At least he showed them how everything that pointed to him in the three major parts of the Hebrew Scriptures, the Law, Prophets, and Writings, was fulfilled in him (Luke 24:44; cf. Acts 1:3). Eventually he appeared to them on a mountain in Galilee, perhaps the mountain on which he delivered his Great Sermon. Finally, when the disciples were next in the vicinity of Jerusalem, he appeared to them at the Mount of Olives and ascended to heaven.

Incidental corroboration of the plausibility of at least part of this sequence of appearances occurs when we understand the length and sequence of Jewish festivals. Passover spanned two weekends, so it was natural for the disciples to have gathered in the same place on consecutive Sunday evenings, the second time just before they would have started home for Galilee. Pentecost came fifty days after Passover, so the disciples would have headed back to Jerusalem just before that time, precisely when we read that the disciples were back at the Mount of Olives. Of course, none of this proves that Jesus ever appeared on these different occasions, but if this is historical fiction, it is more carefully researched to dovetail with everything plausible than any other fiction we know of from the ancient Roman Empire.

Indeed, historical fiction as we know of it was a development of much later centuries.[30] In the Jewish and Roman world of Jesus' day, novels that depicted the lives of exemplary individuals tipped their hats as to their literary genre either by using largely unknown people and places or by inserting deliberate and blatant anachronisms. Writers did pen works of fiction that included a handful of realistic details, but

29. Surveying the proposals and coming to a similar conclusion is D. A. Carson, *The Gospel according to John* (IVP, 1991), 672–73.

30. See esp. Erich Auerbach, *Mimesis: The Representation of Reality in Western Literature* (Princeton University Press, 1953).

usually introduced characters, actions, customs, or locations that were obviously made-up, in order let their readers know what kind of literary genre they were employing (see, e.g., the Old Testament Apocryphal works of Judith and Tobit[31]).

The Gospels and Acts, by way of contrast, have had so many hundreds of incidental details corroborated that if they represent historical fiction, they are unlike any others that we know about in the ancient Mediterranean world, before or during this era, or for many centuries afterward. It is far more likely that they intend to narrate historical and biographical information that would have been considered accurate by the standards of their day.[32]

Here is where both conservatives and liberals often err in the same way. Too many scholars of both the "right" and the "left" judge the Gospels by modern standards of historiography and biographical writing. But the ancient world did not have our modern standards of precision. Topical or thematic arrangement of material was every bit as acceptable as chronological arrangement. Round numbers, approximation, hyperbole, and figures of speech were common. Michael Licona has demonstrated in detail the literary devices that Plutarch used and shown how many of them apply to the Gospels as well.[33]

However, it is patently not the case that the ancients did not judge between good and bad history telling or that they fell for every tall tale that someone might spin. Lucian of Samosata (*How to Write History*) in particular laid out detailed criteria for distinguishing between good and bad historical reporting. Luke's prologue much more resembles the prologues of historical writers like Josephus, Herodotus, and Thucydides (and in some respects more like scientific treatises) than the beginnings

---

31. Daniel J. Harrington, *Invitation to the Apocrypha* (Eerdmans, 1999), 11, 28–29.

32. For detail, see Craig L. Blomberg, *The Historical Reliability of the Gospels*, 2nd ed. (IVP, 2007); and Craig L. Blomberg, *The Historical Reliability of the New Testament* (B & H, 2016). For Acts alone, see throughout the voluminous four-volume commentary by Craig S. Keener (*Acts* [Baker, 2012–15]).

33. Michael R. Licona, *Why There Are Differences among the Gospels: What We Can Learn from Ancient Biography* (Oxford University Press, 2017).

of ancient romance novels.[34] But in a world without quotation marks or any felt need for them, it was every bit as acceptable to paraphrase someone's words as long as you were faithful to their gist. It was perfectly proper to reword one's historical sources by abbreviating, excerpting, selecting, adding, explaining, or combining information together.

In fact, in a world without footnotes or bibliographies, one of the ways that one established one's own literary reputation was by rewording one's sources and making them one's own, complete with distinctive styles and arrangements.[35] But inventing details or episodes out of whole cloth was generally not considered acceptable and the one point where scholars who claim that the Gospel writers at times simply fabricated events have not adequately made their case.[36] So when we see the amount of diversity among the four Gospel writers and compare them with other multiply attested events from ancient Jewish, Greek, and Roman history writing, the combinations of similarities and differences turn out to be remarkably similar.

Even the pervasiveness of miracles in the Gospel narratives does not make them that unique. Miracles occur in other relatively trustworthy histories of the Greco-Roman world. Nor is it the case that Christian historians must reject all of those miracles while accepting the canonical ones. Every claim to a miracle must be evaluated on a case-by-case basis. It is true that the other miracles in Greco-Roman histories and biographies often have far poorer attestation than the Gospel miracles, so that skepticism may be justified on those grounds. But they must not be ruled out *a priori*. The accounts of Hanina ben-Dosa and Honi the Circle Drawer in Jewish circles, for example, dovetail with the Gospels own claims that there were other Jewish miracle workers and

---

34. Loveday C. A. Alexander, *The Preface to Luke's Gospel: Literary Convention and Social Context in Luke 1.1-4 and Acts 1.1* (Cambridge University Press, 1993).

35. Gary Knoppers, "The Synoptic Problem: An Old Testament Perspective," *Bulletin for Biblical Research* 19 (2009): 11–34.

36. R. T. France, "The Authenticity of the Sayings of Jesus," in *History, Criticism and Faith*, ed. Colin Brown (IVP, 1976), 130–31.

exorcists besides Jesus (Luke 11:19).[37] It is also important to point out that miracles are not rampant in Greco-Roman historiography, as some writers would have us think. They are actually comparatively rare. Of course, I am not speaking of mythology here but of historiography, of the kind we find in the Gospels and Acts.

A famous example comes in one of the four accounts of Caesar crossing the Rubicon, the paradigmatic event of ancient history that no one doubts. Miraculous omens appear in one case, but this in no way vitiates the historical value of the narrative even if one is skeptical of the miraculous element.[38] Thomas Jefferson may have wildly misjudged Jesus' reputation as merely a great human teacher, but his approach to the Gospels—cutting the miracles out of them while preserving the rest—was not unlike some classical historians' approach to other ancient historiography.[39] Just because one finds certain supernatural stories embedded within a larger historical account does not destroy those narratives' value in terms of the natural events they recount.

The case can be made, on the other hand, that the miracles in the Gospels fit the overall message of Jesus far more consistently than do the miracles in various other ancient histories or biographies. Indeed, in dramatic contrast from the later New Testament apocrypha, the miracles in the canonical Gospels consistently function to bolster Jesus' claims to have inaugurated the kingdom of God. But if the kingdom had begun to arrive, then a king must be arriving. Or another way of putting it is, if the messianic era is dawning then a Messiah must be present. Isaiah 35:5-6 was a well-known Israelite scriptural prophecy about the miracles that would occur in the messianic age. The Essene sect at Qumran that produced the Dead Sea Scrolls appealed to this same prophecy. Some of the miracles mentioned in Isaiah match exactly those that occurred in Jesus' ministry, at times without any other precedent in Israelite history

---

37. Cf. further Eric Eve, *The Jewish Context of Jesus' Miracles* (Sheffield Academic Press, 2002).

38. Paul Merkley, "The Gospels as Historical Testimony," *Evangelical Quarterly* 58 (1986): 328–36.

39. Revived at the end of the twentieth century by Robert W. Funk, *Honest to Jesus: Jesus for a New Millennium* (HarperSanFrancisco, 1996).

(e.g., giving sight to the blind). Jesus himself replies to the disciples sent by John the Baptist when he was imprisoned to ask Jesus about his identity by telling them to report to John that these miracles are now being performed (Matt 11:26; Luke 7:18–23).[40]

Jesus nevertheless goes on to include "the dead are raised" (Matt. 11:5; Luke 7:22), which was not prophesied in Isaiah. So this cannot be said to be an invention of the Gospel writers, as some have claimed, in order to make it look as if Jesus has fulfilled prophecy when in fact he hasn't. Why would they make their task even more difficult—getting others to believe the Gospel message—by adding this most spectacular miracle of all if it never occurred and never was even prophesied? But if Jesus drew on God's power through the Spirit to reawaken at least three people, even just to more of this mortal life, then some of the objections to Jesus' own resurrection are successfully countered. This time, of course, there is a qualitative distinction between resurrection to mortal life and resurrection to immortal life. But the divine, supernatural world has to exist for even the former to occur and, if it does exist, then there is no reason to deny in principle the possibility of the latter.

Ninth, we have already touched on the issue of mass hallucination. The important element here is not individuals vs. groups but the association with one fixed location. As for how the disciples could have recognized Moses and Elijah at the transfiguration, an event that foreshadowed the resurrection, one needs to have a little historical imagination. Greetings were elaborate and formulaic in antiquity;[41] it is hard to imagine Jesus not greeting the two men by name! We do not have to wonder how they could ever have seen a picture of the men given the Jewish reluctance to create iconography of their heroes (and given the express prohibition against creating any portraits of God). There are other ways to discover who someone is besides having already seen portraits of them.

---

40. For all these points, see esp. Graham H. Twelftree, *Jesus, the Miracle-Worker: A Historical and Theological Study* (IVP, 1999).

41. Part of what makes Luke 9:61 so shocking.

In terms of hearing a heavenly voice, the disciples would hardly have been the first in the history of the world to have had an experience with an unknown voice they had reason to believe belonged to God. Contrary to the fashionable charge among modern, so-called aggressive atheists, such people are not automatically deluded. My own mother, a lifelong German Lutheran without a mystical or charismatic bone in her body, heard a voice in her kitchen after she was widowed telling her first to take her cane and then to take her cell phone as she prepared to take the trash out to the garbage cans by her alley. Black ice that she could not see from the house made both essential as she wound up calling a neighbor for help when she felt "trapped" by the ice and unable to walk safely back to the house, Nothing like that had ever happened to her previously, nor has it since, and I will put her sanity up against anyone's! She just calmly assumed it was God talking and followed the instructions that probably saved her from a serious fall with no way to get help. I have heard other similar accounts from friends and acquaintances whose soundness of mind throughout the rest of their lives is indistinguishable from those who have never "heard voices."

Tenth, Carl's final objections surround the empty tomb. We have dealt with most of these already; here we may add simply that Philo (*Flaccus,* 83–84), Cicero (*Philippics* 2.7.17), and Plutarch (*Antonius 2*) all narrate partial parallels to Joseph of Arimathea's desire to give a victim condemned by Rome a decent burial.[42] So the notion that it was too dangerous for a powerful, leading Jewish figure like a member of the Sanhedrin ever to approach Pilate for Jesus' body is refuted. The idea that Pilate would never have wanted to placate such a powerful Jewish leader when he was already posted to the "hinterlands" of the Roman Empire to keep the peace among a people with the reputation among the Romans for unusual volatility, especially when they believed their purity laws might be violated, is debunked.

---

42. See further Craig S. Keener, *The Gospel of John: A Commentary*, vol. 2 (Hendrickson, 2003), 1159–61. For eleven discrete arguments for the historicity of the Joseph of Arimathea episode by someone who is ultimately ambivalent about the resurrection, see Dale C. Allison, *Resurrecting Jesus: The Earliest Christian Tradition and Its Interpreters* (T & T Clark, 2005), 352–63.

In addition to these two charges, Carl finds the story about Jewish antagonism against Jesus too overblown, especially in the episode in which they request a guard placed at the tomb lest the disciples steal the body and declare him to be resurrected as he had predicted. Carl correctly notes that we don't have a Jewish polemic against Jesus, only a Christian account of a Jewish polemic. But we do have a Jewish polemic against Jesus in the Talmud, codified from earlier oral tradition, and it seems even more vitriolic than anything described in the Gospels.[43] That Jesus was a sorcerer who led Israel astray is the most recurring charge, not unlike the claim made by some Pharisees in the pages of the Gospels that he was possessed by the prince of demons (Matthew 12:24; Luke 11:15). Moreover, despite the disciples' confusion, Jesus had publicly predicted his resurrection. His followers may not have known what to make of such a prophecy. But the opposition could well have imagined them acting on it in some fashion. After his death, his opponents could certainly have worried that his followers might fake something to keep their movement alive. An inscription from Nazareth found later from the first century warns strongly against grave robbing, so the fear could hardly have been unfounded.

As we transition to our conclusion, we must take notice of Carl's discussion of cognitive dissonance. This is one of the more important and significant parts of his case against the resurrection. There is no question that people become convinced of certain foundational truths on which they build their lives over long periods of time, and that the longer they live and the more their lives depend on those truths, especially when they seem to have been vindicated, the harder it is for them ever to imagine changing worldviews. Thomas Kuhn famously created the concept of a "paradigm shift" in the early 1960s, when he demonstrated that sea changes in people's philosophies tend to come through revolutionary rather than evolutionary developments.[44] In other words, one does not usually hold to a deeply entrenched worldview for a long period of time

---

43. See esp. Peter Schäfer, *Jesus in the Talmud* (Princeton University Press, 2009).

44. Thomas S. Kuhn, *The Structure of Scientific Revolutions* (University of Chicago Press, 1962).

and then change it because of tiny, incremental shifts over an equally long period of time. Rather, a person usually encounters a crisis—a whole cluster of events that amount to a philosophical tsunami—and then changes their perspective in a wholesale fashion very quickly.

Those who have studied the processes behind what is today often called "deconverting" from a particular religion that one had earlier voluntarily and personally embraced bear this out. Perhaps the most common pattern is a threefold sequence of events in which (1) one or more very traumatic events happens to a person and they cannot make sense of their experience based on their existing worldview; (2) one or more people who share that perspective on life, from whom the individual would have expected help, consolation, or guidance fails them in a very hurtful way, often by holding them responsible for the trauma because they lacked enough faith to avoid it; and (3) for the first time in their lives, they study an alternative worldview seriously and in detail, and suddenly it makes sense to them in a way their existing world view does not.[45] For example, a young Christian man has a sister who was not a believer take her own life. Instead of falling back on one of several other possible Christian approaches to this scenario, the man, who was previously taught only a restrictivist Christian approach (that believes the deceased must be in hell), cannot cope with the trauma of his loss. Compounding the problem, a fellow Christian tells him it is his fault for not having shared his faith adequately with his dead sister. Finally, for the first time in his life, he studies atheism seriously. He realizes it could relieve him of his burdens and embraces it wholeheartedly, even though he has not really put it to the test with a full critical analysis of its strengths and weaknesses.

Interestingly, another family member may experience the same grief over the loss of the young woman but react in a completely opposite way. This individual may be aware that there are other fully Christian ways of holding out hope for the deceased person, not least the possibility that God would reveal himself in some way to the dying person before

---

45. John W. Loftus, *Why I Became an Atheist: A Former Preacher Rejects Christianity* (Prometheus, 2012), 24. Other studies of "deconversion" have replicated these details.

they completely lost consciousness. Near-death experiences today form a virtual cottage industry of study, with accounts, many of them verified by people of very sober mind, of seeing or hearing what was going on with their bodies or even other places nearby when all around them thought they were dead, only to discover themselves later revived to life in this world.[46] If even a tiny handful of these accounts proves true and thus demonstrates the continued existence of the soul apart from the body after all vital signs have ceased, then who knows how many other people have had similar encounters with God in the liminal state between life and death? We know of the experiences only of those who were remarkably brought back to life, usually through cutting-edge medical procedures. Until recently, such people would have died and we would never have known about their experiences at all. It may be the case that countless people throughout history have had such experiences but, because they were not brought back to life in this world, no one knows what they experienced. And this is just one option consistent with biblical teaching.[47]

Someone with this kind of knowledge, and an equally clear realization that the Bible regularly teaches against the notion that most evil could be avoided if one just had enough faith, might respond very differently to the death of a loved one. I have watched both of these scenarios play out repeatedly in the lives of people I have known. Neither of them demonstrates that atheism is either right or wrong; they just show how people can react remarkably differently to the same set of events. Cognitive dissonance comes into play in both instances. For the first kind of person, there is too much cognitive dissonance between their existing (but limited) Christian beliefs and the reality they have experienced. So, as soon as they discover what appears to be a more viable option they jump at it. Not all opt for atheism; some may opt for a form, say, of pantheistic Zen Buddhism that likewise solves their problems, or so they think. The second person, on the other hand, would

---

46. The pioneering study was Raymond A. Moody, Jr., *Life After Life* (Bantam, 1976).

47. For the full range of options, see John Sanders, *No Other Name: An Investigation into the Destiny of the Unevangelized* (Eerdmans, 1992).

experience too much cognitive dissonance if he abandoned his (broader) Christian beliefs, realizes he doesn't have to, and doesn't find another worldview unambiguously preferable. So while cognitive dissonance is an important element of an individual's spiritual pilgrimage to take into account, it is not the final or most determinative factor.[48]

It is also important for the atheist to take cognitive dissonance into account. The slogan that "foxholes have no atheists" is no doubt exaggerated, but it carries a measure of truth. The two times in life that people are most likely to convert to Christian faith are in young adulthood as they are forming foundational beliefs and deciding what of their parents' convictions they will or will not own for themselves, and when they come face to face with their own mortality, usually though not always at some later stage in life. But again not everyone reacts in the same way. The person receiving a diagnosis of the worst form of pancreatic cancer with almost no chance of survival and the likelihood of living at most a few months and perhaps only a few weeks or days may well be open to the gospel for the first time in their lives. They realize that they are not ready to die, that if the Christian message has even the slightest chance of being true, it would be crucially important for them to put their affairs right with God, and if it is false they have nothing further to lose, and so they become believers virtually on their deathbeds. Others, for various reasons—pride, reputation, relationship with friends or relatives, or whatever—dig their heels in all the more firmly and refuse to countenance even the possibility. Again cognitive dissonance is at work in both scenarios but in a diametrically opposite way. In one case, the dissonance is between the possibility, however remote, that there is life after death and the realization that they are utterly unprepared for it; in the other case, the dissonance would simply be too great between everything they have believed and stood for throughout their lives and a last-minute transformation, even if it could open up to them the glories of an unimaginably happy eternity.[49]

---

48. See further Scot McKnight and Hauna Ondrey, *Finding Faith, Losing Faith: Stories of Conversion and Apostasy* (Baylor University Press, 2008).

49. For these and other generationally related trends, see Elisabeth A. Nesbit Sbanotto and Craig L. Blomberg, *Effective Generational Ministry: Biblical and*

In short, it is equally important for both Carl and me to take cognitive dissonance into account. He says he can't imagine the possibility of becoming a Christian. That surely has to be factored in as one evaluates his arguments, as much as my experience of God colors my approach. But I also have to remind myself that I have experienced what, by any of the standard definitions of the word, are called miracles. I have experienced them, moreover, in distinctively Christian contexts. When one is a part of a concerted prayer effort undertaken publicly by a group of believers to intercede for a longtime friend who has with her the very MRIs showing her cancerous tumor, and she not only feels different immediately afterward but doctors never again find any tumor, one cannot simply write off what one has experienced. When one has witnessed a friend unable to walk without aid for months stand instantly and walk confidently by himself after similar prayer, to what does one attribute that? The same questions could be asked about exorcisms and other kinds of miracles I have witnessed. Even if I doubted every secondhand report of a miracle I have ever encountered, I cannot deny my own personal experience.

Cognitive dissonance goes a long way to explaining the continued existence of sects that set dates for the end of the world and then watch world history continue unchanged. Scholars have applied cognitive dissonance theory to early Christianity in the context of its belief, at times, in the imminent return of Christ.[50] But belief in the resurrection is something quite different; it remains as central and scientifically improbable today as it was in the first century. Something besides cognitive dissonance resolution must be fueling its strength. Cognitive dissonance can help explain the continued existence of sects that have experienced failed prophecy, but the question of the resurrection is something quite different.[51]

It is also interesting that at the end of Carl's chapter he makes

---

Practical Insights for Transforming Church Communities (Baker, 2015).

50. See esp. John G. Gager, *Kingdom and Community: The Social World of Early Christianity* (Prentice-Hall, 1975).

51. Cf. Wright, *Resurrection of the Son of God*, 697–701, who addresses the application of cognitive dissonance theory to the resurrection head-on.

reference to the problem of evil. He did this briefly in the two live debates I had with him in recent years at Oregon State University that spawned our friendship and dialogue. He has done so in email exchanges with me more recently. I suspect that this is the real nub of the problem. There can't be an all-powerful and all-loving God because of the amount of evil in the universe. If there is no God, then there are no miracles. If there are no miracles, there is no resurrection. I suspect that for all of Carl's more sophisticated arguments this is really the reasoning that has led him to his conclusions. If this is the case, then the real issue to be debated is not the resurrection but the problem of evil. And that, of course, would take a different and separate volume.

This project is still worthwhile, however, because others *do* genuinely start with the resurrection as their key issue. But perhaps I may be permitted to suggest just two lines of response that I would want to pursue in such a separate volume. First, where does the concept of evil even come from in the first place if there is no point of reference outside of and transcending humanity to establish it? No other life form in the universe has the ability even to debate about it! Second, we must also deal with the problem of good. How is it that, contra Darwinism, countless people sacrifice what is in their best interests for others because of religious convictions? More appositely, where does the concept of good even come from?[52]

Meanwhile, I welcome Carl's good spirit throughout these exchanges. I am delighted when he describes the relationship he has with his sister. I appreciate his unwillingness to challenge the faith of parents who have lost children in a school massacre. I am glad that he consciously distances himself from the so-called aggressive atheists and only once speaks of people of faith as having a delusion. I suspect we might be able to agree to banish that kind of pejorative language from

---

52. On these issues, which are philosophical and theological, not scientific, see esp. Richard Swinburne, *Providence and the Problem of Evil* (Oxford University Press, 1998); Alvin Plantinga, *God, Freedom and Evil* (Grand Rapids: Eerdmans, 1974); C. S. Lewis, *The Problem of Pain* (Geoffrey Bles, 1940); and Christian Smith, *Moral, Believing Animals: Human Personhood and Culture* (Oxford University Press, 2003).

our conversation altogether. My own take on his good spirit in these matters is that his church upbringing did have beneficial effects. More theologically, I believe this reflects the *imago Dei* (image of God) that historically Jews and Christians have believed God implanted in or impressed on every human being.[53] I trust that the issues discussed and points of view expressed by the two of us, and by our two responders, will be helpful to others who wrestle with these same questions.

---

53. On which, see the numerous helpful perspectives in Beth Felker Jones and Jeffrey W. Barbeau, eds., *The Image of God in an Image-Driven Age: Explorations in Theological Anthropology* (IVP, 2016)

A Rejoinder to Craig

Carl Stecher, Ph.D.

An essential element in my case against the historical resurrection is that many plausible natural explanations are available: grief hallucinations, memory distortion, dreams confused with reality, mistaken identity, disciple rivalry, testimony misheard or misunderstood, cognitive dissonance reduction. And here I might add wishful thinking, a human tendency that we do not need university studies to evince or explain. We all have a tendency to confuse what we wish to be true with what we know to be true.

So there's reason to think that hearing from one disciple that she saw Jesus yesterday but lost him in the crowd, other disciples would believe because they wished to believe. The same thing could happen if a disciple experienced a vivid dream of Jesus, perhaps not making it clear—possibly not knowing himself—that it was a dream. Other disciples hearing this story might also wish to believe it true.

About dream experiences sometimes being confused with real experiences, Craig writes, "There is no doubt that this has happened repeatedly in human experience ... Shared experiences can lead the subconscious to produce similar later nighttime musings." But Craig questions whether five hundred people can have "identical (and not just similar) dreams at the same time," referring to Paul's creed in 1 Corinthians 15:6. But we have no evidence that the five hundred had identical or even similar dreams. All that Paul wrote was that Jesus "appeared" to the five hundred. And as many scholars have pointed out, there's good reason to be skeptical about Paul's claim. Michael Martin, for example, writes:

> If such an event really happened, it would have been the strongest evidence that Christians had for their belief in the Resurrection. Surely they would have used it whenever they could. Furthermore, the fact that five hundred people reported seeing a resurrected man would surely have attracted wide attention in the region and would have come to the notice of the authorities and historians who were writing at the time. Yet this most remarkable phenomenon is neither mentioned in any other part of the New Testament nor confirmed by either Jewish or pagan sources. One must conclude that it is extremely unlikely that this incident really occurred, yet Paul mentions it in the same breath and with the same confidence that he mentions Jesus' post resurrection appearances to Cephas, to the twelve, and to himself. Surely this does not inspire confidence in Paul as a reliable source.[1]

I suggested that at some point Jesus' disciples might have misheard another disciple relating a dream of an encounter with Jesus; Craig amplifies this possibility, writing, "perhaps the reference to the dream dropped out and people who didn't know the original story assumed it was recounting a real event. Or maybe they just didn't hear that part of the story and so began passing it off as if it were real." Returning to a more skeptical perspective, Craig adds, "But again the same objections obtain. 'Gossip' alone doesn't convince people of something as counter-intuitive as a resurrection, and certainly not if it is going to be something that reshapes a person's entire worldview, commitments, how they spend the rest of their lives, and how, in some instances as with some of the original apostles, they are willing to die for their faith."

I have several responses. First, I have never encountered the report-ed testimony of the disciples characterized as "gossip," a word choice

---

1. Michael Martin, *The Case Against Christianity* (Temple University Press, 1991), 90.

that trivializes the disciples' words. I'm unclear why Craig would denigrate the disciples' testimony this way. Second, if we are to trust the Gospel accounts, Jesus' disciples, in response to his teachings, had already abandoned their families to follow Jesus, to learn from his teachings, and to attain eternal reward in heaven. Jesus had promised them, "anyone who has left houses, or brothers or sisters, or father or mother, or children, or land for the sake of my name will be repaid many times over, and gain eternal life" (Matt. 19: 29). The extraordinary demands that Jesus made of his disciples is revealed in this incident: "Another man, one of his disciples, said to him, 'Lord, let me go and bury my father first.' Jesus replied, 'Follow me, and leave the dead to bury their dead'" (Matt. 8:21–22). Given how seriously ancient peoples, and Jews especially, viewed the obligations of the living to the dead, and especially dead family members, Jesus' words are shocking. These disciples had good reason to cling to anything that might support the truth of the resurrection; their belief in Jesus had already reshaped their lives.

Craig argues that words misheard could have contributed to the belief that Jesus had been resurrected only if it could be shown that words exist in the vocabulary of first-century Jerusalem that could be confused because of their similar sound. I think that this very specific confusion is necessary only for a comedy sketch; in my own experience I have often misheard statements, sometimes with comic consequences, but often times with momentary confusion the only consequence. As I age, these miscommunications happen more frequently.

Craig continues, "Another option Carl offers is the case of mistaken identity. At first glance this seems more promising than the previous two and could well be harder to disprove." But Craig seems to misread the point I am trying to make, which is not to prove anything. My contention is that because of the limitations of the evidence, it's impossible to either prove or disprove Jesus' resurrection. The most that I can accomplish is to show that natural causes for the resurrection belief are possible and plausible.

Craig's response to my argument that mistaken identity might have been a factor in the disciples' resurrection belief is, first, to concede that Jesus probably looked like many others: "Most first-century Jewish men

CARL STECHER • 111

wore beards, moustaches, and forelocks. Most had dark hair and dark skin. If Jesus were of average height and weight and if he and his disciples all wore simple, ground-length robes, it could well have been easy to confuse one of the others for Jesus." But, Craig continues, "Jerusalem may have had as few as 25,000–30,000 people when festivals were not in progress" and Jesus' disciples, having heard the reports of someone looking like Jesus being seen in Jerusalem, would have "moved heaven and earth, so to speak, to try to find him."

What Craig has claimed is true, but still misleading. Craig gives us the lowest estimates of the population of Jerusalem in the early first century; other modern estimates are for a city anywhere between 25,000 and 250,000.[2] Moreover, the festivals *were* in progress, and many scholars believe that at these times the population of Jerusalem at least doubled. So the potential Jesus' lookalikes could have numbered in the thousands, and many of these would have been strangers in Jerusalem for only a few weeks, not permanent residents. Besides, Jesus' disciples were terrified and in hiding, not wishing to share Jesus' fate. So Craig's conclusion that "sooner or later these disciples would have had to find out that it wasn't Jesus they had seen after all" is not realistic.

I am confused by Craig's response to my point that disciple rivalry might have been a factor in the resurrection belief. Craig first suggests that disciple rivalry, as reported in the Gospel accounts, might really have occurred later, reflecting late first-century rivalry between Peter's and John's followers rather than rivalry in 30 C.E. Craig then seems to waffle, apparently conceding my point. "But suppose that it also reflected a real rivalry between Peter and John during Jesus' lifetime. Synoptic sayings certainly allude to such competition among various disciples, including James and John versus all the rest" (Mark 10:35–41).

In responding to my inclusion of grief hallucinations as another plausible explanation for the resurrection belief, Craig refers to Gary Habermas' analysis. In Craig's words, "But the one very consistent feature throughout all the otherwise diverse reports [of a miracle] is that *there is some location*, some physical object, often a statue of a revered

---

2. Hershel Shanks, "Ancient Jerusalem: The Village, the Town, the City," *Biblical Archaeology Review*, May/June 2016.

person," in other words, "something tangible that can be identified as the place where these visions, appearances, or hallucinations occur" and "that is why *such shrines often spawn pilgrimages of the faithful* who come to those locations in hopes of a similar experience" (my italics).

And yet proponents of Jesus' resurrection, including Craig, often argue that first-century disciples of Jesus did not treat Jesus' tomb as a sacred place to be venerated, and that this is evidence that the tomb was discovered to be empty! But this argument defies common sense, predictable human behavior, and *Craig's words in the previous paragraph.* Surely if there had been an empty tomb, briefly occupied by the crucified Jesus, the site of this event, in the Christian view the most consequential in the history of the world and the foundational belief of the new faith, would have become the most sacred place on earth where true believers would gather, saying, "Here's the table upon which the broken body of our savior was laid, and here's the stone door to Jesus' tomb which the angels rolled open, not so Jesus could leave the tomb—Jesus not needing such assistance—but so that we could see the location of his miraculous resurrection." That nothing like this happened is powerful evidence that the empty tomb was legend, not history.

Craig next lists all the reported sightings of Jesus at various locations, noting in passing that "the disciples were cowering behind locked doors, understandably fearful for their own lives after Jesus' crucifixion." In doing so, Craig underlines why it is women who are credited with discovering the empty tomb: it was too widely known that Jesus' male disciples were, in Craig's words, "cowering behind locked doors." But this would also have made it very difficult to find Jesus' *Doppelgänger.*

Craig also comments on the limited evidence about Jesus' supposed resurrection: "[T]here are in fact remarkably few first-century sources that address topics that have anything to do with first-century prophetic or rabbinic figures in Israel to begin with. Those that do are largely in the New Testament or the writings of Josephus, which do refer to Jesus' resurrection. So this line of inquiry actually works in favor of the resurrection, not against it." Here Craig and I agree about the scarcity of evidence for Jesus' resurrection, but differ in interpreting its significance. I would argue that, whatever the *cause* of the very limited evidence, this does nothing to improve the *fact* of this limitation nor the consequent inability to know the *truth* in the scant existing and often contradictory evidence. I should also note that Josephus' discussion of Jesus is widely identified to be a Christian forgery.

Craig rejects my various possible natural explanations for the resurrection belief, holding that I would also "need to explain in detail how matters would have unfolded in order to have completely fooled so many people without the truth having ever been discovered." But Craig again misses my point: this is impossible because the evidence is insufficient and conflicting. I can speculate, as I sometimes have, but I cannot know, and given the insufficiencies of the evidence, I don't think Craig can either. Which is not to say that Craig cannot believe quite other than I do, and for Craig perhaps to believe is also to know.

Craig comments on my creation of an imaginary rabbi in our own day with two witnesses no longer available for interrogation. Craig is correct in inferring that I was thinking of Peter and James in the first century and is also correct in reminding me that both were probably still alive when Paul wrote 1 Corinthians. I thank Craig for this correction. But I stand by my larger point: the claim that any of these supposed five hundred could be interrogated to confirm that alleged appearance is completely unrealistic. Corinth is eight hundred miles from Jerusalem; Paul does not indicate where this alleged appearance to five hundred some twenty years previously had happened; he does not name a single one of the five hundred supposed witnesses. In addition to Michael Martin's previously cited assessment of why the claim of five hundred witnesses is extremely unlikely, I am going to quote Craig's own claim, italicizing key words:

> We know that Peter himself *most probably* had been in Corinth . . . because that is the *likely reason* for why some there *claimed* to belong to a faction or party that followed him. He would not settle down in Rome until 60, since he *appears* to have been evangelizing the western and central parts of what is Turkey today (based on the provinces greeted in 1 Peter). So there was *a good chance* he would have been in Corinth again in the late 50s for people to question.

Craig is here drawing inferences based upon speculations, never the best way of determining the truth.

Craig writes that Paul had a different experience than Jesus' disciples had: to the disciples, "he appeared in bodily form, walked on the ground, could be touched, ate food, and so on. To Paul, he appeared in a heavenly vision." And yet Paul used the same verb in relating his own experience and the other disciples' encounters, translated in every Bible I have consulted as "appeared." Craig has a mastery of ancient Greek, the language of Paul and of the New Testament; my question is did Paul's Greek have only one all-purpose verb for the activity in question? Unless this is the case, Paul is equating his experience with that of the other witnesses. His testimony, then, suggests that all the appearances were visions, even though *the much later* Gospel accounts suggest encounters with a reanimated physical body.

I have also questioned why the ascension occurs in only one account, Acts 1:6–11. Craig responds, "The reason the ascension doesn't appear in multiple writers may be as simple as observing that only one of the New Testament Gospel writers wrote a sequel." Aside from labeling the ascension as a "sequel," I view this as a nonanswer. I think Craig inadvertently comes closer to the truth with the first sentence in his paragraph: "Third, Carl raises questions about *the ascension, which completes the story of Jesus' resurrection*" (my italics). To rephrase my original question, why do all the New Testament writers except Luke leave the resurrection stories incomplete? Given the cosmic significance of this alleged event, the fact of Jesus' last words on earth, the spectacular nature of his departure, and that the original Gospel readers were unlikely to have more than one account of Jesus' resurrection, I can't imagine that Mark, Matthew, and John would fail to complete the story—*if they knew this story of the ascension at all.*

As to my query why the resuscitation of Lazarus appears only in John, written decades after the other Gospels, Craig answers, "only John . . . narrates that Jesus regularly headed up to Jerusalem from Galilee at the time of the major annual festivals . . . But the resurrection of Lazarus occurs on Jesus' *second-to-last* trip to Jerusalem, so it simply does not fit in the already chosen outlines of the Synoptic Gospel writers." But the story of Lazarus, true or not, is so much more memorable than the stories of Jairus' daughter and the son of the widow in Nain, the other occasions when Jesus was said to have brought back someone from the dead, that it's hard to credit that the authors of Mark, Matthew, and Luke would have failed to relate this story of Lazarus—*unless the story had not been invented before they wrote their Gospels.* That all these authors would have left this story untold because it happened on the wrong trip to Jerusalem, while they have not at any point indicated that they had taken the considerable liberty of telescoping the three trips into one, seems highly improbable.

As to the question of why the story of "doubting" Thomas is found only in John, Craig writes, "the Fourth Gospel was written so that people might believe that Jesus was the Christ and the Son of God." Craig and I have already agreed that many of those on the scene and in the best position to judge did not come to believe that Jesus was "the Christ and the Son of God." Part of the problem probably was that with Jesus and his first disciples, all first-century Jews, the Gospel accounts of Jesus were not in accord with Jewish expectations, which were for a human representative of God, a great warrior king who would defeat the occupying Romans and establish God's Kingdom on earth, with Jerusalem as its capital and the Messiah as its king. But again, this didn't happen.

It should be remembered that in the first century, unlike in later centuries when the canon had been established, the New Testament as such did not exist. The Gospel authors were writing for audiences that were very unlikely to have multiple accounts of the Jesus story. There's no reason to think that lacking the story of the ascension as related by Luke and only by Luke, first-century Jews and Gentiles who had access to Mark's account, *or* Matthew's *or* John's, would also have access to the Gospel according to Luke or Acts. This first-century situation puts me in mind of Paul Harvey, who years ago had a syndicated radio program that most people of my generation will remember. Harvey was a storyteller, recounting familiar lore from American history, but with a great deal of new and colorful information. At the end of each broadcast, Harvey would sign off, "And now you know—the rest of the story." But for the first-century Christians, who probably had access to only one Gospel, the Gospel written for their community, there was no first-century Paul Harvey to tell them "the rest of the story."

Craig next attempts to answer my question of how the Gospel writers could have learned about conversations between Pilate and Jesus with none of Jesus' followers present. Craig speculates that "it is highly unlikely that any Roman governor would ever be left alone with an accused criminal; other guards would have been present . . . who knows what other acquaintances he might have had among the Roman guard?" Again, this is pure speculation without any evidence. Perhaps I have been too influenced by the movie versions, but I have always pictured Pilate in armor—including a sword—that would identify his rank. Jesus, by contrast, would have had his hands tied. Literally. And we have to remember that this encounter between Jesus and Pilate happened some sixty-plus years *before* John tells the tale. Do we really believe that a Roman soldier survived for six decades, hanging around for twenty years after the Romans destroyed Jerusalem and the magnificent Temple so that he could tell any Christians who had survived and who still lived in Jerusalem how he had overheard the words that passed between Pilate and Jesus?

Craig continues, "Carl's claim that there is no 'method for differentiating the historical from the legendary and fictional elements' in the resurrection accounts is simply false . . . The Institute of Biblical Research's historical Jesus study group, for example, spent an entire decade investigating twelve key events from the Synoptic Gospels and applying the most currently accepted criteria, concluding that in each instance a strong case can be made for historicity." But it would be a shock if this institute had come to any other conclusion. To quote from its Web site: "Our confessional basis to which the Fellows, Associates, Friends and Student Members agree is . . . The unique divine inspiration, integrity, and authority of the Bible . . . The deity of our Lord Jesus Christ . . . The historical fact of his bodily resurrection." In other words, the conclusions found after twelve years of study match exactly the beliefs that members had to attest to in order to become members of the institute and its study group. This unfortunately undermines the credibility of the study and its study group in the first place.

Craig's next point is that the various Gospel accounts of the resurrection are not contradictory; there are many harmonizations. "John Wenham's entire little book, *Easter Enigma*, shows one plausible way that all the information can fit together into a sensible sequence." But I've read Wenham's little book and it does not live up to this claim. Wenham examines the crucial passages in which the empty tomb is discovered by the women and reported to the male disciples who are terrified (not without reason) and in hiding. But instead of showing how they are all in accord, Wenham composes a composite speech combining the two accounts of what the angel tells the women at the tomb. This angelic pronouncement ends: "Go quickly, tell his disciples (and Peter) that he is raised from the dead and is going before you and into Galilee. You will see him there, as he said." But this composite speech glosses over the actual words the women hear at the tomb. Wenham just omits the account in John, which is very different. In John's account, the only words the two angels say is a question that they ask Mary of Magdala, who is alone: "Why are you weeping?" The angels promptly disappear, replaced by Jesus who gives Mary instructions to tell the disciples that he is ascending to his Father. In Luke, by contrast, "two men in dazzling garments" remind the women that Jesus had told them that He would rise up on the third day; it's clear that Jesus makes no tomb-side appearance in Luke's account. Wenham's purported harmonization might hide these contradictions, but it cannot eliminate them.

Likewise, Craig's paragraph of explanation *similarly* glosses over significant contradictions in the Gospel accounts. For example, Craig writes, "*If* Jesus did spend considerable time with his disciples over a forty-day period after the resurrection teaching them . . ." (Acts 1:3; my emphasis). But there is no hint of this in Paul's epistles or in the accounts of the resurrection in Mark, Matthew, or John. I find similar problems with Craig's own harmonization in his paragraph beginning, "This much, however, seems clear." The best way of illustrating this is to quote Craig's account of what happened on Easter morning sentence-by-sentence, noting the problems as they appear: "A group of women went to the tomb" (in John, Mary alone goes to the tomb); "They announced that Jesus was risen" (in John, the angels only ask

Mary, "Why are you weeping?"); "They told them to tell his male disciples to go ahead to Galilee and there they would see him" (not in Luke or John); "The women left trembling, afraid, and silent" (only in Mark); "En route, Jesus appeared to some of them as well" (not in Luke, Mark, or John; Craig leaves this undefined—"en route" to where? By "some of them" is Craig referring to women or to Jesus' male disciples?); "Peter and John rush to the tomb, find the grave empty, and leave again" (not in Luke, Mark, or John); "Mary Magdalene returns with them, lingers, and has an encounter with Jesus in the garden" (all of this is only in John).

Craig writes, "In terms of hearing a heavenly voice, the disciples would hardly have been the first in the history of the world to have had an experience with an unknown voice they had reason to believe belonged to God." Craig then relates an experience reported to him by his mother, who, as she prepared to take out the trash, "heard a voice in her kitchen . . . telling her first to take her cane and then to take her cell phone." He continues, "Black ice that she could not see from the house made both essential as she wound up calling a neighbor for help when she felt 'trapped' by the ice and unable to walk safely back to the house . . . She just calmly assumed it was God talking and followed the instructions that probably saved her from a serious fall with no way to get help." I have never had an experience similar to Craig's mother's. Nor has any family member or friend related such an experience to me. But I do have an experience that might help put this in perspective.

Several years ago my wife and I came across a complete DVD edition of the television drama *NYPD Blue*, a gritty, award-winning series; it struck us as very realistic, often painfully so. In one segment the son of the principal character, Andy Sipowicz, was killed when he intervened in an attempted holdup. Several episodes later, Sipowicz encountered his murdered son and conversed with him. I was dismayed by this turn of events because to me it violated the verisimilitude of what was otherwise a very realistic program. It was only some years later that I discovered in my studies that perceived encounters between the living and the dead are very common; many undoubtedly sane people have had such experiences. The conclusion of the academic studies of this phenomenon is not that the dead return to us, but that the human mind plays strange tricks, which could include a conversation with a recently deceased family member, or, in the experience of his mother that Craig cites, "hearing" the voice of God—these are normal, common experiences and understandable without any supernatural explanation.

Craig continues his account of Jesus' appearances following his execution, concluding, "Finally, when the disciples were next in the vicinity of Jerusalem, he appeared to them at the Mount of Olives and ascended to heaven." The actual passage in Acts reads:

> To these men he showed himself after his death and gave ample proof that he was alive; he was seen by them over a period of forty days and spoke to them about the kingdom of God. While he was in their company he directed them not to leave Jerusalem . . . When they were all together, they asked him, 'Lord, is this the time at which you are to restore sovereignty to Israel? He answered, 'It is not for you to know about dates or times which the Father has set within his own control . . . After he had said this, he was lifted up before their very eyes, and a cloud took him from their sight. They were gazing intently into the sky as he went, and all at once there stood beside them two men robed in white, who said, 'Men of Galilee, why stand there looking up into the sky? This Jesus who has been taken from you up to heaven will come back in the same way as you have seen him go.'" (Acts 1:3–11)

Craig does not make clear how literally we are to take this. N. T. Wright, in his massive *The Resurrection of the Son of God,* wrote:

> We may remind ourselves at this point of two basic rules for modern readers reading ancient Jewish texts. First, two decker language about a 'heaven' in the sky above the earth almost certainly did not betoken a two-decker, let alone a three-decker, cosmology . . . Jews were comfortable with the language of heavenly ascent without supposing that their god . . . was physically situated a few thousand feet above the surface of the earth . . . To speak of someone 'going up to heaven' by no means implied that the person concerned had (a) become a primitive space traveler and (b)

arrived, by that means, at a different location within the present space-time universe.[3]

But having stated on his own authority and without any evidence what first-century Jews did *not* believe, Wright does nothing to explain what they *did* believe.

Whatever Wright believes, I'm under the strong impression that tens of millions of American Christians believe that when good Christians die they go to heaven, which is somewhere "up there." I frequently hear such Christians speaking about departed loved ones, that they are looking down at us, enjoying our triumphs, waiting for us to join them. I recall that when the Red Sox won their first World Series in almost one hundred years, some of their fans expressed gratification that a loved one in heaven must be overjoyed. Wright provides no evidence that first-century Jews were more sophisticated about the cosmos than twenty-first century American evangelical Christians.

Is it Craig's belief that when the Gospels say that God's voice came down from heaven, as it did both when Jesus was baptized and in this transfiguration event, anyone who was there and listening would have heard God's voice? And that Jesus literally ascended up into the sky until he disappeared into a cloud? If not, what actually happened? Craig writes, "Just because one finds certain supernatural stories embedded within a larger historical account does not destroy those narratives' value in terms of the natural events they recount." Does this apply to the story in Acts of Jesus' ascension? Does Craig believe that any of the accounts of miracles in the Bible, and especially the New Testament, are not to be taken as literal and historical truth?

Craig also writes, "the miracles in the canonical Gospels consistently function to bolster Jesus' claims to have inaugurated the kingdom of God." Does this mean that we are now living in the kingdom of God, as has been the case for Christians for the past two thousand years? Or perhaps that Christian believers are living in God's kingdom, but, because I am not a Christian believer, I am not? Were the Jerusalem Jews

---

3. Wright, *Resurrection* (Fortress Press, 2004), 655.

(aside from the adherents of the new Christian faith) also living in the newly inaugurated kingdom of God when the Romans, with their superior legions, were defeating their uprising and destroying their capital city and sacred Temple? If the kingdom of God was inaugurated two thousand years ago, is there any expectation that things will ever be any better in this earthly life?

Near the end of his chapter critically examining the case I made against the resurrection as history, Craig expressed his interpretation of the underlying problem that I have with the idea that Jesus was resurrected by God: "There can't be an all-powerful and all-loving God because of the amount of evil in the universe. If there is no God, then there are no miracles. If there are no miracles, there is no resurrection." Craig is correct, although this has not been part of my argument. I do think this. Millions of Christians believe in a God who is supposedly everywhere, all-powerful, loving of all his children, and morally perfect. Given the disasters that so beset humanity, Christian and non-Christian alike, I cannot share this belief.

PART THREE: THE CASE FOR JESUS'
RESURRECTION AS A FACT OF HISTORY

A Positive Case for the Resurrection

Craig Blomberg, Ph.D.

The New Testament accounts of the resurrection of Jesus of Nazareth in the first century C.E. have provoked vigorous controversy and debate ever since they were first penned. Saul of Tarsus, the Pharisaic Jew and arch-persecutor of the fledgling church comprised of Jesus' followers, identifies the resurrected Jesus' appearance to him as the cause of a dramatic about-face in his religious understanding (Galatians 1:11–16). Throughout the first century, many Jews, Greeks, and Romans likewise turned from their previous religious affiliations to become "Christians," at least in significant part due to their conviction that Jesus was indeed raised from the dead, which would thereby vindicate the claims he made during his life to be a heaven-sent, divinely accredited spokesman for Yahweh, God of Israel, who was revealing the very will and nature of Yahweh himself.[1]

The majority of those in the first century who heard the stories about Jesus and his resurrection, however, did not become believers. Long before the advent of what we would call modern science, people in every culture and location on the planet knew that dead people stayed

---

1. Of the 45 earliest sources for the life of Jesus, in both non-Christian and Christian circles, "18 specifically record the resurrection, while an additional eleven more provide relevant facts surrounding this occurrence." Gary R. Habermas, *The Historical Jesus: Ancient Evidence for the Life of Christ* (College Press, 1996), 253.

dead. Of course, there were the very occasional examples of people having been pronounced dead prematurely, who revived and continued to live on. But they all eventually died and remained that way. On the other hand, ancient Israel, like many of the cultures of the Ancient Near East, believed in the bodily resurrection of people to various forms of unending life sometime in the unknown future, beyond life as we know it now.[2] By the first century, however, Judaism was the only major religious perspective in the Mediterranean World that still held to this conviction (and even their small, aristocratic, and priestly leadership group known as the Sadducees questioned this). To be sure, many different groups and perspectives throughout the first-century Roman Empire believed in life after death in some disembodied fashion—the immortality of the soul—without any bodily resurrection. And occasionally, there were stories about people seeing ghostlike figures ascend to the heavens after the death of someone deemed to be particularly great, or of gods very ephemerally appearing on earth and interacting with mortals.[3]

But the early Christian accounts are unique in that they ascribe a physical, bodily resurrection to a person known to have lived as a real human being within the lifetime of most of his first followers, many of whom personally knew him. No Roman apotheosis, no Greek myth, and no Jewish belief about the end of the ages has a true parallel to this combination of elements. Nor, for that matter, does any other religion or ideology in the history of the world. The accounts that even partially parallel the Christian resurrection stories all originated many centuries after the lifetimes of the people they depict, and in many instances one is unsure if the people in them ever lived real, human lives at all.[4]

---

2. Murray J. Harris, *From Grave to Glory: Resurrection in the New Testament* (Zondervan, 1990), 31–43.

3. Paul Fullmer, *Resurrection in Mark's Literary-Historical Perspective* (T & T Clark, 2007), 58–93.

4. See the surveys in Richard N. Longenecker, ed., *Life in the Face of Death: The Resurrection Message of the New Testament* (Eerdmans, 1998), 21–95; and N. T. Wright, *The Resurrection of the Son of God* (SPCK; Fortress, 2003), 32–206. Cf. more broadly, Gary R. Habermas, "Resurrection Claims in Non-

How then did the New Testament accounts of the resurrection of Jesus first emerge? One may still hear Christian apologists setting up and knocking down largely straw figures, views that almost no bona fide scholars of the Bible or biblical world hold. For example, once in a while someone has imagined that the belief in the empty tomb came about because the first individuals who testified to it—grieving women—went to the wrong tomb and the others followed their lead. But surely someone, including Jesus' opponents, would then simply have produced the correct tomb and identified the coffin and the corpse. Or perhaps the disciples stole the body and hid it and then went around announcing that he was raised from the dead as he had predicted. But then the entire movement would have been based on a known lie, at least to its originators. More importantly, neither of these perspectives explains the accounts of hundreds of people seeing Jesus alive again (1 Corinthians 15:6). No doubt the most incredible of all of these fanciful alternatives is the swoon theory, popularized by Hugh Schonfield in the mid-1960s,[5] that Jesus never actually died on the cross, but recovered in the cool, moist air of the (walk-in) tomb, rolled the huge stone sealing it away, and convinced his followers on multiple occasions over the next forty days that he was not only alive again but healthier than he had ever been, only to then disappear never to be seen again. The obvious, multiple fallacies for anyone familiar with the New Testament accounts are too glaring and numerous even to bother mentioning them here.[6]

But these are not the common scholarly alternatives to the resurrection. The old history-of-religions approach is still popular in some circles, as scholars comb ancient literature still looking for parallels that *are* close enough to the biblical stories to be credible possible sources for the apostle Paul and the Gospel writers.[7] The original history-of-

---

Christian Religions," *Journal of Religious Studies* 25 (1989): 167–77.

5. Hugh Schonfield, *The Passover Plot*, 40th anniversary ed. (Disinformation Co., 2005).

6. But, if they are needed, see George E. Ladd, *I Believe in the Resurrection of Jesus* (Eerdmans, 1975), 134-36.

7. See esp. the continuing monograph series, *Religionsgeschichtliche Versuche und Vorarbeiten* (de Gruyter). At least some of the volumes are now

religions movement arose in the late nineteenth and early twentieth centuries, particularly in Germany, as anti-Semitism was rapidly growing there and elsewhere in Europe. This was the age in which more than one author promoted an Aryan Jesus, to try to "purge" the New Testament of anything that was both positive and Jewish. If key aspects of Jesus' life and ministry could be derived from Greco-Roman beliefs and practices, then one could embrace a form of Christianity that did not have to acknowledge any indebtedness to Judaism.[8] A classic example was the idea that baptism and the Lord's Supper were developments from purification rites and table-fellowship meals in the Greco-Roman mystery religions. The trouble was that even as scholars highlighted partial parallels in the pagan world of antiquity, the far clearer parallels and direct New Testament statements of derivation from Judaism were summarily ignored.[9]

Sometimes supposed parallels in the Greco-Roman world were highlighted, not necessarily in contrast to Jewish parallels, but just because they seemed to be the closest. After World War II, a generation of scholars became enamored with explaining Jesus' incarnation and resurrection/ascension as derived from a so-called Gnostic redeemer myth.[10] Gnosticism was a collection of sects that reached its heyday in the second and third centuries C.E. sympathetic to a neo-Platonic cosmology, in which the material world was inherently evil. In Gnostic creation stories, an emanation from the original Godhead rebelled by creating the universe. Unlike Genesis, therefore, creation was wicked

---

appearing in English as well. For example, see Richard L. Gordon, *Beyond Priesthood: Religious Entrepreneurs and Innovators in the Roman Empire* (2017).

8. Susannah Heschel, *The Aryan Jesus: Christian Theologians and the Bible in Nazi Germany* (Princeton University Press, 2008), 58–64, 202–3.

9. For baptism, see esp. Everett Ferguson, *Baptism in the Early Church: History, Theology, and Liturgy in the First Five Centuries* (Eerdmans, 2009), 25–96. For the Lord's Supper, cf. I. Howard Marshall, *Last Supper and Lord's Supper* (Paternoster; Eerdmans, 1980), 13–29.

10. Reaching its zenith in Rudolf Bultmann, *The Gospel of John: A Commentary* (Basil Blackwell; Westminster, 1971).

from the outset. A redeemer needed to descend from the Godhead to save humanity. This redeemer was *Sophia*, or Wisdom. Redemption or salvation for the Gnostic, therefore, did not occur because God offered himself, in his Son, as a sacrifice for sin, making forgiveness available to all who would accept it and serve him, as in first-century Christian writings. Instead, it came about through the esoteric knowledge imparted by a particular Gnostic sect. It also required a person to fan into flame the spark of divinity that resided within every human soul. Salvation for the Gnostic meant the ability to transcend one's corporeal nature already now in this life and to look forward to disembodied immortality, freed from the fetters of the material forever in the life to come.[11]

Because the fullness of the Godhead, to use Gnostic language, still contains Wisdom as a divine emanation, *Sophia* must have returned to her source after she had finished her work. Indeed, immortality more generally could be referred to as the ascent of the soul. It was a short step from this conglomeration of beliefs to announce the existence and even centrality of a Gnostic redeemer myth and, for those enamored with the history-of-religions approach to Christian origins, to declare the accounts of Jesus' resurrection to have borrowed and modified Gnostic mythology. After a while, however, clearer thinking prevailed. It was observed that there was no existing text, among the plethora of Gnostic literature, to which one could turn and read this story as I have just narrated it. It came from one possible synthesis of disparate texts, supplemented by various assumptions about how to fill in gaps that remained.[12] Some of the reconstructed myth was secure enough, such as the evil of the material world leading to the rejection of the resurrection of the body. But the weakest link was the claim that there were any close parallels to the accounts of Jesus' resurrection. Moreover, even what partial parallels existed were all second- and third-century in origin, so that if anyone borrowed from anyone else, Gnosticism would have had

---

11. For a good introduction to Gnosticism, see Riemer Roukema, *Jesus, Gnosis and Dogma* (T & T Clark, 2010). For several Gnostic approaches to resurrection, see pp. 102–10.

12. Edwin M. Yamauchi, *Pre-Christian Gnosticism: A Survey of the Proposed Evidences*, 2nd ed. (Baker, 1983), 163–70.

to have borrowed from and then modified apostolic Christianity and not the other way around.[13]

Today, Mithraism has replaced Gnosticism in a few scholarly and numerous popular circles as the preferred supposed origin of Christian resurrection (and numerous other things).[14] Mithraism was a Roman mystery religion that rivaled Christianity in popularity in the late third and early fourth centuries C.E. Comprised exclusively of men, many of them retired soldiers, Mithraic rites involved codes of honor and purity practices to prepare its members for war. It is extraordinarily difficult to know what exactly Mithraism taught because, by design, its members were to keep its practices and beliefs secret. Most of our information about it comes from the art and architecture of its shrines as well as from the discovery of a Mithraic "liturgy," although we have no way of knowing how representative it was. What we do know is that Mithras was a god consistently depicted as a bull slayer. He was born out of a rock and the offspring of Isis and Osiris, mythological gods associated with the change of the seasons. Isis had killed her husband, Osiris, and cut his corpse into twelve pieces, consigning them to the underworld. But, at the end of every winter, Osiris was "resurrected," meaning that the pieces of his body were reassembled, in conjunction with spring and the renewed fertility of the earth. But he never left the underworld. Each fall he was killed and dissected again, accounting for winter, until the cycle recurred.[15] One could scarcely guess that this was the "close parallel" to Jesus' resurrection touted by its supporters. Other "parallels" need not detain us, except to say that again when they actually are at all close to Christian practices, we discover they are all post-Christian in origin.[16] So they cannot be the source of the birth of Christianity or of belief in Jesus' resurrection.

---

13. Ibid., 187–249.

14. See esp. Michael Patella, *Lord of the Cosmos: Mithras, Paul, and the Gospel of Mark* (T & T Clark, 2006).

15. Cf. Jack Finegan, *Myth and Mystery: An Introduction to the Pagan Religions of the Biblical World* (Baker, 1989), 203–12.

16. Ronald H. Nash, The Gospel and the Greeks: *Did the New Testament Borrow from Pagan Thought?* rev. ed. (P & R, 2003), 133–38.

The most common and credible alternatives to belief in the bodily resurrection of Jesus in New Testament scholarship today, therefore, involve some kind of "subjective visions" hypothesis, whereby Jesus' first followers genuinely believed they had experienced Jesus raised from the dead, even though in reality they had not.[17] Often times this is combined with an "evolutionary" hypothesis that argues that Jesus' earliest followers saw him merely as a good Jewish rabbi who was tragically martyred. Little by little as his message was spread outside of Jewish territory, it was amalgamated with various Greco-Roman ideas. Those who had followed him slowly began to worship him and ascribe to him loftier and loftier titles. Not until the writings ascribed to John, however, at the very end of the first century or perhaps the beginning of the second century, does full-blown belief in Jesus' divinity emerge. By this time the gospel had become completely Hellenized and the resurrection accounts corresponded to Greco-Roman apotheoses of divine men. What began as Palestinian Jewish Christianity later became Hellenistic Jewish Christianity and finally Hellenistic Gentile Christianity. Maurice Casey aptly epitomized this approach in the title of one of his books, *From Jewish Prophet to Gentile God.*[18]

The edifice of this approach has more recently begun to crumble as well. It is now widely agreed that there was no standard "divine man" portrait in Greco-Roman thought for anyone to borrow.[19] Nor was there anything remotely resembling a linear development of early Christian theology in discrete phases.[20] Most strikingly of all, across all the earliest of the clearly datable letters of the New Testament, and especially in the creeds or confessions of faith that predate them, one finds worship of Jesus. Even apart from contexts that actually ascribe titles to him, Jesus

---

17. A key pioneer of this approach was Willi Marxsen, *The Resurrection of Jesus of Nazareth* (Abingdon, 1969).

18. Subtitled *The Origins and Development of New Testament Christology* (Westminster John Knox, 1991).

19. See esp. Barry L. Blackburn, *Theios Anēr and the Markan Miracle Traditions* (J. C. B. Mohr, 1991).

20. See, e.g., Mark A. Powell and David R. Bauer, eds., *Who Do You Say That I Am?: Essays on Christology* (Westminster John Knox, 1999).

is venerated in manners the ancient Mediterranean world reserved for gods. Larry Hurtado is responsible for a number of seminal writings in this area, and he came to the conclusion that resurrection belief, like Christian origins more generally, was a "revolutionary" rather than an evolutionary hypothesis.[21]

This is the approach that is also taken by famous atheist historian Gerd Lüdemann in his multiple works on the resurrection, though without using this exact terminology.[22] Lüdemann's works are all the more important because he first makes the profoundly convincing case that the resurrection accounts of the New Testament are not late, slowly evolving myths or legends. He points out how Paul in 1 Corinthians 15:3–8 introduces what in Greek looks and reads very much like an early creed or confession of faith with its rhythmic, condensed, and tightly packed succession of clauses which Paul passed along to the Corinthians "first of all" (v. 3; KJV, ASV), or "as of first importance" (NIV, NRSV) or both, just as he had received it, presumably at the beginning of his Christian catechesis as well. The verbs used here for receiving and passing on, moreover, were often used somewhat technically for the reliable transmission of oral tradition.[23]

Lüdemann recognizes that combining biblical and extrabiblical chronology yields a date for Saul's conversion to within two or three years of Jesus' death (32 or 33 if we adopt the most commonly accepted date of 30 for the crucifixion). But Paul was first taught (as far as we know) by Ananias and other Christians in Damascus (Acts 9:10–19), a considerable distance from Jerusalem where the church began. So we

---

21. His largest and most significant work is Larry W. Hurtado, *Lord Jesus Christ: Devotion to Jesus in Earliest Christianity* (Eerdmans, 2003). The article that uses the terminology I have introduced here is his "The Gospel of Mark: Evolutionary or Revolutionary Document?" *Journal for the Study of the New Testament* 40 (1990): 15–32.

22. Gerd Lüdemann, *The Resurrection of Jesus: History, Experience, Theology* (Fortress, 1994); *What Really Happened to Jesus? A Historical Approach to the Resurrection* (Westminster John Knox, 1996); and *The Resurrection of Christ: A Historical Inquiry* (Prometheus, 2004).

23. Anthony C. Thiselton, *The First Epistle to the Corinthians* (Eerdmans, 2000), 1186–87.

must allow time for the first followers of Jesus to craft such a creed or confession, agree on its wording, determine that it was important to teach it to new believers as soon as possible, and then spread the word to other places to which Christians had traveled. The result for Lüdemann, therefore, is that the core testimony about Christ's resurrection that forms the heart of Paul's creed in 1 Corinthians 15 must have been formulated within a year or two at most, and maybe less, of Jesus' death. It arose in thoroughly Jewish soil and it is hard to explain as anything other than what Jesus' earliest disciples genuinely believed they experienced.[24]

Another way of coming at this same issue is to go back to our discussion of Gnosticism. It was scarcely unique to one given Greco-Roman form of religion to reject bodily resurrection. Although Stanley Porter has shown that there may have been some belief in it in a few pockets of Hellenistic thought,[25] it certainly would have remained the exception and not the rule. If Jesus had not been raised from the dead, and if belief in the resurrection did not first emerge until the gospel was securely ensconced in Greek and Roman territory, why would it have developed at all? All such belief accomplished was to make it *harder* for the gospel to be accepted outside of Jewish circles. Had Jesus been an Athenian and taught about the immortality of the soul, and had his followers spread out gradually from Greece, eventually landing in Israel two centuries later, one might imagine his story being recloaked in the clothing of a bodily resurrection. That would appeal to Jewish beliefs and expectations (see Daniel 12:1–4). But the trajectory of early Christianity developed in exactly the reverse direction from that which was needed to have made such a theory plausible.[26]

It is to Carl's credit that he opts for none of the approaches sur-

---

24. Lüdemann, *What Really Happened to Jesus*, 14–16.

25. Stanley E. Porter, "Resurrection, the Greeks and the New Testament," in *Resurrection*, ed. Stanley E. Porter, Michael A. Hayes, and David Tombs (Sheffield Academic Press, 1999), 52–81.

26. Cf. Peter G. Bolt, "Life, Death, and the Afterlife in the Greco-Roman World," in *Life in the Face of Death: The Resurrection Message of the New Testament* (Eerdmans, 1998), 51–79.

veyed thus far. I have already interacted with his specific proposals in my response earlier in this volume. But here I need to acknowledge that the greatest strength in his cluster of suggestions is that none of them requires a long period of time to have elapsed after Jesus' death before resurrection faith began. None of them appeals to development based on parallels that did not exist in Israel or that did not yet exist in the Mediterranean world. None of them requires the rejection of Jesus as a genuine figure of human history—a theory so improbable that it need not detain us here. Carl realizes this, just as he realizes that something most likely happened to Jesus' followers almost immediately after his death by Roman crucifixion to spark what would eventually come to be called Christian faith. Even if we still have significant disagreements, those are two very important points of agreement.

How then do we adjudicate among the remaining options? At this point the issue of preunderstanding, presuppositions, or worldviews looms large.[27] If one is an antisupernaturalist (or, more simply, just a naturalist), then one excludes the possibility of an actual bodily resurrection at the outset. No amount of dialogue, discussion, or debate can change that. Dead men don't rise. Everyone today knows this. Therefore, however we explain the rise of Christian faith, a literal physical resurrection is excluded *a priori*. We can debate the relative merits of the alternatives, but the historic Christian belief simply can't be the correct one. But how do we know that naturalism is true? The eighteenth-century Scotsman, David Hume, famously argued that we *don't* exclude the miraculous at the outset of any investigation; we simply observe that the case is always stronger for a nonmiraculous than for a miraculous explanation of some startling and inexplicable event. Put another way, the chance that all eyewitnesses to a seemingly supernatural event were deluded is always stronger than the case for an actual miracle. The probability that all independent reports of a spectacular event were distorted in transmission is always greater than the likelihood that a miracle hap-

---

27. On which, see William W. Klein, Craig L. Blomberg, and Robert L. Hubbard, Jr., *Introduction to Biblical Interpretation*, 3rd ed. (Zondervan, 2017), 210–43.

pened.[28] Hume is particularly notorious for his blatant racism in rejecting accounts coming back to his homeland, often via Christian mis-
sionaries, from Africans.[29] Hume also claimed that no one has sufficient
reason for believing in something that has no analogy in their personal
experience or in the experience of anyone they know. Already in the
eighteenth century, however, it was pointed out that by this logic no
person living in the tropics should ever believe in ice.[30]

Today, the presupposition of antisupernaturalism is often phrased
a little differently. Nothing may be admitted as genuinely existing, or
as having occurred, unless it can be demonstrated empirically or logically. But the truth of this presupposition is merely asserted; it is never
demonstrated either empirically or logically! Indeed, by its very nature
it cannot be. So the argument is solipsistic, that is, it forms a viciously
circular form of reasoning and therefore has no force. Only slightly different is the claim that unless something can be proven scientifically,
there are no rational grounds for believing it. But again this affirmation
itself cannot be proven scientifically. We are reminded that science is
not omnipotent and cannot be the final arbiter of reality.

Putting it still another way, from time to time individuals or cor-
porations have offered large sums of money to anyone who can successfully predict that an event without an existing scientific explanation (corresponding to their understanding of what people mean by a
"miracle") will occur at a certain time and place. Then they boast that
no one has ever claimed the money, thereby suggesting that miracles

---

28. David Hume, *Enquiry Concerning Human Understanding*, rev. & ed. Tom
L. Beauchamp (Clarendon; Oxford University Press, 2006), section 10.

29. Cf. Charles Taliafero and Anders Hendrickson, "Hume's Racism and His
Case against the Miraculous," *Philosophia Christi* 4 (2002): 219–26.

30. In addition, Richard Whatley in 1819 in a book entitled *Historic Doubts
Relative to Napoleon Buonaparte* applied Hume's method to a study of the
life of Napoleon, a unique individual in many ways, demonstrating by that
method that one has no reason to believe that most of the accounts of his
life are true, a conclusion that is patently absurd. The problem with Hume's
approach is that it excludes everything that is unique about a person, event,
location, or period of time. As the popular saying nicely puts it, "Everything is
unprecedented until the first time it happens!"

can't happen.[31] Even just a little bit of logic, nevertheless, discloses the fallacy here. By definition, a miracle is something unexpected and inexplicable. If one could predict when it would happen, one could analyze the forces that caused it and it would cease to be a miracle. Science is the study of the repeatable, preferably under laboratory conditions. If a miracle could be repeated by a formula of cause and effect, it would cease to be a miracle![32] Philosophers of science, often unlike scientific practitioners, are increasingly realizing this and making more modest claims about the domains of scientific investigation.[33]

The resurrection of Jesus is depicted in every ancient source in which it appears as something miraculous. If a person decides that under no conditions will they ever leave the door open even the slightest crack for the possibility of miracles, then no further conversation about the resurrection as a supernatural event makes any sense. We might as well end our chapter at this point. But leaving the door open does not commit one to believing in the resurrection, any more than belief in biblical miracles commits one to rejecting accounts of miracles in other religions or worldviews. All we are recommending is that people be willing to thoughtfully evaluate the evidence for every account on a case-by-case basis with as much objectivity as they can muster. If the door to the supernatural is not locked and bolted at this juncture, then a raft of additional arguments on behalf of the resurrection of Jesus merits consideration.

First, all four Gospels narrate their accounts of the resurrection by beginning with women as the first eyewitnesses (Matthew 28:1; Mark 16:1; Luke 24:10; John 20:1). No two Gospels give the identical list

---

31. Cf. "List of Prizes for Evidence of the Paranormal," Wikipedia, https://en.wikipedia.org/wiki/List_of_prizes_for_evidence_of_the_paranormal (accessed on August 25, 2017). Three dozen offers are listed!

32. Cf. Terence L. Nichols, "Miracles in Science and Theology," *Zygon* 37 (2002): 703.

33. See esp. Peter Medawar, *The Limits of Science* (Harper & Row, 1984; Oxford University Press, 1985). Cf. Noson F. Yanofsky, *The Outer Limits of Reason: What Science, Logic, and Mathematics Cannot Tell Us* (MIT Press, 2013), esp. 235–96 on metaphysical realities.

(though Mary Magdalene appears in all four), showing that the writers are not in collusion and possibly giving independent testimony at this point. But neither does anyone claim to provide an exhaustive list, so they are not contradictory. Matthew's Gospel mentions "Mary Magdalene and the other Mary." Mark tells us of "Mary Magdalene, Mary the mother of James and Salome." So now we know who the other Mary was. Probably this is the mother of the apostle referred to as James the younger, because Salome was the wife of Zebedee and mother of the more prominent James among the Twelve along with his brother, John. Luke itemizes "Mary Magdalene, Joanna, Mary the mother of James and the others with them," indicating that there was a group of at least five. If Salome was one of the "others" then all the accounts mesh even if none is comprehensive, at least in supplying names. Only John's Gospel mentions just one woman's name—Mary Magdalene. But when she reports to the disciples that the tomb was empty, she says, "we don't know where they have laid him," an odd use of the first-person plural if indeed she were alone. Given the standard ancient narrative practice of often referring only to one person who acted as a spokesperson for a group,[34] it is easy to envision Mary as having gone to and from the tomb with other companions. Claims of hopeless contradiction among the Gospel accounts concerning which women were present are considerably premature.

But if there were no empty tomb for anyone to discover and the Gospel writers simply invented the story, why would they all, seemingly independently of each other, make women the first and primary witnesses to the resurrection in a culture that often didn't allow women's testimony in a court of law?[35] The criterion of embarrassment is one of the standard criteria of authenticity in historical-Jesus research (and elsewhere among classical historians),[36] and the resurrection appear-

---

34. Michael R. Licona, *Why Are There Differences in the Gospels?: What We Can Learn from Ancient Biography* (Oxford University Press, 2017), 20. Licona calls this "spotlighting."

35. See Claudia Setzer, "Excellent Women: Female Witness to the Resurrection," *Journal of Biblical Literature* 116 (1997): 259–72.

36. For a full survey, see Stanley E. Porter, *The Criteria of Authenticity in*

ances to women are a classic case of something that seems too embarrassing for the credibility of the resurrection story in its original milieu to have been created. It is far more likely to be historical. Precisely because women were not perceived to be a threat to male authorities the way other men were,[37] they would have been allowed to stay near the cross, follow the soldiers who buried Jesus to see where the tomb was, and come early in the morning to provide the spices for his burial that Rome would not have given him, all precisely as the Gospels delineate (Matthew 27:56, 61; Mark 15:40–41, 47; Luke 24:55–56; John 19:25–27).

Second, why would Jewish Christians already within the first generation of the movement begin resting and worshipping on Sunday, the first day of the week, in direct violation of one of their ten most foundational commandments which prescribed the seventh day or Saturday as their holy day, unless something earth-shattering and objective enough to be datable to a Sunday morning had actually happened? 1 Corinthians 16:1–4 refers to laying up a sum of money weekly, on the first day of each week (i.e., Sunday), for the impoverished Christians in Jerusalem, so that Paul would not have to take up any collection when he arrived in Corinth. This must be a reference to Christian worship services on Sundays, because, if it were simply a command for believers to save something each week in their homes, a collection would still have been needed when Paul arrived.[38] And we know there were both Jewish and Gentile Christians in Corinth (1 Corinthians 1:12; cf. Acts 18:1–8). In Acts 20:7–12, Paul and Luke gather with the Christians in Troas on the first day of the week to break bread, a probable reference to the Lord's Supper as part of the early Christian worship service.[39] Paul teaches well into the night, because neither Jews nor Greeks had Sun-

---

Historical-Jesus Research: Previous Discussion and New Proposals (Sheffield Academic Press, 2000). On embarrassment, see pp. 106–10, and the literature there cited.

37. Kenneth E. Bailey, *Through Peasant Eyes: More Lucan Parables* (Eerdmans, 1980), 135.

38. Cf. Joseph A. Fitzmyer, *First Corinthians* (Yale University Press, 2008), 615.

39. Carl R. Holladay, *Acts: A Commentary* (Westminster John Knox, 2016), 390–91.

days off work. Meetings or services would have begun after dark. Here we are told nothing about the ethnic makeup of the assembly, but given Paul's consistent practice throughout Acts of going to gatherings of Jews first, before preaching to Gentiles (cf. also Rom. 1:16), it is probable that the converts were a mixture of Jew and Gentile in background. Finally, the Jewish author of Revelation speaks about being "in the Spirit" on "the Lord's day" (Rev. 1:10), an early reference to Sunday as a day of worship.[40]

From early church history we know this pattern continued. Christians, even Jewish ones, who insisted on continuing to worship on the Sabbath (Saturday) were called Judaizers (followers of Jesus who were overemphasizing the Jewish Law) and severely criticized.[41] It would not be until the fourth century when Christians would have a legal day of rest—on Sunday. Constantine, the first Christian emperor of Rome, would legalize the practice of Christianity and set aside Sunday as a day of rest, allowing adherents of multiple religions to worship at that time. For the preceding three centuries, Christians had to gather at their own peril. Even during the times when Rome was not officially persecuting them, they still had to carve out time after working a full day on Sunday (unless a local holiday happened to fall on that day). It does not seem likely that they would have created all this additional difficulty for themselves unless there was some fairly dramatic, objective, and foundational experience that actually occurred on a Sunday that they felt bound to commemorate on that day rather than any other day. A bodily resurrection, of course, would fit those criteria well, whereas it is much less clear that the alternatives to the resurrection suggested would do so.

Third, what led the original Jewish followers of Jesus to continue to revere him after his death when their own law declared that anyone hanged on a tree was cursed by God, and their own religious teachers had already determined that a crucifixion was similar enough to also

---

40. For more detail, see Craig L. Blomberg, "The Sabbath as Fulfilled in Christ," in *Perspectives on the Sabbath: 4 Views*, ed. Christopher J. Donato (B & H, 2011), 309–11, and the literature there cited.

41. Craig R. Koester, *Revelation* (Yale University Press, 2014), 243.

imply God's curse?[42] It is one thing to allow a new, charismatic leader to raise the anticipation of a messianic movement. Josephus, the Jewish historian who wrote in the late first century, describes a dozen or so such movements between the time of Judah the Galilean in 6 C.E. and the destruction of Jerusalem by Rome in 70.[43] In every case, small groups of revolutionaries were hoping to overthrow Rome so that Israel could again live independently in their land. The Gospels give numerous signs that the Jewish crowds hoped Jesus would be just such a messiah (cf. esp. John 6:15). But the longer his ministry progressed, the clearer it became that he had no interest in playing this role. The crowds became more and more disenchanted. Finally, the Sanhedrin convicted him on a trumped-up charge, phrased it in terms of sedition in order to interest the local Roman prefect, Pontius Pilate, and called for his crucifixion until Pilate finally acquiesced (Mark 14:55–65; 15:1–15 and parallels).

The very nature of this gruesome form of execution made it extremely discourteous even to talk about in public. It was a repulsive scourge that defiled the land of Israel in the eyes of law-abiding Jews. That Rome by 30 C.E. had crucified literally thousands of criminals and insurrectionists this way, at public crossroads as a deterrent to others, made Jesus' execution even more shameful than it was agonizing.[44] And all this was true even without recalling Deuteronomy 21:23, which includes the declaration that "anyone hung on a tree is under God's curse" (NRSV). Add in God's legal condemnation of such a victim, and it would have taken some spectacular event to convince Jesus' first followers to ignore all this and still declare him to be the Messiah and liberator of Israel. A bodily resurrection would do the trick, but it is hard to imagine what else could have provoked such a response.

How then did the first Christians handle Deuteronomy 21:23? The

---

42. See David W. Chapman, *Ancient Jewish and Christian Perceptions of Crucifixion* (Mohr Siebeck, 2008), 117–77.

43. Richard A. Horsley with John S. Hanson, *Bandits, Prophets, Messiahs*, rev. ed. (T & T Clark, 1999).

44. For full details, see Chapman, *Ancient Jewish and Christian Perceptions of Crucifixion*, esp. 43–96.

apostle Paul shows us in Galatians 3:13: "Christ redeemed us from the curse of the law by becoming a curse for us—for it is written, 'Cursed is everyone who hangs on a tree'" (NRSV). In other words, he was not cursed by God for his own sins but bore the punishment we deserved to suffer.[45] Whether one finds that response theologically satisfying is not the point here. It convinced enough of Jesus' first followers to keep the movement growing. But what prompted *anyone* in the years immediately after Jesus' horrific death even to look for such alternate explanations? A crucified messiah was foolishness to everyone in the first-century world (1 Corinthians 1:18–25).

Fourth, and closely related to this last point, why did the Jesus movement even survive much less thrive, when every other first-century messianic movement in Israel collapsed entirely after the death of its founder? One may make a comparison with al-Qaeda today. When Osama bin Laden was killed, the *theological* as well as practical reasons that led Muslims to support him vanished; he was not the apocalyptic figure in the chain of imams leading up to the end of the age that they had hoped he would be. ISIS became a plausible alternative in the minds of these Muslims only after al-Qaeda was discredited. Of course, the analogy to first-century revolutionary movements is only partial because al-Qaeda continues, even if in a much reduced and less theological role. But the point that transcends specific differences from one culture to the next is that few people want to follow defeated and executed freedom fighters, whether their quests are for physical or spiritual freedom. Something highly unusual must have occurred to make the Jesus-movement the lone first-century exception in Israel.

Fifth, to reuse the title of one of Hurtado's most recent works, "why on earth did *anyone* become a Christian in the first three centuries" of Christian history at all?[46] This was the era in which believers were frequently persecuted for their faith, had no power base, and had nothing to gain economically or socially but often much to lose. If the heart of

---

45. See further Douglas J. Moo, *Galatians* (Baker, 2013), 210–14.

46. Larry W. Hurtado, *Why on Earth Did Anyone Become a Christian in the First Three Centuries?* (Marquette University Press, 2016).

their message had been Jesus' teaching, one might reconstruct a plausible scenario. Various groups of people throughout history have tried to follow the ethical teachings of founders of religions even at significant personal cost. But the heart of the earliest Christian literature both inside and outside of the New Testament was not about Jesus' teachings. One can find scattered allusions to them in the letters of Paul, even though these letters predated the written form of the Gospels, showing that Paul was relying on oral tradition that was close in form to what was later written down by the four Evangelists.[47] But the overwhelming majority of the references to Jesus in the New Testament letters highlight his death and/or resurrection. Clearly this was the most important thing about the founder of Christianity in his followers' minds.

Paul's logic in 1 Corinthians 15:12–19 summarizes early Christian convictions powerfully:

> But if it is preached that Christ has been raised from the dead, how can some of you say that there is no resurrection of the dead? If there is no resurrection of the dead, then not even Christ has been raised. And if Christ has not been raised, our preaching is useless and so is your faith. More than that, we are then found to be false witnesses about God, for we have testified about God that he raised Christ from the dead. But he did not raise him if in fact the dead are not raised. For if the dead are not raised, then Christ has not been raised either. And if Christ has not been raised, your faith is futile; you are still in your sins. Then those also who have fallen asleep in Christ are lost. If only for this life we have hope in Christ, we are of all people most to be pitied. (NRSV)

The idea that liberal Christians have introduced over the last two hundred and some years, that Jesus is worth following as a great human teacher and leader even if he were not raised from the dead or the divine

---

47. For the full range of plausible references, see Craig L. Blomberg, "Quotations, Allusions, and Echoes of Jesus in Paul," *Studies in the Pauline Epistles: Festschrift for Douglas J. Moo*, ed. Matt Harmon and Jay Smith (Zondervan, 2014), 129–43.

Son of God,[48] would never have dawned on the first Christians. It was all or nothing. Either Jesus was God incarnate or he was irrelevant. There was no middle ground, as far as we can tell.

Sixth, 1 Corinthians 15 likewise discloses a relationship between the resurrection of one person and the resurrection of all people at the end of this current age of human existence, which is unparalleled in the history of religion. Judaism, as already noted, believed in the resurrection of all people, some to everlasting life and some to everlasting judgment, at the end of human history. Whether we are to take the account literally or metaphorically, that is what the enigmatic little passage about the resurrection of selected Old Testament "saints" in Matthew 27:52–53 is intended to teach.[49] Those who encountered the resurrected Jesus would have expected this to be the beginning of a quickly unfolding series of events that would usher in Judgment Day and the end of this old, sinful world. Within weeks, if not days, it would have become clear that this was precisely what was *not* happening. Indeed, if people had been listening to Jesus' teaching more carefully, they would have known that he never predicted the timing of his return, despite a few somewhat striking declarations that at first glance could sound like he was (Mark 9:1 and parallels; Mark 13:30 and parallels; and Matthew 10:23).[50] After all, it was Jesus who also said that no one knows the day or hour, not even he (Mark 13:32 and parallels), and that it was not for his followers to know the times or seasons of his coming (Acts 1:7). Even if the first of these two passages could be pedantically read as allowing for someone to know the week, month, or year, the second passage excludes any estimate of the time frame between Jesus' first and second comings, no matter what unit of temporal measurement one introduces.

---

48. Classically preserved and updated in the work of the Jesus Seminar in the 1990s and well expressed in Robert W. Funk, *Honest to Jesus: Jesus for a New Millennium* (HarperSanFrancisco, 1996).

49. For options, see Michael R. Licona, *The Resurrection of Jesus: A New Historiographical Approach* (IVP, 2010), 548–53.

50. See further Craig L. Blomberg, *The Historical Reliability of the New Testament: Countering the Challenges to Evangelical Christian Beliefs* (B & H, 2016), 93–94, and the literature there cited.

What this boils down to, then, is that the early church was insisting the last days of human history had begun, but they might continue indefinitely for any period of time, however short or long.[51] At least one man had been raised from the dead, but the general resurrection of all people had not occurred in conjunction with that one resurrection. Nothing in the Old Testament had predicted such a separation of resurrections, so where did the idea come from? The Greco-Roman world did not look for resurrection at all, with rare exceptions. The only logical alternative is that the concept actually came from the personal experience of the first followers of Jesus with their resurrected Lord.[52]

Seventh, the fact that the same Jewish and Roman authorities who authorized Jesus' crucifixion never produced a body or pointed people to the tomb where his corpse still lay, even as claims of resurrection began to circulate within days of his death, suggests that his tomb really was empty. 1 Corinthians 15:3b–4a stresses "that Christ died for our sins according to the Scriptures, that he was buried, [and] that he was raised on the third day according to the Scriptures." Why add that he was buried? The important truths for Paul were that Jesus' death provided atonement for humanity's sins and that his resurrection vindicated his ministry and foreshadowed his followers' resurrections. There was no need to give the burial special attention. If verses 3–7 form a pre-Pauline creed, hymn, or confession of faith, then the question becomes even more acute. Creeds or confessions are by nature succinct; one includes only the very most important material. The reason for including Jesus' burial in this ancient confession of faith now becomes apparent. The first-century Roman Empire was predominantly Gentile, so its inhabitants would have naturally thought of some spiritual, disembodied form of life after death. Paul, like the tradition he inherited, had to stress that he was talking about a bodily resurrection. Burial, *in this context*, implies an empty tomb once resurrection has come into view.[53]

---

51. As thoroughly demonstrated in A. L. Moore, *The Parousia in the New Testament* (Brill, 1966).

52. Cf. N. T. Wright, *What Saint Paul Really Said: Was Paul of Tarsus the Real Founder of Christianity?* (Eerdmans, 1997), 141.

53. William L. Craig, "The Empty Tomb of Jesus," in *Gospel Perspectives*, vol.

William Lane Craig has repeatedly demonstrated that the story of Joseph of Arimathea's allowing Jesus to be buried in Joseph's own unused tomb passes all the standard criteria of authenticity with flying colors.[54] It is narrated independently in both the Synoptic (Mark 15:42–47 and parallels) and Johannine traditions (John 19:38–42) and so satisfies the criterion of multiple attestation. It fits the double dissimilarity criterion by being distinctive from conventional Jewish expectation as well as from early Christian emphases. One would not have expected a secret disciple of Jesus serving on the Sanhedrin, so that it is not likely to have been invented by a *Jewish* Christian. And the only Gentile Christian document in which anything more is narrated about Joseph is the very late, sixth-century apocryphal Gospel of Nicodemus.[55] But the account of the burial also satisfies the criterion of Palestinian environment. It is the type of thing we could have expected to have happened in early first-century Israel. Any governor appointed to Judea was caught between a rock and a hard place. He had to show himself sufficiently loyal to Rome so as not to be deposed, or worse. But he also had to keep the peace among the Jews in the land, who had a reputation for rebelling at Roman offenses against their law. A proper burial, even for convicted criminals, was hugely important in ancient Israel; Rome would have had no reason not to grant Joseph's desire that Jesus' body be properly interred so that the land would not be defiled in Jewish eyes. We even have records of Roman rulers doing precisely this for other victims of execution.[56] The idea popularized by Dominic Crossan that Jesus' body would have been dumped in some shallow trough somewhere and left

---

2: *Studies of History and Tradition in the Four Gospels*, ed. R. T. France and David Wenham (JSOT Press, 1981), 173–200.

54. Beginning with William L. Craig, *Assessing the New Testament Evidence for the Historicity of the Resurrection of Jesus* (Edwin Mellen, 1989), 173–76.

55. Felix Scheidweiler, "The Gospel of Nicodemus: Acts of Pilate and Christ's Descent into Hell," in *New Testament Apocrypha*, vol. 1: *Gospels and Related Writings*, rev. ed. (James Clarke; Westminster John Knox, 1991), 501–36.

56. John G. Cook, *Crucifixion in the Mediterranean World* (Mohr Siebeck, 2014), 429 and n. 69.

to be eaten by dogs or wild animals is far less probable.[57]

Eighth, since Jesus would likely have been given a decent burial and various individuals could have guided people to the location of his tomb, the fact that none of the Jewish or Roman authorities hostile to the early Christian claims ever produced, claimed to produce, or even tried to produce a body to squelch the notion of Jesus' resurrection, is remarkable. Had they done so, the direction the Jesus movement would have taken, if it would have survived at all, would have been quite different. Even if evidence of their production of the body was lost or destroyed, which would explain why we have no record of it today, Christianity could scarcely have survived in the form that still claimed that Jesus was bodily resurrected.

Ninth, the accounts of the resurrection in the various Gospels are all remarkably restrained. The original ending of Mark (16:8) in the oldest and most reliable manuscripts concluded without an actual resurrection appearance of Jesus to anyone, only the prophecy by the young man at the tomb that Jesus' followers would see him.[58] Matthew, Luke, and John all do narrate a variety of those appearances but no one ever describes Jesus actually leaving the tomb. He just appears to people in other places. If the notion of Jesus' bodily resurrection were an invention, one would expect a description of someone actually seeing Jesus come out of the tomb and what that looked like. The late-second- or early-third-century apocryphal Gospel of Peter does precisely this. It narrates that the guards at the tomb saw two angels, whose heads touched the clouds, descend from heaven, move the stone, enter the tomb, and emerge again with Jesus in between them. His head rose above the clouds. All the time the vision of a cross followed them. Then a voice spoke from the cross asking if Christ had preached to those who were dead and he answered, "Yes" (Gospel of Peter 35–42)! When one

---

57. John Dominic Crossan, *The Historical Jesus: The Life of a Mediterranean Jewish Peasant* (HarperSanFrancisco, 1991), 216.

58. What have come to be called vv. 9–20 of Mark 16 are almost certainly later scribal additions. The other viable option if Mark did not originally intend to end at verse 8 is that his ending got "ripped off" the end of the scroll on which the Gospel was written and thus became lost.

compares this story with the canonical accounts, the differences far outweigh the similarities.[59]

What is also fascinating in the canonical accounts is how they independently depict Jesus as at first unrecognizable, only to have those who see him eventually reach a point of recognition. In Matthew, Jesus appears to the Eleven in Galilee, where some immediately worship him while others at first "doubted" (28:16–17). The only logical thing for them to doubt was that it was really Jesus, suggesting that he looked different enough that not everyone immediately recognized him.[60] In Luke, Jesus walks a long way with Cleopas and his unnamed companion on the road to Emmaus before they realize who he is as they eat dinner with him in town (Luke 24:15–35). Their comments made it clear they were distraught over Jesus' death and never expected to see him again. This probably also prevented them from recognizing him any sooner than they did. In John, Mary Magdalene thinks Jesus is the gardener until he speaks tenderly to her and she identifies him by his voice (John 20:11–17). Nothing is made theologically of any of these details, so they are not likely to have been invented. But a person restored to a glorious new life after a traumatic, agonizing death should look sufficiently distinct as to not be recognizable immediately.

A tenth and final point is quite different from these first nine because it involves modern events. David Hume had some legitimate concerns when he heard accounts of the miraculous from foreign countries that corresponded to nothing he or any other Scots had ever experienced or heard of in their world. But today we live in a global village. All manner of media make access to quantities of information (and misinformation, and the debunking of misinformation), that would have themselves seemed like science fiction throughout most of world history. Craig Keener's massive two-volume work on miracles documents literally hundreds of modern-day miracles from every continent on

---

59. David F. Wright, "Apocryphal Gospels: The 'Unknown Gospel' (Pap. Egerton 2) and the Gospel of Peter," in *Gospel Perspectives: The Jesus Tradition outside the Gospels*, vol. 5, ed. David Wenham (JSOT Press, 1985), 207–32.

60. Licona, *Resurrection of Jesus*, 358–66.

the planet and of every major category represented in the New Testament. By his own admission he has applied such stringent criteria to the accounts he has collected that he has probably omitted many more hundreds of genuine miracles simply because they were not sufficiently documented to satisfy his criteria.[61]

Keener supplements the brief references in his monograph to resurrections with a follow-up journal article, in which he highlights some of the best-documented modern-day resurrections.[62] Of course, this is somewhat of a misnomer; all these people will go on to die again in later years. Some prefer, therefore, to speak of them as revivifications, reawakenings, or reanimations. But the nomenclature is unimportant. The point is that people whose bodies should have started to decay have remained without vital signs for hours on end and then been brought back to life, sometimes through medical procedures and sometimes through concerted Christian public prayer (or both). Hume's criterion for at least a partial analogy in human experience is therefore satisfied.

One of the important principles to remember throughout this entire conversation is that history is based to a large degree on personal testimony, not on science or philosophy. Historians have to determine on a case-by-case basis if the transmitters of the tradition that passed on a given story appeared to be reliable, if the testimony fit conditions of the time and place in which the purported events are set, if the people who told the stories had something to gain by falsifying the historical record, if it was an embarrassing story that they would have preferred to modify or cover up if they felt free to alter the facts, if the tradition could be traced back to someone who experienced the events narrated, if there was any independent testimony to those events, and so on. This is how historians operate.[63]

---

61. Craig S. Keener, *Miracles: The Credibility of the New Testament Accounts*, 2 vols. (Baker, 2011).

62. Craig S. Keener, "'The Dead Are Raised' (Matthew 11:5//Luke 7:22): Resuscitations Accounts in the Gospels and Eyewitness Testimony," *Bulletin for Biblical Research* 25 (2015): 55–79.

63. See, classically, Marc Bloch, *The Historian's Craft: Reflections on the Nature and Uses of History and the Techniques and Methods of Those Who*

It may still be objected that if the resurrection really happened, something so spectacular should have left behind much more evidence than we currently have. But that is a modern perspective, in light of what the Jesus movement has become over almost twenty centuries. Ancient history and biography were almost entirely written about kings and queens and their reigns, military leaders and their exploits, the wealthy and aristocratic class, or people in prominent positions of officially recognized religious or philosophical leadership. Jesus fit none of these categories. That we have approximately a dozen references to him in the non-Christian Jewish, Greek, and Roman worlds in the generations immediately after his life is the most we could reasonably expect in that day.[64] No one had any way of knowing in the pre-Constantinian era that Christianity would grow into the world's largest religion centuries later and that its founder would become the household name that he has become (even when used only as a swear word!).

A related observation proves even more relevant. Every person whom the ancient accounts of the resurrection claim saw Jesus were either already one of his followers or, like Saul of Tarsus (1 Corinthians 15:8) and Jesus' own half-brother, James (v. 7), became a follower after seeing him alive again. It is hard to imagine someone having such an experience and *not* becoming a believer! Conversely, it was commonplace for individuals in antiquity not to refer to that which painted them in a negative light or proved particularly embarrassing. So anyone who might have had reason to refer to the resurrection who was an opponent of Christianity in its earliest years would most likely just have suppressed knowledge of the tradition. In other words, the question often asked as to why we don't have non-Christian evidence for the resurrection from the earliest days of the faith is fairly disingenuous. Everyone we know of who was not a Christian before encountering the Risen Christ became a follower when they saw him. No one who heard about the resurrection in the earliest days who did not become a believer would have had any

---

Write It (Alfred A. Knopf, 1953).

64. For details, see esp. Robert E. Van Voorst, *Jesus outside the New Testament: An Introduction to the Ancient Evidence* (Eerdmans, 2000).

reason to preserve information about it.

In addition, we simply have very few documents from the first century that say anything about the history of Israel in the 20s and 30s. Lists of first-century writers who say nothing about Jesus typically mislead, inasmuch as they include geographers, botanists, philosophers, and others whose books had nothing to do with recent events in Israel. The vast majority were Greek and Roman writers whose purview was to discuss their own nation's history![65] The only writer we know of whose works have been preserved who does depict this period and this place in any detail is the late-first-century Jewish historian Josephus, and he does make mention of Jesus and says that he performed "wondrous deeds" and that his followers claimed to have seen him alive after his death.[66]

It is also somewhat inaccurate to say that only Paul and the four Gospel writers teach us anything about the resurrection within the New Testament. They are the only ones who refer to the people to whom Jesus appeared. But most of the twenty-seven books of the New Testament reflect theologically on the significance of the resurrection, which would be impossible if there had not been one. If one turns to the second century, moreover, then testimony to the resurrection grows exponentially in early Christian writings, and this new religion's opposition begins to do so as well. To be sure, by this time everyone is responding to and/or building on the first-century testimony, so we cannot speak of extra independent attestation. But, again, that is simply the way history writing works. It *would* be notable if there were some significant gap in discussion about the resurrection only to have it reemerge a century or two later. Then one might wonder if the later writers had misunderstood what the first-century events had actually been. Instead, we

---

65. Excelling at this deception is Michael Paulkovich, *No Meek Messiah: Christianity's Lies, Laws and Legacy* (Spillix, 2013), who lists 126 "first-century" writers who say nothing about Jesus, in spite of the fact that they cover pre-Christian times as well as going well beyond the first century, include writers who do in fact mention Jesus, and list a host of writers whose topics gave them no reason to say anything about any first-century Israelite rabbi.

66. On the most probable original version of Josephus' testimony, see John P. Meier, "Jesus in Josephus: A Modest Proposal," *Catholic Biblical Quarterly* 52 (1990): 76–103.

have an unbroken tradition of reflection on the meaning of the resurrection from the pre-Pauline confession of faith in 1 Corinthians 15, most likely composed no later than a year or two after Jesus' death, all the way through to the twenty-first century today. And countless lives have been changed for the better because of it over those centuries.[67] Christianity, based on the resurrection of Jesus, has also formed a disproportionate amount of the foundation of modern education, science, medicine, law, relief efforts, and other forms of humanitarian aid.[68] The most plausible explanation of all these phenomena is that Jesus was in fact bodily raised from the dead.

---

67. This is not to deny the existence of those who have "gone bad," but rather to remind ourselves that they are a small minority of all Christians around the world and throughout church history.

68. See esp. Jonathan Hill, *What Has Christianity Ever Done for Us?: How It Shaped the Modern World* (IVP, 2005).

A Reply to Craig

Carl Stecher, Ph.D.

Craig prefaces his ten-point positive case for the resurrection of Jesus as a fact of history with an excellent scholarly essay surveying various skeptical responses in the past century or so, and explains why he finds none of them convincing. Having accomplished this, he writes, "It is to Carl Stecher's credit that he opts for none of the approaches surveyed thus far." This being the case, I will comment on these opening pages of Craig's only in so far as they seem relevant to the question of Jesus' resurrection as we are debating it. I will then respond to the positive case that Craig makes for the resurrection as history.

In his first paragraph, Craig writes of "the claims [Jesus] made during his life to be a heaven-sent, divinely accredited spokesman for Yahweh, God of Israel, who was revealing the very will and nature of Yahweh himself." Two comments. First, as Craig knows, the authenticity of this claim, that Jesus identified himself as God incarnate, has been hotly debated. In fact, in October 2015, Craig and I debated this question for the Socratic Club of Oregon State University; that debate can be found on YouTube. Furthermore, a strong case can be made that Jesus believed himself to be Christ, the Messiah of Jewish expectations. If that were the case, Jesus was not claiming divinity, but instead that he was the one who would be God's human representative, the king who—like his ancestor David—would rule over God's kingdom on earth once Roman rule was overthrown.

It should always be remembered that Jesus and all his original disciples were first-century Palestinian Jews. "Think not that I am come to destroy the law, or the prophets," Jesus is depicted as saying, "I am not come to destroy, but to fulfill. For verily I say unto you, Till heaven and earth pass, one jot or one tittle shall in no wise pass from the law, till all be fulfilled" (Matt. 5:17–18, KJV). The Romans are long gone from Jerusalem, but many faithful Jews are still awaiting this Messiah. As either Cleopas or the other, unidentified disciple said to the unrecognized Jesus on the Road to Emmaus, "we had been hoping that he was to be the liberator of Israel" (Luke 24:21). Bart Ehrman has explored the significance of Jesus' probable belief that he was the Messiah that many Jews were awaiting:

> What he meant by "messiah" has to be understood within the broader context of his apocalyptic proclamation. This is where one of the sayings of Jesus . . . almost certainly authentic comes into play . . . Jesus told his disciples—Judas Iscariot included—that they would be seated on twelve thrones ruling the twelve tribes of Israel in the future kingdom . . . But who would be the ultimate king? Jesus was their master (=lord) now. Would he not be their master (=Lord) then? He is the one who called them, instructed them, commissioned them, and promised them thrones in the kingdom. It is almost unthinkable that he did not imagine that he too would have a role to play in that kingdom, and if he was the leader of the disciples now, he certainly would be the leader of the kingdom of God soon to be brought by the Son of Man. And what is the typical designation for the future king of Israel? Messiah. It is in this sense that Jesus must have taught his disciples that he was the messiah.[1]

I think a strong case can be made that Christianity misappropriated the title "Messiah."

Craig continues, "Long before the advent of what we would call modern science, people in every culture and location on the planet knew

---

1. Ehrman, *How Jesus Became God* (Harper Collins, 2014), 119.

that *dead people stayed dead.*"² I find this statement problematic just in terms of its factuality. Surely Craig does not mean this statement to include Jesus and his disciples. Witness Jesus commissioning his disciples to "Heal the sick, *raise the dead*" (Matt. 10:8). When John the Baptist had his disciples ask Jesus, "Are you the one who is to come [presumably the Messiah] or are we to expect someone else?" Jesus answered, "Go and report to John what you hear and see . . . *the dead are raised*" (Matt. 11:5). "At that time Herod the tetrarch heard of the fame of Jesus, and said unto his servants, 'This is John the Baptist; *he is risen from the dead*'" (Matt 14:1). According to the Gospels, Jesus himself raised three people from the dead, the widow of Nain's only son (Luke 7:12–15), Jairus' daughter (Matt. 9:18–24), and of course Lazarus, whose story is told only in John (11:1–53). Jesus repeatedly tells his disciples in the clearest possible language that he will be executed but that three days later he will be raised from the dead. "From that time forth began Jesus to show unto his disciples, how that he must go unto Jerusalem, and suffer many things of the elders and chief priests and scribes, and be killed, *and be raised again* the third day" (Matt 16:24). Jesus told his disciples, "Tell the vision to no man, until the Son of man *be risen again from the dead*" (Matt 17:10). "And while they abode in Galilee, Jesus said unto them, 'The Son of man shall be betrayed into the hands of men: And they shall kill him, and *the third day he shall be raised again.*'" (Matt. 17: 22–23). "And the Son of Man shall be betrayed unto the chief priests and unto the scribes, and they shall condemn him to death, and shall deliver him to the Gentiles to mock and to scourge and to crucify him, *and the third day he shall rise again*" (Matt. 20:18–19). Curiously, none of his disciples reminded Jesus that everyone knows the dead stay dead.

In his next paragraph, Craig writes, "The majority of those in the first century who heard the stories about Jesus and his resurrection, however, did not become believers." Craig is probably right in this assertion, but he does not explore its implications. My question is, if those in the best position to establish the truth, those Jews alive and on the scene in the first century, if they did not become Christian believers,

---

2. My emphasis here and throughout paragraph.

we must wonder why not? If they found the tales of Jesus' resurrection unbelievable, why should we believe?

Craig's paragraphs discussing the atheist historian Gerd Lüdemann also require some discussion, since they focus especially on 1 Corinthians 15:3–8, a passage which I refer to in my case *against* the resurrection as history. Regarding this passage, Craig writes:

> It looks and reads very much like an early creed or confession of faith with its rhythmic, condensed, and tightly packed succession of clauses . . . So we must allow time for the first followers of Jesus to craft such a creed or confession, agree on its wording, determine that it was important to teach it to new believers, and then spread the word to other places to which Christians had traveled.

As a skeptical non-Christian, I am familiar with the Nicene Creed and the Apostles' Creed, both repeated countless times by millions of believers, but I have never previously heard of Paul's Creed, or whatever this would be called. Perhaps Craig can explain why, if this is an early creed, the only place it seems to have survived is in this single passage in 1 Corinthians.

Before turning to his positive case for the resurrection as a fact of history, Craig turns back to the question of "preunderstanding, presuppositions, or worldviews," the focus for the opening chapters of this exploration. "If one is an antisupernaturalist (or, more simply, just a naturalist), then one excludes the possibility of an actual bodily resurrection at the outset," Craig writes. I detect a note of frustration in these words. But this is not my position, as I had hoped to make clear in my "Horizons" chapter. I am certainly willing to consider the evidence for the resurrection, just as I call upon Craig to consider the evidence for natural explanations and the problems with the evidence for the resurrection as a fact of history. Both of us, certainly, have presuppositions, but the hope is for both of us to make the strongest possible cases for and against the resurrection as history (given the limitations of the format and the voluminous arguments on both sides), then to clarify where and why we differ and to discover, if possible, where we are in agreement.

My position is not that Jesus' resurrection did not happen, but that the evidence is scant and deeply flawed, contradictory in almost every possible way, and therefore insufficient to establish Jesus' resurrection as a fact of history. Furthermore, I argue, there are many plausible natural explanations to explain why some of Jesus' disciples might have come to believe that Jesus had been raised from the dead.

Turning to Craig's ten arguments to support the historicity of Jesus' resurrection, he surprisingly begins with the fact that, "all four Gospels narrate their accounts of the resurrection by beginning with women as the first eyewitnesses." But it is only in the Gospels of Matthew and John, written decades after the event, that women were the first eyewitnesses, or were even witnesses at all. In Mark's account, the women at the tomb see only a young man wearing a white robe who tells them that Jesus has been raised (16:3–8). In Luke, the one young man has been replaced by two in "dazzling garments," who tell the women that Jesus has been raised. But the women clearly do not see Jesus (24:4–7). And in the supposedly creedal statement in 1 Corinthians, Paul does not mention *any* women witnesses. Craig holds that women were not allowed to testify. However, as the Rev. R. T. Beckwith testified, "women were allowed to give evidence on matters within their knowledge if there was no male witness available . . . [this] would mean that Mary Magdalene was on rabbinical principles entitled to give witness to an appearance of Christ which was made only to her or to her and other women."[3]

Craig writes a long paragraph defending the consistency of the Gospel accounts, concluding, "neither does anyone claim to provide an exhaustive list [of the women who go to the tomb] so they are not contradictory." This is not in response to any argument I have made; I agree that differences about which women saw Jesus would not be significant. But Craig does query, why would all four Gospel accounts "make women the first and primary witnesses to the resurrection in a culture that often didn't allow women's testimony in a court of law?" Again, this is not completely accurate because in Paul's account and the Gospels of Mark and Luke there's no indication that any women ever see the risen

---

3. As quoted in Robert M. Price and Jeffery Jay Lowder, ed., *The Empty Tomb: Jesus Beyond the Grave* (Prometheus, 2005), 283.

Jesus. Perhaps the answer to this question is that the failure of the male disciples, at this moment, was notorious. When Jesus was arrested they had all fled in panic and went into hiding. Even Peter, according to the Gospel accounts, had denied Jesus three times.

In Craig's own words:

> Precisely because women were not perceived to be a threat to male authorities the way other men were, they would have been allowed to stay near the cross, follow the soldiers who buried Jesus to see where the tomb was and come early in the morning to provide the spices for his burial that Rome would not have given him.

The author of Mark—and the authors of Matthew and Luke, who use Mark as their source—might be providing whatever details they include for literary verisimilitude. Craig concedes that the authors of the Gospels might at times have been more concerned with artistic considerations than with historical accuracy. In Craig's analysis, for example, Matthew, Luke, and Mark all telescope Jesus' teaching and healing ministry from three years to one; for this reason, according to Craig, they are unable to narrate some important events because these happened on the wrong years. I see this differently, of course: the willingness of the authors of these Gospels to place literary considerations above historical accuracy calls into question, at the very least, the historical reliability of their Gospels.

Craig's second evidence for the historical reliability of the resurrection accounts is that "already within the first generation of the movement" Jewish Christians began "resting and worshipping on Sunday, the first day of the week, in direct violation of one of their ten most foundational commandments which prescribed the seventh day or Saturday as their holy day." Craig is referring to the years 30–70; in the last year the Romans essentially destroyed the Jewish community in Jerusalem and demolished their magnificent temple. But unless I am mistaken, the only evidence about when and where Jesus' original disciples in Jerusalem *worshipped* during these years are these few words in Acts: "And they continuing daily with one accord in the temple." (2:46).

Craig quotes 1 Corinthians 16:1–4, saying, "Upon the first day of the week let every one of you lay by him in store, as God hath prospered him, that there be no gatherings when I come." According to Craig, "This must be a reference to Christian worship services on Sundays, because, if it were simply a command for believers to save something each week in their homes, a collection would still have been needed when Paul arrived." To this, I make two points. First, these are not the Jerusalem disciples, but instead the attendees at the synagogue in Corinth, eight hundred miles away, which had a significant number of Gentile worshippers, attracted to the synagogue there because of Jewish monotheism and the Jewish moral code. As Craig admits, "there were both Jewish and Gentile Christians in Corinth." These pagans would have had a long history of Sunday worship, and no prior commitment to Saturday worship. Second, Craig continues, "Paul and Luke gather with the Christians in Troas on the first day of the week to break bread, a probable reference to the Lord's Supper as part of the early Christian worship service." Or maybe they were just hungry. Most folks break bread every day. Witness Acts 20:11: "When he [Paul] therefore was come up again, and had broken bread, and eaten, and talked a long while, even till break of day." As evidence that Jesus' Jerusalem disciples switched from Saturday to Sunday worship, abandoning or at least modifying one of the Ten Commandments, this bread is sliced very thin.

Craig carries his argument based upon Sunday worship ahead to the fourth century when Constantine legalized the practice of Christianity, prohibited pagan worship, and set aside Sunday as a day of rest. "It does not seem likely," Craig writes, "that they would have created all this additional difficulty for themselves unless there was some fairly dramatic, objective, and foundational experience that actually occurred on a Sunday," one "that they felt bound to commemorate on that day rather than any other day. A bodily resurrection, of course, would fit those criteria well." I would argue that a teaching *and a belief* in Jesus' resurrection might just as well, several centuries after the reported event, be sufficient.

Craig continues his case for the resurrection as history by asking "what led the original Jewish followers of Jesus to continue to revere him after his death when their own law declared that anyone hanged on a tree was cursed by God, and their own religious teachers had already determined that a crucifixion was similar enough to also imply God's curse?" As a response to this question, he notes, "Rome by 30 C.E. had crucified literally thousands of criminals and insurrectionists this way ... [I]t would have taken some spectacular event to convince Jesus' first followers to ignore all this and still declare [Jesus] to be the Messiah and liberator of Israel."

My answer to Craig's query is three-fold.

First, cognitive dissonance reduction could account for this response to the disciples' continuing worship of Jesus, as I have argued in my chapter challenging the sufficiency of the evidence for the resurrection: think Rebbe Schneerson and William Miller (examples I gave earlier in this volume). As Kris Komarnitsky explains:

> Today, many New Testament scholars doubt the historicity of the Gospel accounts of Jesus predicting his own death ... If Jesus' followers had no expectation of his death, then like any human beings, they would have been subject to the powerful influence of cognitive dissonance and the desire to reduce that dissonance through rationalization ... A sustaining rationalization for Jesus' death would most likely have emerged very quickly and in the presence of others who could offer mutual encouragement ... [W]e know that the imminent return of Jesus and the ushering in of a new kingdom was widely believed throughout the early Christian community.[4]

Second, after Jesus' execution, and after the crushing defeat of the Jewish uprising and the destruction of the Temple, it's difficult to imagine how anyone, and especially any first-century Jerusalem Jew, could continue to think of Jesus as the Messiah and/or the liberator of Israel. But some of Jesus' disciples believed that Jesus had risen from the dead: this belief, whether or not Jesus' return to life had actually happened, might well have been sufficient, but only if *Messiah* was radically rede-

---

4. Komarnitsky, *Doubting Jesus' Resurrection*, 59–60.

fined. It's unimaginable how, in 70 C.E., with the Temple a smoldering ruin and the Jewish revolutionaries completely defeated, anyone could have thought that Jesus had liberated Israel. But our self-imposed task is to consider carefully and with as much objectivity as possible, given our varied backgrounds and presuppositions, whether there is sufficient evidence to validate the belief that Jesus was God, miraculously resurrected.

Third, if God (the Father), assuming for the moment his existence, wished to communicate Jesus' divinity and his own omnipotence, why did he not perform some truly spectacular event for all to see, instead of limiting his revelation to a few favorites? "And we are witnesses," the disciples are made to say, "of all things which [Jesus] did both in the land of the Jews, and in Jerusalem; whom they slew and hanged on a tree," and, "Him God raised up the third day, and showed him openly; *not to all the people, but unto witnesses chosen before of God, even to us, who did eat and drink with him after he rose from the dead*'" (Acts 10:39–41; my emphasis). As Richard Carrier has argued, for millions of potential believers God is silent. "If God wants something from me, he would tell me. He wouldn't leave someone else to do this, as if an infinite being were short on time," and "he would certainly not leave fallible, sinful humans to deliver an endless plethora of confused and contradictory messages."[5]

Before turning to Craig's fourth argument, I would like to question this statement of Craig: "Finally, the Sanhedrin convicted him on a trumped-up charge, phrased it in terms of sedition in order to interest the local Roman prefect, Pontius Pilate." But if the Gospel accounts are to be believed, Jesus had no defense against the charge of sedition:

> "Are you the king of the Jews?" Pilate asked him. "The words are yours," [Jesus] replied . . . Pilate questioned him again: "Have you nothing to say in your defense? You see how many charges they are bringing against you." But, to Pilate's astonishment, Jesus made no further reply. (Mark 15:2–3)

---

5. Richard Carrier, *Why I Am Not a Christian* (Philosophy Press, 2011), 7.

Note that Pilate does *not* ask Jesus, "Are you God incarnate?"

But if, as the Gospels indicate, Jesus did claim to be the Messiah, the expected King of the Jews, Jesus was guilty as charged. The Romans decided who was accorded royal power; for any Jew to claim royal power for himself the Romans would consider treason.

Craig's fourth argument for the resurrection as history is that "few people want to follow defeated and executed freedom fighters . . . Something highly unusual must have occurred." I concur. The unusual event was that some of Jesus' disciples came to believe that Jesus had been miraculously resurrected from the dead; that belief became the central teaching of Christianity, which evolved radically from its Jewish origins. But it should be pointed out that despite the catastrophic military defeat by the Romans and the destruction of the Temple in Jerusalem, Judaism also survived and, despite the Holocaust, eventually returned to Palestine, its adherents today numbering more than fourteen million.

History records many occasions when true believers have carried on the fight long after any chance of a military victory has disappeared. As Craig notes, in first-century Palestine the defeat and execution of one Jewish claimant to be the Messiah led to the emergence of another claimant, and then another and another. In our own time, militant Muslim fanatics, as hateful and morally repugnant as their cause might be, have demonstrated remarkable resilience. And one last thought on Craig's fourth point: If anyone who is hanged is thereby cursed by God, doesn't this put in the hands of the Roman executioners the determination of who is going to suffer God's curse? What sense does this make?

Craig's fifth evidential support for a literal understanding of the resurrection as a historical event is as follows: "This was the era in which believers were frequently persecuted for their faith, had no power base, and nothing to gain economically or socially but often much to lose," and yet "the overwhelming majority of the references to Jesus in the New Testament letters highlight his death and/or resurrection. Clearly this was the most important thing about the founder of Christianity in his followers' minds." I find it difficult to understand how this attests to the *truth* of Jesus' resurrection, since much the same can be said for other faiths and only one—if that many—can actually be true. Certainly, inspired by the revolutionary fervor of Osama bin Laden, thousands have died a martyr's death in support of the teachings of al-Qaeda; thousands more have died to advance ISIS. The followers of Joseph Smith were often persecuted; some died for their faith. History abounds in faiths that people have died for—including many varieties of Christian faiths. Many who have died for one understanding of Christian faith were killed by other Christians with a different understanding of the faith. It is not a proud record.

Craig's sixth argument for the historicity of Jesus' resurrection is apparently that "1 Corinthians 15 . . . discloses a relationship between the resurrection of one person and the resurrection of all people at the end of this current age of human existence, which is unparalleled in the history of religion." I've been carefully studying the two paragraphs in which Craig develops this idea; however, I have not succeeded in understanding Craig's point. Many first-century Jews clearly did believe that the end times were upon them; God would not long tolerate Roman rule over his chosen people. A messiah would appear, the Roman legions would be defeated under his leadership, and God's kingdom would be established here on earth, with Jerusalem as its capital. These expectations were firmly grounded in the prophetic books of the Bible, which to first-century Jews meant, of course, only what Christians would later call the Old Testament.

I could see Craig's point here, if there had been a "resurrection of all people at the end of this current age of human existence." But this clearly has not happened. And I really do wonder just what Craig meant when he referred to "the end of this current age of human existence." Have there been other ages of human existence? Is there another age, or perhaps several ages, yet to come? But I do find it interesting that Craig, without actually quoting the relevant passages, insists that Jesus did not predict when he would return. Here are those relevant passages (greatly condensed):

Then Jesus asked him, "Do you see those great buildings? Not one stone will be left here upon another; all will be thrown down." . . . Peter, James, John and Andrew asked him privately, "Tell us, when will this be, and what will be the sign that all these things are about to be accomplished?" (Mark 13:2–4)

Jesus responds by listing disasters that are about to happen, both natural and man-made:

"And ye shall hear of wars and rumors of wars . . . For nation will rise up against nation, and kingdom against kingdom . . . and there shall be famines, and pestilences, and earthquakes in divers places. Then they will see the Son of Man coming in clouds with great power and glory. And then shall he send his angels, and shall gather together his elect from the four winds, from the uttermost part of the earth to the uttermost part of heaven. Now learn the parable of the fig tree: When her branch is yet tender, and puteth forth leaves, ye know that summer is near: So ye in like manner, when ye shall see these things come to pass, know that it is nigh, even at the doors. *Truly I tell you, this generation will not pass away until all these things have taken place* . . . But about that day or hour no one knows, neither the angels in heaven, nor the Son, but only the Father." (Mark 13:7–32; my emphasis)

Also to the point:

"Whosoever therefore shall be ashamed of me and of my words, in this adulterous and sinful generation, of him also shall the Son of man be ashamed, when he cometh in the glory of his Father with the holy angels. And he said unto them, Verily I say unto you, that *there be some of them that stand here, which shall not taste of death, till they have seen the kingdom of God come with power.*" (Mark 8:38–9:1; my emphasis)

Yet Craig claims:

Indeed, if people had been listening to Jesus' teaching more carefully, they would have known that he never predicted the timing of his return, despite a few somewhat striking declarations that at first glance could sound like he was. . .After all, it was Jesus who also said that no one knows the day or hour, not even he (Mark13:32 and parallels), and that it was not for his followers to know the times or seasons of his coming (Acts 1:7). Even if the first of these two passages could be pedantically read as allowing for someone to know the week, month or year, the second passage excludes any estimate of the time frame between Jesus' first and second comings, no matter what unit of temporal measurement one introduces.

At the risk of seeming pedantic, I would like to look more closely at Craig's statement that Jesus "never predicted the timing of his return." Craig examined these passages, and the question of whether Jesus proved to be a false prophet on the question of his Second Coming, in his book, *The Historical Reliability of the Gospels*. There he declares:

> Several of Jesus' very solemn pronouncements *sound as though he believed that he would return within the lifetime of at least some of his disciples* . . . But at least three key observations weigh against it. (1) None of the verses cited above should be taken to mean that Jesus mistakenly believed that he would return to earth in the first century. In fact, each has several alternative interpretations that are more likely. *Perhaps the best* are that in Mark 9:1 Jesus was referring to his subsequent transfiguration as an important foreshadowing of his final coming 'with power. . .'[6] (my emphasis)

But as Craig himself notes, "others argue that an emphatic proclamation that some would not die before an event [the transfiguration] only a week away makes no sense." I agree. What Craig has identified as the best explanation for the delay of the promised Second Coming "makes no sense." Craig notes that others also argue "that in Mark 13:30 the 'all things' do not include his return but only the signs leading up to his return." But Jesus makes this distinction in none of the passages in which he predicts he will return in this generation. Furthermore, Jesus' words portrayed the Son of Man coming "in the glory of his Father with

---

6. Craig L. Blomberg, *The Historical Reliability of the Gospels*, 2nd ed. (IVP Academic, 2007), 64.

the holy angels" just before he states, "Truly I tell you: there are some of those standing here who will not taste death before they have seen the kingdom of God come with power" (Mark 8:38). This hardly sounds like a prediction of the transfiguration, which does not portray Jesus as returning in glory accompanied by angels.

Craig further states, "Even if the disciples had interpreted Jesus' teaching to mean that he would return in their generation, they would not have been the first Jews to have believed that the end of the age would come quite soon." I fail to see the relevance of what Jews other than Jesus' disciples believed. And I fail to see how this history of failed prophecy in Judaic history strengthens the case that Jesus' promise was somehow misunderstood.

In yet another argument, Craig advances that Jesus did not mistakenly predict an imminent return:

> Christians need not have changed their theology or invented alleged teaching of Jesus to mask his original claims when the delay in his return became apparent; rather, they simply underlined the vast chasm between God's and humanity's perspectives on time: 'With the Lord a day is like a thousand years' . . . this interpretation of God's delay, based on Psalm 90:4, had already been applied by Jews in pre-Christian times to their questions concerning God's "tardiness".[7]

I would argue that this characterizes God as deceitful, devious. Imagine that you desperately needed a medication and were promised by your pharmacy that you would be able to fill the prescription very soon. But days and weeks pass, then months and years. Long after your eventual demise, would your family be satisfied by the pharmacy's explanation, "Here at Haveadrug Pharmacy, a day is like a thousand years"? Or would your family be satisfied if the pharmacy explained that if only you had been listening more carefully, you would have realized that the pharmacy had never actually predicted the timing of the availability of your needed medication? If this were the treatment

---

7. Ibid., 66.

that you received from the pharmacy, you'd fill all your prescriptions at Walgreens. But in waiting for Jesus' return—the glorious return of the Messiah, accompanied by angels—we are not talking in terms of months or years or even centuries. We are dealing with an unexplained delay of two thousand years!

If we are to believe Matthew, Jesus clearly expected that his return was imminent, not many millennia in the future:

> And the high priest answered and said unto him, "I adjure thee by the living God, that thou tell us whether thou be the Christ, the Son of God." Jesus saith unto him, "Thou has said; nevertheless I say unto you, Hereafter shall ye see the Son of man sitting on the right hand of power, and coming in the clouds of heaven." (Matt. 26:63–64)

This never happened.

It's clear, at any rate, that Paul, certainly the most influential voice in the developing theology and Christology of the first centuries, believed that Jesus had predicted his return within the time frame of the first century:

> For this we say unto you by the word of the Lord, that *we which are alive and remain unto the coming of the Lord* shall not prevent them which are asleep. For the Lord himself shall descend from heaven with a shout, with the voice of the archangel, and with the trump of God, and the dead in Christ shall rise first: *Then we which are alive and remain* shall be caught up together with them in the clouds, to meet the Lord in the air: and so shall we ever be with the Lord. (1 Thessalonians 4:15–17; my emphasis)

If Paul can't get this right, perhaps those of us who share his confusion will be forgiven.

One final response to Craig's sixth point. Craig writes:

> Judaism, as already noted, believed in the resurrection of all people, some to everlasting life and some to everlasting judgment, at the end of human history. Whether we are to take the account literally

or metaphorically, that is what the enigmatic little passage about the resurrection of selected Old Testament "saints» in Matthew 27:52–53 is intended to teach.

The passage in question reads as follows:

Jesus, when he had cried again with a loud voice, yielded up the ghost. And, behold, the veil of the temple was rent in twain from the top to the bottom; and the earth did quake, and the rocks rent; And the graves were opened; and many bodies of the saints which slept arose, And came out of the graves after his resurrection, and went into the holy city, and appeared unto many.

Craig does not explain the connection he sees between this passage, found only in Matthew—I think of it as the parade of the zombies—and the promised resurrection of all people. Without Craig's guidance I find the passage baffling.

Moving on to Craig's seventh point evidencing the resurrection:

the fact that the same Jewish and Roman authorities who authorized Jesus' crucifixion never produced a body or pointed people to the tomb where his corpse still lay, even as claims of resurrection began to circulate within days of his death, suggests that his tomb really was empty.

There are many reasons why this argument lacks force. To mention one, a point that I have made elsewhere (as have many others), there are many arguments against the very existence of an empty tomb, so many that I can't possibly do justice to their variety and substance. A starting point for anyone really interested in exploring this question is *The Empty Tomb: Jesus Beyond the Grave,* a 544-page collection of articles by nine credentialed scholars sharing a skeptical perspective; our colleague in this debate, Dr. Richard Carrier, is a major contributor. Robert M. Price, one of the volume's editors, writes in the introductory chapter:

> The arguments of this book are not attempts to debunk the Bible but to understand it better as what it is: a great ancient text of mythology ... But have we not, in arguing against the factual veracity of a belief in the resurrection of Jesus, argued against Christian faith ... Not at All! The whole problem that haunts these discussions is the failure of some religious believers to separate issues of historical scholarship from personal investment in the outcome of the investigation.[8]

The following brief excerpts suggest the focus and scope of this collection:

1. Richard Carrier: "In the ancient world, to experience supernatural manifestations, of ghosts, gods, and wonders was not only accepted, but often encouraged, and consequently hallucination occurred more often and more openly—most people of the time were enculturated to have them, respect them, and believe them." (p. 184)

2. Peter Kirby: "[T]he post-Markan gospel narratives of the resurrection are legends and fictions built up around the empty tomb story in the Gospel of Mark ... Since all accounts of the empty tomb are dependent on Mark, the story hangs by a slender thread indeed." (p. 236–237)

3. Roy Hoover: "[T]he location of Arimathea has not (yet) been identified with any assurance; the various 'possible' locations are nothing more than pious guesses or conjectures undocumented by any textual or archaeological evidence." (p. 237)

4. Roy Hoover: "Is it very likely that a pious Sanhedrinist [Joseph] would be rushing about on the day before the Sabbath during the Passover to have the bodies of the crucified properly buried?" (p. 244)

5. Roy Hoover: "it is hardly plausible that Pilate would have allowed Jesus to be given an honorable burial, as this would be tantamount

---

8. Price and Lowder, *Empty Tomb*, 16.

to an admission that Jesus was crucified without just cause." (p. 244)

6. Peter Kirby: "[The distinguished Catholic historian Raymond Brown] . . . notes the following passages where the phrasing suggests that Jesus was buried by Jews who had condemned Jesus, not by the otherwise unknown Joseph of Arimathea: "Those who lived in Jerusalem and their rulers . . . requested Pilate to have him killed; and when they had fulfilled all that was written of him *they* [Brown's italics] took him down from the tree and placed him in a tomb" (Acts 13:27–29). (p. 247) [If this biblical account is accurate, it's unlikely that Jesus' disciples would know the location of this mass tomb, which would be reserved for criminals dying without honor, not for someone honorably buried by family members.]

7. D. H. van Daalen: "what were the disciples doing fishing in Galilee (John 20:21–23) if the Lord had already appeared to them in Jerusalem and sent them to proclaim the Gospel? The answer now becomes obvious: in the story as it was originally told they had not seen the risen Lord in Jerusalem." (p. 253)

8. Peter Kirby, quoting William Lane Craig: "'Indeed, is it too much to imagine that during his two week stay Paul would want to visit the place where the Lord lay? Ordinary human feelings would suggest such a thing.'" Raymond Brown states, 'A particular reason for remembering the tomb of Jesus would lie in the Christian faith that the tomb had been evacuated by his resurrection from the dead. Thus, it is extremely likely that an empty tomb would become a site of veneration from the very start of Christianity . . . the fact that there was no tomb veneration indicates that the early Christians did not know the location of the tomb of Jesus.'" (p. 256)

9. Jeffery Jay Lowder: "Most Jewish burials were honorable ones. In contrast, dishonorable burial was reserved for criminals condemned by the Jewish court; it lacked the rites of mourning and burial in a family tomb. Instead, the condemned were buried in a public graveyard reserved by the Jewish court. There is, therefore, a

high prior probability that the Jews would bury an executed criminal like Jesus dishonorably." (p. 266)

10. Keith Parsons: "As far back as 1852, when Charles Mackay published his classic study *Memoirs of Extraordinary Delusions and the Madness of Crowds*, it was known that people in crowds are often more susceptible to visual or auditory delusions than they are individually. Mass hallucinations are extremely well-documented phenomena. In 1914, British newspapers were flooded with reports of the 'Angels of Mons', supposedly seen in the sky leading the troops against the godless Huns. The 'miraculous' manifestations of the Virgin Mary at Fatima, Portugal, were witnessed by thousands." (p. 436)

Craig, further developing the story of the empty tomb, refers to William Lane Craig's arguments for support. I have studied W. L. Craig's published works and watched some of his debates on YouTube and discovered that he can't always be trusted. For example, in a lecture delivered on October 25, 2011, at the Sheldonian Theatre in Oxford, he claimed that nowhere in the Old Testament does God order the extermination of the Caananites and, indeed, that "there is nothing in the narrative to suggest that any women or children were killed.—there is no narrative whatsoever that says that anybody other than combatants were killed."[9] But this is plain misinformation if not a flat lie. "Now listen to the voice of the Lord . . . Go now, fall upon the Amalekites, destroy them, and put their property under the ban. Spare no one; put them all to death, men and women, children and babes in arms, herds and flocks, camels and donkeys." (1 Samuel 15:1–3) See also Joshua 6:16–17, 6:21, 8:2, 8:24–25, 10:28, 10:40 ("So Joshua conquered the whole region . . . He left no survivor, destroying everything that drew breath, as the Lord God of Israel had commanded"), 11:14–15, 11:20, 23:4; 1 Samuel 15:3, 15:8–9, 15:17–19; and Deuteronomy 2:34.

Given W. L. Craig's dishonesty about God-commanded genocide,

---

9. See the video titled "Did God Command Genocide in the Bible?" uploaded to YouTube on April 30, 2013, by DrCraigVideos, www.youtube.com/watch?v=9FGv9aOCcyU.

CARL STECHER • 171

his claims related to other biblical questions should be greeted with skepticism—for example, when he points out that "the order of events is identical" in the resurrection accounts in 1 Corinthians, Acts, and Mark and argues that "[t]his remarkable correlation shows convincingly that the burial mentioned in the summary statement quoted by Paul refers to the event that is described in the gospels as Jesus' burial in the tomb." In this case, what is this "remarkable correlation" with the identical order of events? Jesus died, he was buried, he was raised, he appeared. But what other order of events could there have been? Jesus would not have been buried before he died, nor could he be resurrected. And it would be a strange tale indeed if he were resurrected before he was buried, tomb or no tomb. W. L. Craig's claim of a "remarkable correlation" has no substance.

Craig's eighth argument supporting the historicity of the resurrection is:

> Since Jesus would likely have been given a decent burial and various individuals could have guided people to the location of his tomb, the fact that none of the Jewish or Roman authorities hostile to the early Christian claims ever produced, claimed to produce, or even tried to produce a body to squelch the notion of Jesus' resurrection, is remarkable . . . Christianity could scarcely have survived in the form that still claimed that Jesus was bodily resurrected.

In fact, as I have previously evidenced, it's very unlikely that someone convicted and executed for sedition would be given a lavish honorable burial, especially since there was the alternative of a dishonorable interment specially reserved for those who had challenged the authority of the Roman provincial government. Buried with many others who had in some way offended the Romans, Jesus' body would soon have decayed beyond recognition.

Craig's ninth argument for the truth of the resurrection accounts is that they are remarkably restrained:

The original ending of Mark (16:8) in the oldest and most reliable manuscripts concluded without an actual resurrection appearance of Jesus to anyone, only the prophecy by the young man at the tomb that Jesus' followers would see him. Matthew, Luke and John all do narrate a variety of those appearances but no one ever describes Jesus actually leaving the tomb. He just appears to people in other places. If the notion of Jesus' bodily resurrection were an invention, one would expect a description of someone actually seeing Jesus come out of the tomb and what that looked like.

But I am not arguing that the narratives in the Gospels about the appearances to the disciples are wholly inventions. I agree, if they were, there would probably be more fantastic elements. My argument is that in all probability some of Jesus' disciples did believe that Jesus appeared to them alive shortly after his crucifixion. But this does not necessitate a miraculous resurrection, since numerous and plausible natural explanations could account for this belief. Thousands of people alive today are convinced that they have been abducted by aliens, but this does not mean they actually were. According to one Gallup poll, 4 percent of Americans believe that Elvis has been seen alive and well in the years following his death and burial, even though the vast majority of Americans are convinced that such reports are mistaken and accept that he died in 1977. In both cases, the evidence for the believers is far more substantive than the evidence for the resurrection of Jesus.

I am willing to grant, certainly, Craig's point that the Gospel accounts of Jesus' appearances do not include an account of Jesus' dead body returning to life. This is a simple statement of fact. I don't see how this evidences the truth of the appearance accounts that the Gospels provide, given that those disciples who thought they had seen the risen Jesus might well have been mistaken for the many reasons that I have already argued.

Craig's tenth and final argument for the historicity of Jesus' resurrection is, if I understand it correctly, that Jesus' resurrection is probably a fact of history because miraculous events, including resurrections from the dead, are actually common occurrences. Craig evidences this point two ways: from his own personal experiences and observations of miracles, and with Craig Keener's massive study.[10] As it happens, Craig and I corresponded on this topic several years ago. Craig then wrote:

> Extrapolating from a 2006 Pew Forum survey, Keener conservatively estimates that as many as 200 million people alive today have personally experienced or witnessed an extraordinary event, unaccounted for by the current state of scientific understanding, and in direct response to Christian prayer.

I responded that there were so many problems with this sentence I hardly knew where to start. First, I cannot believe that any competent social scientist would accept a single religious survey as the basis for extrapolating the experience of 200 million people. Second, the statement would certainly be more accurate if it read that [whatever number of people] "have personally experienced or witnessed *what they thought to be* an extraordinary event, unaccounted for by *their scientific understanding*, and *directly following* Christian prayer." I note that the original survey focused on Pentecostalist and Charismatic Christians; almost all Christians in these faith groups also believe in the six-day creation and the worldwide flood. As a skeptic, I do not think this segment of the population to be particularly credible. Third, the statement also contains another classic logical fallacy: *post hoc propter hoc*. The fact that what was considered to be an extraordinary event happened after Christian prayer is not evidence that it was caused by this prayer.

As to apparently miraculous cures (a major part of Keener's evidence), it took me only about ten minutes on Google to find the following information: according to CBS News, a recent survey estimated that physicians in the United States make approximately 12 million misdiagnoses a year. I suspect many of the reported miracles Keener cites were simply cases of misdiagnosis. Craig writes from his own experience: "On two occasions, patients with previously diagnosed cancerous tumors went to their doctors shortly [after prayers and anointing], and the medical experts could find no trace of any tumors ever having

---

10. Craig Keener, *Miracles: The Credibility of the New Testament Accounts* (Baker Academic, 2011).

existed. " Again, *post hoc propter hoc*. And given the frequency of misdiagnosis and the sometimes unpredictable behavior of cancer, things like
this are going to happen; prayers and heavenly intervention are possible
but not required.

Considering this fact of medical misdiagnosis, and on a personal
note, I went to my personal-care physician several times two years ago
with a complaint of pain in my back. I was not unduly alarmed, as I
am 77 years old, and by that age many people, perhaps most people,
experience back pain—especially common for anyone working, as I had
been, in a garden. The diagnosis was mild back strain. I was prescribed
some pain medications and physical therapy. It was only when I didn't
experience any relief that I was given a whole battery of tests just to
make sure nothing else was wrong. The result was a sky-high PSA score
and a diagnosis of stage 4 prostate cancer; my oncologist tells me my
whole skeleton is affected. Since then I've had two kinds of radiation
therapy, hormone therapy, and seven sessions of chemotherapy, which,
I am thankful, had only minor side effects. I even have a brand new
head of hair! I'm doing very well, thank you, and the prognosis for a
few more years seems quite good. It occurred to me one night recently
that my goose might be cooked, but the pop-up timer has not stirred.
My point: medical science, with as many advances as have been made in
recent years, still is far from perfect in making diagnosis and prognosis.

Craig suggests that my disbelief in Jesus' resurrection might be
caused by frustration with the fact that it is a straightforwardly supernatural religion. He also points out that if someone excludes the supernatural *a priori*, then of course the resurrection didn't happen. He
thinks my highlighting improbabilities in the accounts after this is then
unnecessary. But I believe that my case has been built solely upon those
improbabilities, and the many other deficiencies of the evidence for a
supernatural explanation for that belief and upon the greater probability of the many plausible natural causes for the disciples' belief that they
had witnessed the resurrected Jesus. Craig thinks that antisupernaturalism is neither rational nor scientific, but the same, certainly, can be
said for supernaturalism. And if the criteria to be consulted must be
the strength of the testimony and the trustworthiness of those giving it,

this is exactly the evidence that I have examined and found wanting to provide a compelling case for the resurrection.

Craig continues, "It may still be objected that if the resurrection really happened, something so spectacular should have left behind much more evidence than we currently have." I am in complete accord with this statement. In fact, I think it touches a fatal weakness in the historical case for the resurrection. Consider the situation. Traditional Christianity claims that a God exists who is morally perfect, who loves all the people he has created, and who longs for them to love him in return. This God has unlimited power and complete omniscience. Yet two thousand years after the execution of Jesus, convicted of sedition by the Romans, billions of people have lived, some of them with fortuitously good lives, but many of them suffering grievously, some of them embracing Christian teachings, but billions of them never having heard of Jesus, or hearing nothing about him which convinced them that Jesus was the son of the only God, or that he died so that those who believed in him would have an eternal and glorious life with Jesus and his Father and the Holy Ghost, all of whom are really one.

There is another consideration here, and perhaps this is the best opportunity to briefly explore it. The question is, does the claimed resurrection of Jesus provide part of a larger picture which itself makes sense? It is at this point that the picture becomes murky at best. The larger picture asserts—what? As far as I can see, traditional Christian belief can find no consensus, no answer that makes any sense to nontheists, or even to Christians of other denominational persuasions. From the very beginning Christians divided into numerous sects with different theologies; today such sects number in the thousands.

To use another metaphor, the belief in the resurrection of Jesus is a building block, but certainly not the only building block, in most all traditional versions of Christianity. The other building blocks include a God who is claimed by the major Christian faith confessions to be omniscient, omnipotent, and morally perfect. Moreover, this God is claimed to be the only God. But I do not see any way of reconciling these claimed attributes of God with the reality that surrounds us, with the clear facts of the world we live in.

Craig is nevertheless on the mark when he suspects that the question of Jesus' resurrection and of the truth of Christianity is not the only or even the most important reason why I reject Christian belief. As I explained in my "Horizons" chapter, disbelief in the Christian idea of God is not a choice for me. I find the Christian idea that an invisible but ubiquitous spirit, with both infinite power and perfect morality, rules this world to be impossible to believe in, as impossible as belief in Wotan or the tooth fairy.

Another compelling reason for my disbelief is the problem of evil. Turn on the nightly TV news, or read the daily paper, and death, suffering, destruction seem almost ubiquitous—car accidents, painful fatal diseases, earthquakes, droughts, and floods. It's not always easy to remember the appalling pain visited upon unoffending children, both from injuries and from the loss of parents and siblings. They have done nothing to deserve such suffering. I have often read and heard that God has a plan for each of our lives. But are these disasters all part of God's plan? What kind of God would be responsible for such calamities? Or for the thousands and millions of similar disasters wherever one looks? This is the part of the puzzle that I cannot find, the building block of Christian belief that seems to be missing.

This is not a god that I can believe in, much less worship.

The underlying problem, as I see it, is twofold.

On the one hand, if Craig Keener and Craig Blomberg are right, there are an incredible number of miracles, millions and millions of them, miracles being understood as the intervention of God to contravene the ordinary course of nature to provide some result desired by God. We might use the example of the alleged resurrection of Jesus, or the unidentified voice that Craig's mother heard warning her of a slippery and dangerous pavement. But why does God construct a world in which millions are tormented, many of them having no knowledge of Jesus and Christianity?

The Christian teaching that all will be made right in the next life, in the eternity that God's people will spend in heaven, is not an answer to the problem of evil because it depends upon the belief that God can indeed create a world without diseases and natural disasters like hurricanes and earthquakes, but that God created instead the world we all live and die in; a world wonderful in many ways, but a world in which innocent, unoffending children and certainly some very good adults suffer hideously and unnecessarily. The promised compensation of eternal heaven doesn't justify the unnecessary suffering of innocent children, or the unavoidable suffering of the child's parents who are helpless to assuage the pain visited upon their child. Nothing can justify this.

Craig concludes his case for the resurrection, writing:

> [C]ountless lives have been changed for the better because of it over those centuries. Christianity, based on the resurrection of Jesus, has also formed a disproportionate amount of the foundation of modern education, science, medicine, law, relief efforts, and other forms of humanitarian aid. The most plausible explanation of all these phenomena is that Jesus was in fact bodily raised from the dead.

In so writing, Craig does not differentiate between the positive effects of *belief* in the resurrection and the historic *truth* of the resurrection. I have, from the very beginning of this exploration, acknowledged the *utility* of Christian belief; what I have disputed is the evidence of Jesus' resurrection as a *fact of history*.

It should also be noted, at least in passing, that the positive accomplishments of historic Christianity need to be balanced against the sometimes catastrophic failures of the faith: from the earliest years the suppression and persecution of Christian groups that did not conform to what became Christian orthodoxy, including the Gnostics, Marcionites, Montanists, Arians, Sabellians, Nestorians, Monophysites, and Copts. Also to be kept in mind are the heresies surrounding Pelagius, Origen, the Donatists, and the Manichaeans, the Crusades, the Inquisition, the Thirty Years' War, the witchcraft persecutions, the pogroms, even the Holocaust—which took place in one of the world's most deeply Christian countries, with the pope never excommunicating Hitler nor declaring the crime anathema. Most recently, the Roman Catholic Church has been is deep disgrace for decades for its failure to protect

178 • RESURRECTION: FAITH OR FACT?

children from the sexual assault of predatory priests.

Keeping this in mind, I would like Craig's help in answering several questions about Christian belief. Craig writes about "God's people," referring to Christians like himself. How does one become one of God's people? On the one hand, Jesus seems to say that admittance into the kingdom of God is determined by human behavior: Jesus tells his disciples, "When the Son of man shall come in his glory, and all his holy angels with him," and "before him shall be gathered all nations," and "he shall set the sheep on his right hand," then "shall the King say unto them on his right hand, 'Come, ye blessed of my Father, inherit the kingdom prepared for you from the foundation of the world; For I was ahungered, and ye gave me meat; I was thirsty and ye gave me drink; I was a stranger and ye took me in'" (Matt. 25: 31–35). Jesus here says nothing about what those who are to be saved must believe.

On the other hand, Jesus elsewhere tells his disciples that admittance into God's kingdom is determined by belief, not by behavior: "The Father loveth the Son, and hath given all things into his hand," so "He that believeth on the Son hath everlasting life; and he that believeth not the Son shall not see life; but the wrath of God abideth on him" (Matt. 3:35–36). The Gospel of John is particularly insistent on this point: "For God so loved the world, that he gave his only begotten Son, that whosoever believeth in him should not perish, but have everlasting life"—indeed, "He that believeth on him is not condemned, but he that believeth not is condemned already, because he hath not believed in the name of the only begotten Son of God" (3:16–18). And again: "no one can come to me unless it has been granted to him; by the Father" (6:65). And again, "I am the resurrection and the life . . . no one who lives and has faith in me shall ever die" (11:25–26).

Consider also the idea of demons and demonic possession. Craig writes, "it is important to add here that contemporary experience is making it more and more difficult to deny the reality of demon possession, even in Western society today."[11] But if demons exist, as Craig believes, they owe their existence to an allegedly morally perfect God.

11. Blomberg, *Historical Reliability of the Gospels*, 122.

And like Satan in the book of Job, the awful things that demons do they do with God's permission. I can neither believe in nor worship a God who unleashes demons on the world. Presumably they do terrible things—but do they, can they, do these terrible things without the powers that God has given them? Can they do anything that God does not want them to do? If they can, God has surrendered some part of his power to them. If they can do only that which God desires them to do, how is God any better than a demon?

I am grateful that at least to this point in our debate, Craig has never attributed my skepticism about Christian belief to my secret sinfulness. Even if this is what he really believes. And I do wonder what Craig believes about the moral nature of nonbelievers and those who adhere to other faith traditions. What will be the ultimate fate of good people who have little or no knowledge of Christianity, who were born into a community and family of Muslims, or Buddhists, or skeptics? What will be the eternal fate of those who have considered all the evidence for the resurrection but remain unconvinced that it actually happened? Are any such, in Craig's view, good people? God's people? Are the people of Scandinavia and other countries dominated by secularists doomed to suffer the everlasting wrath of the God worshipped by Christians? I have a very dear Danish friend who is also a Lutheran pastor, but not a true believer in the sense that Craig is. Perhaps in his final statement Craig will address these related questions.

A Rejoinder to Carl

Craig Blomberg, Ph.D.

Many thanks to Carl for his response to my positive case for the resurrection. Just as he proceeded more or less sequentially through my chapter I will do the same for his response.

I actually worded my statement about Jesus carefully so that it would correspond to what many nonevangelical scholars would accept: "a heaven-sent, divinely accredited spokesman for Yahweh, God of Israel, who was revealing the very will and nature of Yahweh." That is quite different from saying he was God incarnate. It could mean he was the climactic prophet in a long line of Jewish prophets, as a fair cross section of historical Jesus studies grant, including Bart Ehrman's.[1] One does not need to be God incarnate to be resurrected to eternal life. Otherwise the Judeo-Christian belief that all God's people will one day be resurrected to eternal life makes no sense.[2] My case for the resurrection does not depend on Jesus as God; quite the reverse. It is the resurrection that makes one look on him as more than merely human.

---

1. Bart Ehrman, *Jesus: Apocalyptic Prophet of the New Millennium* (Oxford University Press, 1999).

2. Cf. the striking acknowledgment of the probability of the resurrection by the non-Christian, Jewish rabbi, Pinchas Lapide, *The Resurrection of Jesus: A Jewish Perspective* (Fortress, 1982). The book was so stunning that it made a featured review in *Time* magazine, May 7, 1979 (after the original German edition was published).

Did Christianity misappropriate the title "Messiah"? In later centuries to be sure. People today sometimes think Christ was Jesus' last name, as if his parents were Joseph Christ and Mary Christ! But first-century Christians did not misappropriate the title; they simply added others into the mix—Son of man, Son of God, Lord, Son of David, and so on. Messiah referred to the anointed liberator, repeatedly prophesied in the Hebrew Scriptures.[3]

When I said people knew that dead people stayed dead, I was making a generalization that was intended to counter the idea that one sometimes hears about the virginal conception, the healings, exorcisms, nature miracles, and resurrection of Jesus—that people in the first century believed in such things because they didn't understand modern science. My point was not that there were never claims that such things happened. My point was that reactions would have been similar to our own—disbelief, demand for evidence, alternative explanations for what happened, and the like. My point remains that if the average teenage girl came home in first-century Israel and told her parents she was pregnant but not to worry because there was no boy involved, there was no greater reason to expect her to be believed without overwhelming evidence than there would be today. And even if there were accounts of people having been brought back to life only to die again (the people whom Elijah and Elisha in the Old Testament and Jesus in the New Testament raised to life), there was no precedent for resurrection to unending, glorified, bodily existence.

This ties in directly with Carl's next question. He accepts my observation that the majority of people who heard about Jesus' resurrection did not become believers. What he doesn't realize is that in accepting this observation he is implicitly granting my previous point that he disputed. There was no greater reason to accept claims of Jesus' resurrection then as now. So the real question is not why so many people disbelieved, but why anyone believed at all.[4] If accounts of Jesus appearing

3. Cf, Michael Bird, *Jesus Is the Christ: The Messianic Testimony of the Gospels* (IVP, 2012).

4. Again, cf. Larry W. Hurtado, *Why on Earth Did Anyone Become a Christian in the First Three Centuries?* (Marquette University Press, 2016).

directly, repeatedly, and clearly to the disciples, demonstrating to them that he was an embodied person and not a ghost, failed to convince many who heard the stories, how can Carl imagine that people would have believed if the reports were based on a fleeting glimpse of someone they thought might have been Jesus, or something that at best could be described only as a subjective vision or mass hallucination? Carl's skepticism undercuts his own alternative explanations for resurrection belief.

Why then *did* anyone believe? Initially it was because they had undeniable personal experience of the resurrected Jesus.[5] Subsequently, it was because they recognized the impeccable integrity of the people describing their experiences and observed continued miracles worked by the apostles.[6] As they believed, they sensed the power of the Holy Spirit coming on them, sometimes to speak boldly about their experiences despite persecution and threat of imprisonment and even execution, and often to give them a new peace and assurance that they were right with God.

Carl next asks for more information about early Christian creeds. There is a significant body of scholarship that analyzes the structure and contents of various passages in the New Testament, in the original Greek, where a lot of Christological doctrine is jam-packed into a small, condensed text, often with signs of poetry, especially synonymous and antithetical parallelism and sometimes meter as well. These are typically referred to as creeds, confessions of faith, and even hymns.[7] The clear-

---

5. Larry W. Hurtado, *How on Earth Did Jesus Become a God? Historical Questions about Earliest Christian Devotion to Jesus* (Eerdmans, 2005).

6. Cf. esp. Graham H. Twelftree, *In the Name of Jesus: Exorcism among Early Christians* (Baker, 2007); and Graham H. Twelftree, *Paul and the Miraculous: A Historical Reconstruction* (Baker, 2013).

7. See esp. W. Hulitt Gloer, "Homologies and Hymns in the New Testament," *Perspectives in Religious Studies* 11 (1984): 115-32; Robert J. Karris, *A Symphony of New Testament Hymns* (Liturgical, 1996); Lawrence DiPaolo, Jr., *Hymn Fragments Embedded in the New Testament: Hellenistic, Jewish and Greco-Roman Parallels* (Edwin Mellen, 2008); and Clemens Leonhard and Hermut Löhr, eds., *Literature or Liturgy? Early Christian Hymns and Prayers in Their Literary and Liturgical Context in Antiquity* (Mohr Siebeck, 2014).

est example is Philippians 2:6–11, which divides into two halves, one about Christ's descent from heaven all the way to a human death and the other about his ascent and return to his exalted position next to God the Father. Each half divides into three stanzas of three lines with three accented syllables each. The one phrase that destroys the perfect parallelism is "even death on a cross" (v. 8), which adds a fourth line with two accented syllables to the third stanza of the first half. But given that the crucifixion is at the very heart of Paul's message (1 Corinthians 2:2), it makes sense to envision Paul adopting a preexisting creed, confession of faith, and/or hymn and adding this climactic phrase at its very center.[8] Other examples, besides 1 Corinthians 15:3–6, that are widely acknowledged as similar creeds include Colossians 1:15–20; 1 Timothy 3:16; and 1 Peter 1:18–21, 2:21–25 and 3:18–22.

With these introductory issues behind us, it is time to respond to Carl's treatment of my ten main points. To the first point, Carl properly chides me for having called the women the first eyewitnesses in all four of the canonical Gospel accounts. He naturally assumes that I meant they were the first to see the risen Jesus in all four accounts. What I should have said and what I intended was that they were the first eyewitnesses to the empty tomb in all four accounts. Later when I do reference the resurrection, I speak of the women solely as "witnesses," not "eyewitnesses," meaning that they are the ones who testify to the event as the reason for the empty tomb. I did not make this nearly plain enough, and will readily concede this.

I was, however, consciously more careful in expressing myself with respect to the legality of the women's testimony. What I wrote was: "But if there were no empty tomb for anyone to discover and the Gospel writers simply invented the story, why would they all, seemingly independently of each other, make women the first and primary witnesses to the resurrection in a culture that often didn't allow women's testimony in a court of law?" My choice of the word "often" was deliberate because

---

8. See esp. Ernst Lohmeyer, *Kyrios Jesus: Eine Untersuchung zu Phil. 2,5-11* (Winter, 1928); endorsed and elaborated by Ralph P. Martin, *A Hymn of Christ: Philippians 2:5-11 in Recent Interpretation and in the Setting of Early Christian Worship,* rev. ed. (IVP, 1997).

I was aware of the kind of exceptions that Beckwith acknowledges and that Price and Lowder cite. But that doesn't vitiate my point. If I wanted to invent a story and make it as credible as possible I still wouldn't put the women in the roles the Gospel writers did. First, there *were* male eyewitnesses who could testify to the resurrection, so it is not the case that the women were the only options, as in the Beckwith reference. Second, there was plenty of cultural, informal, and legal prejudice against women's beliefs in the ancient Mediterranean world (cf. the "old wives' tales" of 1 Timothy 4:7). There just isn't any reason to introduce this distracting and detracting information unless it is based on solid historical fact. And, even when it is so based, it isn't needed to make one's point. Thus, the creed or confession of faith that Paul cites in 1 Corinthians 15 can omit it. By definition a creed attempts to give a succinct but impressive list of the most important information on a topic. There was plenty of male eyewitness testimony and no need to mention the women at all. This is exactly what we would expect in a highly patriarchal culture. It's not the way we would do it today but we are very different. In addition, we must always remember that the absence of evidence is not evidence of absence.

We turn, secondly, to the transition from Sabbath to Sunday worship. Here it is important to stress that, *contra* Carl, there was no tradition whatsoever of pagans worshipping on Sundays in the first century. The Jews were the only people of that time who had a rhythm of one day a week for rest and worship. Greeks and Romans and the others they subjugated had annual calendars of festivals so that there were two, three, four, or five holidays per month, giving people days off work and opportunities for worship at the many temples dotting the larger cities of the empire. But these were attached to specific days of each month not to a fixed day of the week. So if Gentile Christians wanted to build on pagan practice (as they would later come to do in the third century by celebrating Christmas on a day that was already a holiday—Saturnalia—so that they would be left alone by those who might otherwise persecute them), they would not have established Sunday as a weekly day of worship. They were following the Jewish practice of Sabbath worship but changing the day of it. And that the minority of Jewish Christians in each community outside of Israel adopted this as well proves telling. Even John, one of the original twelve apostles, and steeped in Judaism, does so when he is in his own private worship on the Lord's Day on the island of Patmos (Revelation 1:10). It is, of course, true that all that is technically needed to explain this is a deeply seated belief that Christ was resurrected on a Sunday morning, not that he really was resurrected, but that just pushes the debate back a stage. Would subjective visions that lots of different people had on different days of the week have ever coalesced around the united conviction that it all began on a specific date and day of the week? Could it have convinced Jewish followers of Jesus to transgress one of the ten most inviolate commands of their law?[9]

Regarding my third point about people worshiping Jesus despite his crucifixion as one cursed by God, Carl appeals to cognitive dissonance, but he does not explain why Jesus is the only one of the numerous would-be liberators of Israel in the first century with whom this happened. Of course, Jesus can't have claimed that he would liberate Israel physically, but the sum total of his ministry, as N. T. Wright stresses, highlights that Satan and sin are the far more powerful oppressors than Rome from whom people need liberating.[10] As for disclosing himself in an irrefutable display of power, this would foreclose on human freedom to accept or reject him. Besides, when one sees the persistence of unbelief even in the face of the spectacular, one wonders what would have qualified as such an event. Some of those who experienced the miraculous feeding of the five thousand and others who heard about it wanted a sign from heaven to confirm the miracle (John 6:30). One really wonders what would have counted in their eyes! Richard Carrier's assertion (quoted by Carl) that "if God wants something from me he would tell me" is precisely that—sheer assertion. It is affirmed but not argued. It is certainly not self-evident. After all, it has been told to him, in Scripture,

---

9. For more on the transition from Sabbath to Sunday, see esp. D. A. Carson, ed., *From Sabbath to Lord's Day: A Biblical, Historical, and Theological Investigation* (Zondervan, 1982).

10. See esp. throughout N. T. Wright, *Jesus and the Victory of God* (Fortress, 1996).

but he rejects it anyway (cf. Luke 16:31—"if they do not listen to Moses and the prophets, they will not be convinced if someone rises from the dead"). Finally, the historic explanation of Jesus' silence before Pilate is that he realized it was his destiny to die for the sins of humanity rather than to defend himself. His silence proves nothing about his actual guilt or innocence.

My fourth point is rather more specific than Carl acknowledges. It is not that religions withstand great adversity. It is that there was something dramatically different about Jesus' supposed Messianic movement within first-century Israel compared with all the others. Of course other claimants could arise; that is exactly what we would expect to happen. My point is instead that none of these Messianic claimants ever had followers after their deaths. Attention turned to someone else. Why continue to think Jesus could be any kind of meaningful liberator, physical or spiritual, if he had been executed and his body were decomposing in some unknown location?

I was afraid that the response to my fifth point would follow the line Carl took. Haven't lots of people suffered and died for all kinds of faith that no Christian would acknowledge as true? I tried to forestall that tack by writing explicitly:

> If the heart of their [early Christians'] message had been Jesus' teaching, one might reconstruct a plausible scenario. Various groups of people throughout history have tried to follow the ethical teachings of founders of religions even at significant personal cost.

But no one has ever claimed that Muhammad died for the sins of humanity and was resurrected to vindicate his claims. Nor have the vast majority of Buddhists, Hindus, Shintoists, Taoists, Confucians, Jews, or Mormons ever made such claims for their founders. Nor did the neo-Platonists, Stoics, Epicureans, Cynics, Gnostics, Mithraists, neo-Pythagoreans, or emperor worshipers in pagan Greece and Rome in the first century. Nineteenth-century books and modern blogsites that claim otherwise have been discredited many times over as in part grossly exaggerated and in part completely untrue.[11] So, in fact, Carl has not replied to my fifth point at all.

I apologize that my sixth point was unclear. I perhaps tried to say too much before coming to the heart of it, which was:

> At least one man had been raised from the dead, but the general resurrection of all people had not occurred in conjunction with that one resurrection. Nothing in the Old Testament had predicted such a separation of resurrections, so where did the idea come from? The Greco-Roman world did not look for resurrection at all, with rare exceptions. The only logical alternative is that the concept actually came from the personal experience of the first followers of Jesus with their resurrected Lord.

I understand the problem of two thousand years elapsing since Jesus' first predictions, too. Can cognitive dissonance really explain the persistence and, indeed, the phenomenal growth of resurrection belief over the centuries? Carl and I can dispute the meanings of the key passages he cites. I have written on these elsewhere and, with a large body of evangelical scholars, do not see them teaching that Jesus or Paul thought the second coming was immediate, only that it might be.[12] But I happily grant that neither of them was thinking in terms of millennia either. My point was simply that the early Christian claims matched neither conventional Judaism (there is bodily resurrection of all people and it happens when Messiah comes) nor conventional paganism (there is no bodily resurrection), but rather it claimed that the Messiah came and was resurrected without the general resurrection of all people beginning. If the story were invented, who got this idea from where and why did anyone think it was better or more convincing than the existing options unless it corresponded to their own objective experiences?

---

11. See, e.g., Maurice Casey, *Jesus: Evidence and Argument or Mythicist Myths?* (Bloomsbury T & T Clark, 2014). For what we can say about genuinely pre-Christian Greco-Roman belief and the resurrection, see N. T. Wright, *The Resurrection of the Son of God* (Fortress, 2003), 32–84.

12. For example, in Craig L. Blomberg, *The Historical Reliability of the Gospels*, 2nd ed. (IVP, 2007), 64–66.

My comments on the delay of Christ's return also pointed out that it *does* have an analogue in the recurring Jewish prophecies about the coming Day of the Lord (or Judgment Day).[13] If the question is not why would somebody have a Messiah resurrected but not everyone else resurrected, but rather is why continue to believe after so long a period of nonfulfillment, then we *do* have Jewish precedent. Isaiah and Amos began prophesying eight centuries before Christ that the Day of the Lord was at hand (e.g., Isa. 13:6, 9; 34:8; Amos 5:18, 20). Partial fulfillments repeatedly occurred, but subsequent prophets predicted still more to come, and continued to do so down through the centuries (e.g., Jer. 39:17, 46:10; Ezek. 30:3; Joel 1:13; Obad. 15; Zeph. 1:14; Zech. 14:1; Mal. 4:5). It was Jews during the Second Temple period who appealed to Psalm 90:4 that God's timing is not human timing. Whether or not that satisfies Carl in the twenty-first century is not the issue; the issue is that there was a body of first-century individuals who did find that logic compelling, even after eight centuries, and could have transferred it from the Day of the Lord more generally to the return of Christ more specifically.[14] To Carl's question about "the parade of the zombies" in Matthew 27:52–53, I suspect they looked more like the resurrected Jesus, and the point was to say, "It's not just Jesus; the resurrection of all people really is coming down the road." But whether these two verses were intended to be taken as a straightforward historical narrative or, as Mike Licona has suggested, an apocalyptic symbol is another question. I am quite sure that when Paul wrote in Romans 10:9, "If you declare with your mouth, 'Jesus is Lord,' and believe in your heart that God raised him from the dead, you will be saved," it never even crossed his mind to add, "Oh, and you have to believe in the literal, bodily resurrection of those other lucky Old Testament saints too"!

Lest anyone think that I must stand my ground and defend every one of my previous points with equal tenacity, let me say that before I

---

13. Cf. esp. Richard Bauckham, "The Delay of the Parousia," *Tyndale Bulletin* 31 (1980): 3–36.

14. See also Charles L. Holman, *Till Jesus Comes: Origins of Christian Apocalyptic Expectation* (Hendrickson, 1996); and A. L. Moore, *The Parousia in the New Testament* (Brill, 1966).

ever wrote my seventh point about no one pointing out Jesus' actual grave I was aware that it was arguably the weakest of my ten. I stand by it, but I will not pursue it any further here. I do certainly understand, with Carl, how some of the same arguments can cut two different ways. On the other hand, to my eighth point—that it is eminently reasonable that Jesus would have been given a decent burial—let me just reiterate that I actually cited the ancient Jewish and Roman sources that support this, to which Carl made no reply.

Ninth, Carl says he does not understand how the remarkably restrained pictures in the canonical Gospels of the resurrection compared to the obviously legendary nature of the apocryphal gospels' accounts support the truth of the resurrection. They do so at least to the extent that if the disciples originally had no actual experience with an empty tomb but imagined seeing Jesus in one of the many different scenarios that Carl suggests, they would have been free to invent the story of the empty tomb any way they liked. Surely they would have created an account to satisfy the very natural human curiosity that the later apocryphal stories were addressing when they portrayed how Jesus came out of the tomb. Did the angels roll the stone away so that he simply walked out? Did the stone remain in place while Jesus suddenly just appeared on the other side of it? Did it happen some other way? The canonical accounts leave no clue.

Tenth, and finally, Carl rejects Craig Keener's presentations of modern-day miracles and even resurrections, which I cited. Here is where he refers back to an informal private exchange we had that I never expected to appear anywhere in print. I know full well the dangers of extrapolating from one survey to the experience of Christians worldwide. Two hundred million modern people who have experienced miracles may be a wildly inflated and unwarranted figure. My point does not depend on whether there are two hundred million or just two hundred. I have personally experienced a half-dozen for which I know of no remotely plausible scientific or medical explanation and which cannot be explained as a misdiagnosis of anything. I know of a couple dozen more that close friends have experienced and the same holds true for them. Carl has no explanation for any of these, much less the fact that the one consistent feature among them is that they occurred shortly after concerted public Christian prayer. That is not the *post hoc, propter hoc* fallacy; I will leave others to speculate about any causal relationship. It is just an observation of relative chronology.

At the end of his response it finally becomes clear. The resurrection of Jesus is not the main issue after all. It is above all the problem of suffering and evil in the world, and secondarily the question of the unevangelized, those who have never had a chance to hear the gospel. And now I can happily announce that I am in fundamental agreement with some of the things Carl says! He catalogs some of the world's horrors and then asks, "What kind of God would be responsible for such calamities?" He adds that he cannot believe in or worship such a god.

Let me say as forthrightly as I know how that this is not a god that I can believe in or worship either. But it is not the God I *do* believe in and worship. Despite numerous distortions of the Bible's message over the centuries, the heart of it is that God is love (1 John 4:8). In his love, he created free human beings with the freedom to rebel against him and they did. And that rebellion led to the entire universe becoming drastically out of whack. James 1:13–18 states unequivocally that God is not the author of evil and that he causes only good things. One may argue from that and say, "but then that means that God must . . ." in all kinds of ways. Some of those inferences may be true; others are not. But if one imagines a god who is to blame for the evil in our world, whether directly or indirectly, one is imagining something other than the biblical God. So Carl and I agree on the kind of God we don't believe in. I just don't know if Carl has ever seriously considered the God I do believe in.[15]

As for those who have never heard the gospel, it is sad that there are Christians who say that everyone who has never heard the gospel is damned or lost for all eternity. There are plenty of people in the Bible who never heard of Jesus who are called God's people—many of them are Old Testament Jews, but some are Gentiles also who come to hear about the God of the Jews. May we not extrapolate from these examples

---

15. Cf. further D. A. Carson, *The Difficult Doctrine of the Love of God* (Crossway, 2000).

and leave it in God's hands to judge those who have never heard? Abraham asked God, "will not the Judge of all the earth do right?" (Genesis 18:25) and the context suggests the answer is that he indeed will. One frequent way to interpreting Romans 2:14–16 is that God will judge everyone according to the "light" that they have received.[16]

In short, I still think there are good reasons to believe historically that Jesus of Nazareth was bodily raised from the dead. Carl's responses either miss nuances of my argument, move slightly off topic, or are based on approaches that some but not all Christians take and don't really defeat the main thrust of my positions. At least those are my opinions. But now we must hear other voices, and so we turn to Richard Carrier's and Peter Williams' reactions to our interchange.

---

16. For a thorough survey of the numerous, diverse approaches to the issue in the history of Christianity, see John Sanders, *No Other Name: An Investigation into the Destiny of the Unevangelized* (Eerdmans, 1992). Sanders presents and thoroughly discusses a half-dozen major, historic Christian options, not merely the "restrictivist" view that holds that all such persons are lost.

PART FOUR: COMMENTARY BY A LIBERAL
ATHEIST AND A TRADITIONAL CHRISTIAN

A Skeptic's Analysis

Richard Carrier, Ph.D.

Carl Stecher's Case

I've been asked to assess this debate, as I've researched and written extensively on the topic before. My chapter "Why the Resurrection is Unbelievable" in *The Christian Delusion* (edited by John W. Loftus) is most representative of my findings. Here, as there, I'll assume for the sake of argument that Jesus indeed existed and was crucified, and some other mundane historical facts.

Carl's case against Jesus' resurrection as a fact of history can be summarized succinctly as follows:

1. Paul, our only contemporary source and the only contemporary witness to the risen Jesus we have any record from, does not report any facts about the nature or circumstances of the risen Jesus' appearances, and certainly none that establish he was encountered in any way outside of momentary private visions, dreams, or hopeful confusions.

2. The Gospels appear decades later, their authors anonymous, and manifestly fictionalize and invent details and whole episodes; and no one to our knowledge verified or fact-checked anything in them, so we cannot know that any of their content dates to the time of Paul.

When we add the first fact to the second, there is no way to *know* that Jesus rose from the dead, only that he was *believed* to have. But strongly held false beliefs are common in all ages and societies. The founding events of Mormonism are a potent example. The evidence for the angel Moroni and his magical gold plates (including multiple eyewitness accounts, and martyrs) is stronger on every measure than the evidence we have for the raising of Jesus. Carl cites other examples such as the witch trials at Salem in 1692, another potent analogy (see, indeed, Matt McCormick's chapter in *The End of Christianity*, also edited by John W. Loftus). In antiquity, Lucian of Samosata famously made fun of such things happening often among the devout in *The Death of Peregrinus* and *The Lover of Lies*.

Carl's argument requires us to distinguish and not confuse two different things: what Paul thought happened when he wrote 1 Corinthians 15:3–8; and the stories the Gospels tell.

In 1 Corinthans Paul wrote (NIV translation):

> . . . that Christ died for our sins according to the Scriptures, that he was buried, that he was raised on the third day according to the Scriptures, and that he appeared to Peter, and then to the Twelve. After that, he appeared to more than five hundred of the brothers at the same time, most of whom are still living, though some have fallen asleep. Then he appeared to James, then to all the apostles, and last of all he appeared to me also, as to one abnormally born.

We have no connecting evidence that establishes anything of Paul's Epistles overlaps with the later Gospel accounts. Paul, for all we can ascertain, had never heard the resurrection tales in the Gospels nor any of the details in them. Nor, so far as we can know, had any Christian for many decades. Not even, so far as we can tell, had the author of the first Gospel (Mark) ever heard them. Mark's narrative has no account of the risen Jesus. What he heard besides, could be *anything*.

It is not difficult to explain the Gospel narratives as legend, fiction, or propaganda. Carl notes a lot of amazing invention got placed in those Gospels. His list, limited to the ascension, the raising of Lazarus, and the tale of "doubting" Thomas, is charitably short (compare my own survey in chapter 10 of *On the Historicity of Jesus*, and even that is not complete). And we do not have access to the opinion or report of anyone who could have fact-checked or verified those things, or challenged them. It is a well-established fact that such enormous fabrications do arise, and are believed without challenge, within mere decades or even years.[1] The Luddites of the early nineteenth century and the cargo cults of the early twentieth century afford apt examples.[2] And because we don't get to hear Paul's opinion of or reaction to any story or detail appearing in the Gospels, nor that of *anyone* who was really there, we can't trust these stories.

So all we actually have to explain is why Paul would write 1 Corinthians 15:3–8. What experiences was he aware of and thus intending when he wrote? Paul specifically mentions only *revelations* (1 Corinthians 9:1; 2 Corinthians 12; Romans 16:25–26; and, of course, Galatians 1:11–12, "I want you to know, brothers, that the gospel I preached is not something that man made up. I did not receive it from any man, nor was I taught it; rather, I received it by revelation from Jesus Christ."). That is, Paul writes exclusively of *inner* experiences. He says, "God . . . was pleased to reveal his Son in me so that I might preach him among the Gentiles" and "I did not consult any man, nor did I go up to Jerusalem to see those who were apostles before I was" (Galatians 1:15–16). Paul conveys to us no knowledge of anyone ever experiencing the risen Jesus in any other way. Even on the one occasion he reports a group experience to hundreds of brethren (1 Corinthians 15:6), this is the only experience Paul says happened "all at once"; we must conclude all the other experiences were to individuals and not groups. These cannot be identified as anything more substantial than is recorded in Acts 2:1–4: "suddenly there came from heaven a sound as of the rushing of a mighty wind, and it filled all the house where they were sitting. And there appeared unto them tongues parting asunder, like as of fire; and it sat upon each one of them."

---

1. See the examples and scholarship I cite in chapter 6.7 of *Historicity* and chapter 3 of my prequel to that, *Proving History*.

2. Carrier, *Historicity*, 9–10, 159–63.

This led to an inner feeling of encountering the Lord.

This sounds not unlike mass sightings of the Virgin Mary, as Carl points out, which include the Fatima sun vision, reported as "an appearance of the Virgin Mary" to and by hundreds. Yet when we hear the actual facts, what was actually seen was nothing of the kind. The only difference between that case and that of Jesus, is that for Jesus, *we don't get to hear* the facts by which to judge. Paul does not tell us what the "hundreds" of brethren *specifically* saw—nor, incidentally, do the Gospels, which fail to even mention any such encounter. The only event at all parallel is the mass ecstasy of the brethren on Pentecost reported in Acts, as I just related, and this sounds exactly like a literarily embellished account of more mundane phenomena: each brother whipped up into an ecstatic state and convincing himself he was seeing a magical light, and "feeling" the presence of the Lord. It was impossible for the disciples to discover they each were producing their own visionary light and feeling. They also had no motivation to make such a discovery, since they all *wanted* to be seeing the same thing, and thus would encourage the others to believe this. They might also feel anyone's doubts in the matter as damnable (see Galatians 1:9, "If anybody is preaching to you a gospel other than what you accepted, let him be eternally condemned!" Cf. James 1:6–8 and 2 Peter 2).

The psychology of ecstatic religious movements is well established scientifically, unlike such supernatural powers as raising the dead. I cite and survey a whole bibliography on this fact in *Historicity* (pp. 124–37). That the author of Acts tends to embellish mundane phenomena into the marvelous is already evident in how he treats the now well-scientifically-studied phenomenon of glossolalia in Acts 2:4–13 . Our only actual *eyewitness* account of it, from Paul (1 Corinthians 13–14), accords instead with the science, not with the fantasy related in Acts (I survey a whole bibliography on *that* fact in *Historicity*, pp. 124–25).

So there remains no difficulty in explaining what Paul reports to us, either. And we are left with no reliable way from this information to be confident Jesus rose from the dead. We can't access eyewitness accounts, nor vet them in any way. And that leaves us with no other conclusion we can claim probable except that what most likely happened is what *usually* happens when the marvelous comes to be believed and is embellished over time. That means phenomena we have well and securely documented—not phenomena that have never been documented, like corpses restored to life.

That's Carl's argument. And he is correct.

Carl also addresses the question of what happened to the body, hence the "empty tomb." No such discovery is attested by Paul, so we can no more establish such a thing happened than anything else in the highly fictionalized Gospel narratives. There are plenty of reasons to conclude no such story of a missing body existed in Paul's day.[3] And even if such stories did then exist (though we have no way to establish that), we know how bodies usually go missing, and it isn't by reanimating a corpse.[4] Indeed, any *natural* cause of a missing body could have *triggered* belief in a resurrection that in turn caused the dreams, visions, delusions, or mistakes Carl proposes led to a belief that Jesus was "seen" on various isolated occasions by the very people expecting or hoping to see him. Again, this conforms to well-established psychology and human nature; reanimating a corpse does not.

Carl has valid points to make about those scholars who believe there was an empty tomb: they are required to believe that for their faith, salvation, or employment. But also, the only data ever collected (but still never published) by Gary Habermas on how many experts believe there was an empty tomb, though purported to show three-quarters do, actually show *less than half do*—when we remember to exclude *non*experts, and to *not* exclude empty tomb *agnostics*.[5] So that an empty tomb was discovered is probably *not* the majority opinion of experts, which is why Gary Habermas has dropped the empty tomb from his ever-shrinking "minimal facts" apologetic.[6]

---

3. See Carrier, *Proving History*, 31, 128, 156–57.

4. Again, "Why the Resurrection is Unbelievable," 304–05.

5. See my discussion in "Innumeracy: A Fault to Fix," richardcarrier.info/archives/4857.

6. See Taylor Carr, "Gary Habermas Shows Why the 'Minimal Facts' of Jesus' Death Can't Establish the Resurrection," at godless-skeptic.blogspot.com/2015/08/gary-habermas-shows-why-minimal-facts.html.

I do, however, disagree with Carl's argument that Pilate releasing the body to a Jewish elder for burial is implausible. To be fair, Carl isn't alone. John Dominic Crossan and Bart Ehrman have both made similar arguments. But neither seems aware that under Judea's treaty with Rome at the time, Pilate was *required by law* to release such a body for burial—a fact attested by both Josephus and Philo.[7] And if Jesus did indeed die before day's end, the Sanhedrin was required by law to bury his body before sundown in a graveyard reserved for executed convicts.[8] Notably, the first account we have, in Mark—of which we know all later accounts are embellished redactions—never says Joseph buried Jesus in his own tomb, or a tomb that had never been used before, or in any lavish way. Those legendary accretions were only added later.[9]

So even if based on any truth (though we have no evidence it was), Mark is more likely relating a garbled account of Jesus' corpse being deposited as law required in the arcosolia of the Sanhedrin's grave complex, where it could easily have been lost, misplaced, or denied to be there even against contrary evidence. Or it could have been stolen (for which I've shown a good case can be made, in "The Plausibility of Theft," in *The Empty Tomb*). Or it might not have been regarded as relevant: many Jews believed resurrection was accomplished by abandoning the old body and taking up residence in an entirely new one. Paul appears to have believed this. I document this in "The Spiritual Body of Christ and the Legend of the Empty Tomb" (also in *The Empty Tomb*). Numerous scholars have concurred with this possibility, including even N.T. Wright.[10] We can't rule *any* of these things out, and if we can't rule them out, we can't rule anything else in—least of all something far more

---

7. See the evidence and scholarship I cite in "The Burial of Jesus in Light of Jewish Law," in *The Empty Tomb*, ed. Robert M. Price and Jeffery Jay Lowder; and I'm not the first to point this out: Byron McCane made the same point in "Where No One Had Yet Been Laid," in *Authenticating the Activities of Jesus*, ed. Bruce Chilton and Craig A. Evans (Brill Academic, 2002).

8. As proved in the same chapters just cited.

9. As Byron McCane aptly points out in "Where No One Had Yet Been Laid."

10. See "Spiritual Body FAQ," richardcarrier.info/SpiritualFAQ.html#othersupport and richardcarrier.info/SpiritualFAQ.html#wrightsupport.

incredible. When you don't have the evidence you need to know which thing happened, by definition *the least likely thing. . .is* not likely to be it.

The same logic operates for the other half of the equation. Carl proposes any one, or indeed *combination,* of eight ordinary things that could have caused an early belief among Jesus's close circle that he had "appeared" to them: "grief hallucinations, dream experiences, misheard or misinterpreted testimony, unconscious appropriation of another's experience, mistaken identification, memory distortion, disciple rivalry, [or] cognitive dissonance reduction." Unlike corpse reanimation, every single one of these is a phenomenon *we know for a fact* happens. Everything on this list is common in the context of thousands of years of billions of human lives. Indeed, the probability of a combination of these known natural phenomena (explaining the appearance beliefs *and* disposition of the body) is far higher than the probability of a single never-verified phenomenon. We would need evidence that rules them out, to rule the latter in. And we just don't have access to any of the relevant evidence we'd need to do that. All we have is Paul, who tells us next to nothing, and decades-later legends based on no sources we can establish, and vetted by no one we know who would have known the truth. That's not enough for any confidence.

So Carl's conclusion holds.

Craig Blomberg's Response

Major Problems

What does Craig have in reply? Nothing that conforms to the logic of evidence.

First, Craig cannot claim resurrection has the highest *prior* probability of explaining any set of facts; to the contrary, it's the one explanation for which we have no scientific evidence it *ever* occurs, much less that it did then. By definition, without evidence proving otherwise, that which usually happens is most likely what did happen. So we need *evidence* to conclude Jesus is the one exception in human history to how bodies *usually* disappear or come to be disregarded, or to how people *usually* come to believe they've seen the dead, or angels or gods or UFOs, or anything uncanny. Carl's point is that we just don't have that evidence.

Second, for evidence to increase the probability of a hypothesis, it has to be more likely on that hypothesis than on any alternative. So Craig argues that the evidence we have is *not* likely in any of Carl's scenarios, but *is* likely on the supposition of a reanimated corpse. Craig, however, produces no such evidence. So how does he get around that? By misrepresenting Carl's arguments, and the facts.

Craig starts with "dreams" and asks how likely it is for people to have experienced not just shared but "identical" dreams. This is a straw man. Carl said nothing about "identical" dreams; nor about *every instance* being a dream. On the dream-vision hypothesis, each percipient dreamt *or hallucinated* an encounter with what he believed to be Jesus. In no way did each such vision or dream have to be identical. Moreover, there is no evidence of their having these dreams and visions all on the same night (contrary to later Gospel legends, Paul does not say any of these revelations occurred "on the third day," only that *the resurrection* did). Only one event, Paul says, happened all at once: the mass ecstasy of the brethren (which, as I already noted, may have been as unexceptional as generic hallucinated lights and a feeling of being in touch with Jesus— Craig can present no other evidence). So all the others might have been one-off, momentary, individually experienced events. Quite in accord with dreams. Or hallucinations. Or both. And being in sequence, inspired by a movement leader (Cephas, aka Peter, the first to "receive" the momentous revelation), we even have a causal explanation of how each of the others was inspired to have a similar or corroborating dream or vision (particularly as their continued membership and authority in the Christian movement required they do so). Paul, after all, does not give us details. Some of the appearances he lists may have been dreams, some bereavement hallucinations, some ecstatically imagined lights, some misidentifications of other persons resembling Jesus (as in John 20:14 and 21:4 and Luke 24:16 and as even alluded in Matthew 28:17, as Craig fully admits). And so on. Any of a million combinations is possible. We can't rule out any on the poor evidence we have.

Context is also crucial. We know the Christians were regular hallucinators, reporting and readily believing visions and voices and spirit communications very frequently, compared to modern Western societies.[11] So we already know they were prone to it—and indeed would have been self-selected that way: the first believers were believers, precisely *because* they were ecstatics or schizotypals.

But we also know in antiquity, "revelations" of the numinous experienced when waking, though indeed common (reported by many pagans and Jews of the time), were not typically distinguished from "revelations" of the numinous experienced when asleep. Quite often, when someone claimed to have "seen" a divinity or had a "vision" or "revelation," they were speaking of something they dreamed—and to their own mind, they were being entirely honest.[12] It would never have occurred to them that its being in a dream made it less real than a waking vision. And consequently, they often wouldn't mention what to them would be an irrelevant distinction. A revelation from the gods was a revelation from the gods. Any combination of dreams and hallucinations is therefore as likely as any other. All would be called visions. All would be called seeing Jesus. And there is no difficulty in explaining this from known facts of human nature and the history of religions.[13]

So is there any evidence we have that is unlikely on the dream-vision hypothesis as Carl *actually* argued? None that Craig points to. All the evidence we have is entirely consistent with the psychological explanations that Carl explored. None of it is improbable.

---

11. Carrier, *Historicity*, 124–37.

12. For a full survey of the evidence on this point, see William Harris, *Dreams and Experience in Classical Antiquity* (Harvard University Press, 2009), and James Tabor, *Things Unutterable: Paul's Ascent to Paradise in Its Graeco-Roman, Judaic and Early Christian Contexts* (University Press of America, 1986).

13. See: Jack Kent, *The Psychological Origins of the Resurrection Myth* (Open Gate, 1999); James Crossley, "Against the Historical Plausibility of the Empty Tomb Story and the Bodily Resurrection of Jesus," *Journal for the Study of the Historical Jesus* 3 (June 2005): 171–86; and Michael Goulder, "The Baseless Fabric of a Vision," *Resurrection Reconsidered*, ed. Gavin D'Costa (Oneworld, 1996).

And this is based on objectively documented evidence from science and history, not the circular logic of citing Christianity's own unsourced teachings. When Craig says, "we see how unwilling Thomas was to believe the collective report of all the other ten without his own personal eyewitness experience," he is failing to refute the evidence that no such thing ever happened, that it's a made-up story. As Carl points out, that's why we find no trace of it in earlier texts—not in Paul, and not in any of the other Gospel writers. One can't use fiction as a point of scientific data about how people really behave, least of all fiction written specifically to persuade people of the very fact Craig wants to establish (the explicitly stated purpose of the inventor of that story: "these are written, that ye may believe that Jesus is the Christ, the Son of God" [John 20:31]). Craig can't establish that that story is true. Our only available witness, Paul, makes no mention of it. So Craig can't establish anyone ever actually behaved like Thomas. Or that there even was a Thomas. And when we look at Paul's own reports of Christians (including himself and his congregations) hallucinating time and again, we see no evidence of any "doubting" Thomases who weren't simply expelled as infidels (as per Galatians 1:6–9, James 1:6–8, and 2 Peter 2).

So once again, is the production of a late fabricated tale about a "doubting" Thomas consistent with Carl's thesis and all the other evidence we have? Yes. Is it at all improbable? No. Is there even any *evidence* it wasn't fabricated? No. Indeed, if Jesus really did rise from the dead, we should expect tales like that *to already be in Paul*, and certainly in the earlier Gospels. That it instead appears only close on *a century* after the events in question, in the last of many revisions of the same canon of Gospels, is actually *improbable* on the reanimated corpse hypothesis. But it's very probable indeed on the "they made this stuff up" hypothesis.

Craig similarly straw-mans Carl's argument by calling his "misheard or misinterpreted testimony" thesis mere "gossip." This is not a term that Carl used, nor does it seem appropriate. Carl's point was that mundane experiences (like "feeling" the presence of Jesus) convinced the original percipients but was *misreported by others* as "Jesus appeared to them." Carl is not saying gossip convinced the apostles to believe

Jesus appeared to them. He is saying something *else* convinced the apostles to believe Jesus appeared to them. Misheard or misinterpreted testimony might have caused them to have those experiences, including those acquired through false memories. They might have called their actual experiences an appearance of Jesus, when really, that's not what *we* would call it—just as we would not call the Fatima sun vision an appearance of the Virgin Mary, yet those who had the experience did. What evidence do we have that *that's* improbable in the case of Jesus? None. So Craig has no argument against Carl's actual point here, either.

Craig also has the order of evidence backwards when he claims Carl must prove such confusions occurred. To the contrary, *the evidence is gone.* Yet such confusions are normal, common, and consistent with the little evidence we have. So it is Craig who has to prove such confusions *didn't* occur—because only by proving they didn't occur, can Craig get any closer to proving it was a corpse's reanimation *instead.* But as Carl points out, all that evidence is lost. Unlike the Fatima sun miracle, we don't get to access what anyone actually was saying or claiming. If all the eyewitness testimony in the Fatima sun miracle were destroyed, and all we had was someone twenty years later saying the Virgin Mary "appeared to hundreds all at one time," would it make any sense to conclude she really did in fact appear—simply because we can't prove how the confusion from "hallucinating a bouncing sun" to "Virgin Mary appeared" came about? No. We can't prove that Jesus' resurrection happened because no eyewitness testimony now exists. *That leaves Craig as much in the dark as we are.* And honesty demands admitting that.

Craig similarly misrepresents Carl's argument about mistaken identity, imagining an impostor trying to convince the apostles he was Jesus. Another straw man. Carl's point never requires such a scenario. He very clearly described the very scenario *the Gospel authors themselves found credible,* an encounter with a stranger who resembled Jesus. So Craig can hardly find it *in*-credible. If the Gospel authors *themselves* imagined this a plausible way to be convinced Jesus had been seen risen, then clearly *it was.* In both the Magdalene and Tiberias tales in John *and* the Emmaus tale in Luke, some complete stranger is mistaken for Jesus . . . not because he was trying to pretend to be Jesus, but simply because the percipients convinced themselves it must have been him in supernatural disguise—and indeed, in those days, angels and divinities were thought to frequently appear in disguise. After this "apparition" of Jesus left, they would have no reason to look for him . . . they would well know he was taking any guise he wished; if he wished them to see him, he'd visit *them*.

And again, as Carl explains, we should not be assuming these tales are 100 percent accurately related. Just as Luke "embellishes" luminous visions and glossolalia in Acts into things more patently fabulous (a voice from the sky, Jesus ascending into a cloud), we can expect him to just as easily embellish the Emmaus narrative to have the peculiar "vanishing hitchhiker" details we find in it. Likewise the other stories. Carl's point is that mistakenly believing that a gardener or a stranger on the road to Emmaus was Jesus, fully explains *both* the belief they had seen Jesus *and* the later embellished and fictionalized legends of those experiences in the Gospels. Matthew 28:17 even tells us that "some of the disciples doubted" it was Jesus they were meeting, suggesting they had to be persuaded after the fact that indeed it was him—yet another indication of what may have originally happened.

So is any of the evidence we have improbable on *this* scenario, the one Carl actually proposed? No. It's consistent with every piece of evidence we have. In fact, that we'd have preserved multiple tales of the eyewitnesses sincerely believing complete strangers were Jesus, and that this amounted to "seeing Jesus," is improbable *on the reanimated corpse* hypothesis. Even if those tales are wholly fictions, they prove this is what even those authors would have believed real, which makes those stories evidence *for the plausibility* of Carl's hypothesis. Either way, he wins the point.

Craig continues his circular logic with such claims as that "the disciples were cowering behind locked doors" or "there were no consistent factors in the circumstances" of where they saw Jesus (and many other like claims), which are all based on the fictions invented by the Gospel authors long after Paul was dead. Carl's argument is precisely that none of this can be established as having been what anyone was claiming in Paul's day. And Craig has not established that any of it was.

So he can't use these assertions to explain what happened that Paul is relating in 1 Corinthians 15. That's the point.

Carl is saying that what happened back then could have been any number of *other* things that *aren't* what we are told in the Gospels; and that what we are told in the Gospels is highly fictionalized, embellished, redacted, creatively manipulated—or wholly fabricated. It's because we can't establish that anything in the Gospels goes back to Paul's day that we can't have any confidence in what happened based on what's in them. And what's in Paul, is not what Craig says. There is nothing there about where or when the diverse appearance events occurred or what triggered or anchored them, or whether *anyone* was "cowering" or, as actually typifies other cults we know, that they weren't consumed by a defiant expectation of vindication and a desperate search for some way to convince themselves they were right. Paul tells us nothing. And that's that.

It's also simply not true that those visions all had to occur in the same geographical space. Each percipient, *being a different person*, would have his own anchors and triggers. It would not even be likely that they'd all have the *same* one. So where some might have bereavement hallucinations, what would have triggered them would not be anchored the same way in every case. And again, Carl is not assuming every single appearance claim was *of the same thing*. Some may have been bereavement hallucinations. Some dreams. Some inner feelings. Some ecstatic visions. Some mistaken identity. And so on. *A million different combinations are possible.* And Craig cannot rule out any of them—because the evidence he would need *to rule them out* doesn't exist anymore. He can't access it to check. And that's why, two thousand years later, we can't know what actually happened.

It's also not valid to cite Josephus here, and not only because most scholars are uncertain that he ever mentioned the resurrection of Jesus. Nearly everyone now agrees the passage in question, which Josephus would have written sixty years after Jesus' crucifixion, was fabricated or heavily doctored by later Christian editors.[14] Furthermore, Josephus'

---

14. See my survey of the scholarship and evidence in *Historicity*, 332–42, and my update, based on what I presented at the 2017 Society of Biblical

obvious source would have been the Gospels—but sources derived from the Gospels cannot corroborate claims made in them. Because Josephus tells us nothing more about how anyone came to believe they'd "seen" Jesus than Paul does, or how he knows even that. Josephus is therefore of no use to Craig's case.

It's similarly not valid for Craig to argue Carl is wrong because "if someone in Corinth didn't believe Paul's word about seeing the Risen Lord, they could ask him where to find James, Peter or any of the five hundred who were still alive." That begs the question of *what they then would have been told.* And this is apart from what Carl already pointed out in his rejoinder, that such confirmation would involve enormous cost of time and money and would be utterly impractical, since Paul identifies not a single one of these alleged five hundred witnesses, and gives no indication of where this appearance supposedly happened, nor any indication of what these alleged witnesses actually witnessed some twenty years previously. Furthermore, there is no evidence that anyone Paul was addressing had any skill or inclination to do such fact-checking.[15] Not surprisingly, there is no evidence that anyone *did* undertake such fact-checking, much less that anyone was able to confirm this five hundred–witness claim. Carl's point is that *we cannot establish* what stories were circulating *when* Paul wrote 1 Corinthians 15, or that they resembled anything in the Gospels written decades later. So, sure, aside from the alleged five hundred witnesses, people could "corroborate" that the witnesses Paul refers to did indeed claim Jesus "appeared" to them. But exactly what would they have corroborated? Appeared how? *That is precisely what we don't know and what Craig Blomberg can't establish.*

Confusing what actually happened that Paul is attesting, with the fabulous tales later told in the Gospels, is precisely what we cannot justify. That's Carl's argument. I do not see any rebuttal to it in the whole of Craig's reply. For example, when Craig says of Paul:

Literature Midwest Region Meeting: "Josephus on Jesus? Why You Can't Cite Opinions Before 2014," summarized at richardcarrier.info/archives/11958.

15. All as I explain and document in chapters 7, 13, and 17 of *Not the Impossible Faith.*

He is like one "abnormally born" (1 Corinthians 15:8), who didn't get to have the kind of experience the Eleven had when Jesus was still appearing on earth. Then [Jesus] appeared in bodily form, walked on the ground, could be touched, ate food, and so on. To Paul, [Jesus] appeared in a heavenly vision.

Craig is assuming facts not in evidence: that when Paul was alive thirty to seventy years before the Gospel accounts were written, anyone was claiming Jesus "appeared in bodily form, walked on the ground, could be touched, ate food." And you can't base confident beliefs on facts not in evidence. Speculation is not fact.

Paul also never says his experience was in any way different from anyone else's. In Romans 16:25–26 he only says revelations were how anyone experienced Jesus. He never says anyone had experienced the risen Jesus in any other way. So Craig, despite trying, cannot conjure evidence that isn't there. For example, the word Paul uses for "abnormally born" is *ektrôma*, "an abortion, a miscarriage" (literally, "from a wound"), meaning one *rejected*. Not one who had a different experience. One who was chosen despite being a monster. Why a monster? In the very next verse Paul explains: "for I am the least of the apostles, who is not fit to be called an apostle, because I persecuted the church of God" (1 Corinthians 15:9). Craig reads the preceding line out of context as somehow Paul saying his *encounter* with Jesus was different. No. Paul says no such thing. He tells us himself that he means he was different solely in having been an enemy of the church before he got to see Jesus. He was not deserving, yet God elected him. There is no evidence here that Paul had ever heard of anyone eating with Jesus or handling his body or anything different from experiencing Jesus *within*, as Paul tells us *he* did.

Much of Craig's reply consists of just inventing what he thinks happened but not presenting any *evidence* for his speculations. That gets us nowhere. We still don't have any good reason to be confident the Gospels tell us what was known to Paul and those of Paul's time. And Paul tells us nothing that corroborates any of what's in the Gospels.

This is why we cannot have any confident belief in what happened. And when we lack evidence for what happened, it is logically necessary that what happened is most likely *what usually happens*. Not what never does. Meeting reanimated corpses is not what ever happens. And this statement is true even if naturalism is false, because it's simply a plain statement of fact. *It requires no worldview commitment.* The natural explanations Carl proposes? Those are things we've *confirmed* happen, and happen a lot. And those things fit all the evidence we have.

And that's all we have. It would be nice if there were evidence, if we could read what the actual eyewitnesses said they had experienced, what actually had convinced them; if we could hear from Paul what he was describing in 1 Corinthians 15:3–8, or even what "Peter" and "James" related to him when he finally met them years after evangelizing the faith across Arabia. But we don't get to. And we can't build a belief on evidence we can't access.

Craig also incorrectly claims "in the Jewish and Roman world of Jesus' day," historical fiction used "largely unknown people and places or [inserted] deliberate and blatant anachronisms." The Kings literature contains whole dubious and fabulous narratives about Elijah and Elisha widely agreed to be mostly if not entirely legendary, yet is padded with real places and facts; it is the mainstream consensus that Exodus and Deuteronomy are not historical texts, but present themselves as such, and reference real personages and places. Daniel, widely agreed to be a forgery, attempts to include real historical background facts (and fails only through error). Most historians do not credit many of the legends in the Maccabean literature to be authentic either, yet those are surrounded by real events and details.[16] The first century *Biblical Antiquities* engaged this practice in elaborate detail. In pagan literature, examples abound that do this as well: the *Satyricon* of Petronius, the *Lives of Aesop*, the *Golden Ass* of Apuleius, and numerous novels and story collections.[17]

---

16. See Sara Johnson, *Historical Fictions and Hellenistic Jewish Identity: Third Maccabees in its Cultural Context* (University of California Press, 2005).

17. See G.W. Bowersock, *Fiction as History: Nero to Julian* (University of California Press, 1997); Alan Cameron, *Greek Mythography in the Roman*

In fact, much of ancient biography of historical persons was fictional;[18] and some was even of fictional persons, yet presented as sober fact (like Plutarch's *Life of Romulus*). Faking histories was indeed so common, it was regarded as a crisis, as attested in the very source Craig himself cites: Lucian of Samosata's *How to Write History* (similarly in Plutarch's *On the Malice of Herodotus*). And modern historians note many episodes contained even in otherwise proper histories of the day, are fictions (as documented by Michael Grant in *Greek and Roman Historians: Information and Misinformation*—just for a start, but examples are endless, and extend all the way from Tacitus to Josephus). So we cannot rescue the fabulous and unverified tales of encountering a risen Jesus in the Gospels as fact by appealing to the claim "no one did that back then."

It's conspicuous that the original story in Mark doesn't contain any appearance narratives, nor hardly any of the "historical details" Craig is so impressed by, but in fact notoriously depicts confused geography and limited understanding of Judean customs. Not even Matthew added much to the resurrection evidence, other than to fix those mistakes, and tack on an appearance narrative. Only when Luke decided to redact Mark and Matthew (or Matthew's *other* lost source, if such there was), do all these markers of "historical genre" suddenly appear: Luke adds tons of background color (none of which actually relates to Jesus or Christianity), the dating of events, and a pseudo-historical preface, all where never such things existed before. John later tacked on more. That does not look like an honest activity. The veneer of history was *added* to the structure of Mark and Matthew, not introduced by them or by anyone with any other identifiable source on Jesus *but* them.

Finally, when it comes to establishing the body went missing—at all,

---

World (Oxford University Press, 2004); Jo-Ann Brant et al., *Ancient Fiction: The Matrix of Early Christian and Jewish Narrative* (Society of Biblical Literature, 2005).

18. See Mary Lefkowitz, *The Lives of the Greek Poets*, 2nd ed. (Bristol Classical Press, 2012); and Ava Chitwood, *Death by Philosophy: The Biographical Tradition in the Life and Death of the Archaic Philosophers Empedocles, Heraclitus, and Democritus* (University of Michigan Press, 2004).

much less by supernatural means—Craig does not answer hardly any of Carl's original points. So my previous summary stands unrebutted.

As if somehow to effect a response, Craig mentions the Jewish polemic against Jesus in the Talmud but fails to point out that none of it involved explaining an empty tomb or missing body. That argument evidently remained unknown to Rabbinical Jews. Even the fictional Jew Trypho, invented by Justin Martyr as a foil for his Christian dialogues, never mentions any Jewish polemic about a missing body. Nor do any Jews anywhere in the whole of Luke or Acts (or Roman authorities either for that matter . . . despite graverobbing being a capital crime). Is Luke omitting something uncomfortable to his case? Or was there no empty tomb for the authorities to discover, explain, investigate, or prosecute anyone for? It has to be one or the other. This is a serious problem for Craig.[19] No such polemic was mentioned by Celsus, either, who nevertheless did know, and reported, Jewish polemic against the virgin birth and the appearance claims. So we can't even establish any Jews ever heard of a missing body, prior to the Gospels contriving it. So we can't establish that that was evidence in Paul's day, either. And with no evidence, we have no knowledge.

Finally, Craig attempts to answer Carl's point about cognitive dissonance with an elaborate *tu quoque* fallacy that is irrelevant to the argument he made. Carl explained sensibly that the well-established psychology of cognitive dissonance is a fully adequate explanation for the disciples' belief Jesus was raised, and we have no evidence that would rule that out. To which fact Craig has no reply. He claims that the resurrection of Jesus is relevantly "different" than all the other documented examples of history and science, but he never explains how. It's not. The disciples desperately needed to believe their man was the Messiah, and that contradicted the fact of his death. The science of cognitive dissonance tells us that when persons are confronted with two contradictory beliefs, they will find some way to rationalize one away, so they can continue believing wholeheartedly in the other. (In fact, science establishes they will then believe it with even greater confidence

19. See Carrier, *Historicity*, 368–71.

than before.) So when confronted with two contradictory beliefs—that Jesus was the promised Messiah, and that Jesus was a rotting corpse—it's almost obvious which of those beliefs had to go. And resurrection, confirming the end has begun as their messiah had promised it would (1 Cor. 15:20–23), was definitely a culturally available solution to any group of apocalyptic Jews.

Maybe some did abandon the faith—after all, Matthew 28:17 implies this, and we don't get to hear about defectors, so we can't confirm there were none. But in the right conditions, more likely they'd do what true believers often do: refuse to believe that their faith had failed a*s soon as anyone suggested a solution.* Like, for example, Peter having innovated it as a potent idea to recover his faith, and finding confirmation of it "hidden" in the scriptures, in the same way Paul says in Romans 16:25–26: "my gospel and the proclamation of Jesus Christ" is "according to the revelation of the mystery hidden for long ages past, but now revealed and made known through the prophetic writings by the command of the eternal God." Peter then charismatically convinced the others it must be what happened; cognitive dissonance would then do the rest, inspiring each (as it did Peter) to have whatever experience they needed to come to the same conclusion (hence 1 Peter 1:8: "though you have not seen [Jesus], you love him; and even though you do not see him now, you believe in him and are filled with an inexpressible and glorious joy"). To accomplish that, there were numerous cultural and psychological tools available to them, particularly in that time and context, where visions were respected as real encounters with the divine, and even "seeing" someone in someone else (as the Gospels relate) was accepted, owing to widespread belief at the time that gods and angels made appearances in just this way. The reality is, we can't rule this in or out, because we cannot access the evidence we would need in order to do so.

Minor Problems

That's enough to conclude the case. But there were an assortment of minor points that can't be left unquestioned.

For example, when Craig attempts to rescue the Gospel appearance narratives from the accusation of being contradictory, he attempts a harmonization that ignores nearly all the actual contradictions Carl called attention to: why the Easter appearances change location from one city to entirely another one three days away (no, the Gospels do *not* place them weeks apart); why the guards vanish in all but one version of the story; why there is no angel descending from the sky. Only one other—the absence of so marvelous an event as the ascension—Craig attempts to explain, but Carl has already noted this explanation doesn't make sense. Carl points out additional problems in his rejoinder. Here's the thing: Any fictions in *any* religion's literature, *any* collection of sagas, *any* film, novel, or comic book canon, that contradict each other can be rationalized away with made-up harmonizations for which no evidence exists. That does nothing to argue that those contradictions aren't still evidence of fiction. They are. And honesty demands admitting this. If Craig weren't writing about his own sacred texts, I wouldn't have to tell him this. He'd be telling *me* this.

Craig also defends the use of "accepted criteria" from the Institute of Biblical Research to extract history from the Gospels; Carl rightly notes Craig's only cited source in defense of their effectiveness on the resurrection is hardly one anyone would trust who isn't already committed to the conclusion. In the actual *peer-reviewed* literature of *mainstream* journals and publishers, every single study dedicated to evaluating the efficacy of those criteria has found them commonly ineffective, fallacious, or abused.[20] In no case does a logically valid and factually sound application of any of those criteria support any detail

---

20. For example: Chris Keith and Anthony Le Donne, *Jesus, Criteria, and the Demise of Authenticity* (T&T Clark, 2012); Stanley Porter, *The Criteria for Authenticity in Historical-Jesus Research* (T&T Clark, 2004); Gerd Theissen and Dagmar Winter, *The Quest for the Plausible Jesus: The Question of Criteria* (Westminster John Knox Press, 2012); Christopher Tuckett, "Sources and Methods," in *The Cambridge Companion to Jesus*, ed. Markus Bockmuehl (Cambridge University Press, 2001); John Gager, "The Gospels and Jesus: Some Doubts about Method," *Journal of Religion* 54, no. 3 (1974); Morna Hooker, "Christology and Methodology," *New Testament Studies* 17 (1970); for a full analysis, see chapter 5 of my book *Proving History*.

of the resurrection narratives in the Gospels. Accordingly, Craig gives no example of their doing so. For instance, his attempt to deploy an argument from embarrassment to prove women found the tomb empty rests on factually false premises about ancient women (as I'll explain shortly).

Likewise, many pagan bodily resurrection stories predate Christianity; several are about divine saviors akin to Jesus. Inanna, Zalmoxis, Bacchus, Romulus, and Osiris are just the short list; and Craig's account of them is not factually correct.[21] The features Christianity adapted from those religions are too numerous to be coincidence.[22] And that does indeed provide an available explanation for where the novel idea of inventing a risen Jewish savior came from. Beliefs about Jesus combined that "risen savior" concept with Jewish models of eschatological resurrection. For belief in Jesus's resurrection was closely tied not only to his ability to grant salvation to those who mystically commune with him (and thus was *necessary* to what Christians wanted to preach: 1 Corinthians 15:13–19), but also to his apostles' belief that the general resurrection of Israel and the end of the world had indeed begun as Jesus promised (hence he was "the first fruits" of the general resurrection: 1 Corinthians 15:20, 23–24). This is why they needed to believe him bodily raised. This does not establish that anything narrated in the Gospels ever happened, or was ever even claimed to have happened by anyone in Paul's day.

And there is a lot more that could be said that there is too little space for.

For example, there is a great deal more evidence that the Lazarus narrative, and the unnamed "witness" John claims for some scenes, were fabricated than Carl mentions.[23] And the Gospels did *not* independently

---

21. See chapter 3 of *Not the Impossible Faith* and pp. 168–73 (with pp. 36–48 and 56–58) of *Historicity*; but for a quick look at what Craig gets wrong about them, see Richard Carrier, "Dying-and-Rising Gods: It's Pagan, Guys. Get Over It," at *Richard Carrier Blogs*, March 29, 2018, richardcarrier.info/archives/13890.

22. See Carrier, *Historicity*, 96–108.

23. See ibid., 500–5.

place women at the tomb; they all just get that idea from Mark, and simply change up how they wanted it to go. There are ample reasons why, not least being to reify the gospel: the haughty will be humbled, and the least shall be first. There is no evidence they had any sources for any of that, or that any such tales existed in Paul's day. And what we cannot establish, we cannot believe with any confidence. It's also *false* that Jewish or Greco-Roman culture "didn't allow women's testimony in a court of law" (and the evidence is far more decisive than even Carl attests: see chapter 11 of *Not the Impossible Faith*). Christian apologists need to stop using that argument.

And not just facts, but also logic needs to be respected. Craig makes much of Jesus' resurrection being special because he didn't die again— but where do we have evidence of that? After scattered, momentary visions to the apostles, he vanishes, never to be seen again. If you insist someone who died is *still* alive, you are required to produce him. Otherwise, we have no reason to believe you. "I feel it in my heart" or "he answers me when I pray" is simply not evidence that would be accepted by any court of law or peer-reviewed history journal. Nor even "I saw him once." As Carl said: does this work for Elvis or Michael Jackson? Similarly, when Craig argues that he will believe any strange story, so long as he can imagine an even stranger version of it, because if the actual story told "were an invention, one would expect" its author to have rendered it even more fabulous . . . I must hope no reader of this volume requires me to explain why his reasoning is illogical.

As to why a new sect would change what day they reserve for rest and worship, a reanimated corpse is still the least likely explanation. No such thing was required of the Seventh-day Adventists to reject traditional Christian teachings and revert to Saturday worship. Nor would such have been required for a breakaway sect of ancient Jews. Likewise, believing Jesus was raised by God pretty much eliminates any concern over how he was killed. And Carl's entire point is that no supernatural event is required to explain why they believed he was unjustly killed. Likewise, that no other sect vindicated their man with a resurrection is simply how religions work: every religion and sect comes up with new, innovative ways to resolve their cognitive dissonance and distinguish themselves. It is unreasonable to expect every religion and sect to have identical historical claims and theologies. If they did, there would be only one religion or sect, not thousands. And why would Paul's creed say their dying messiah was buried? Because scripture said their dying messiah would be buried (Isaiah 53:9).[24] No other explanation is required. Paul *conspicuously* never says that Jesus' grave became empty or that anyone verified it was empty or that anyone even knew where it was. And as Carl says, when we lack evidence, we cannot know with any confidence.

In just the same fashion, Craig cites Keener . . . who, contrary to what he and Keener assert, has produced no scientific evidence that any of the miracle stories he collected *are true*. Believers—including Craig—still tell miracle tales, and there are unscientific witnesses who swear by them, yet engage in no scientific controls to vet what they think happened. This is not evidence corpses rise from the dead. That's why Keener can't get a single instance of resurrection published in any peer-reviewed *science* journal: his evidence is no better than what we get for magic crystals and homeopathy. The Scientific Revolution was defined by humanity finally, honestly admitting that we cannot base our beliefs on unverified stories. We really need to remember that. Otherwise, it's back to snake oil, mesmerism, and Salem 1692.

Conclusion

When it comes to the resurrection, Paul, our only witness, doesn't give us any details; and we can't prove the Gospels actually come from any witnesses. We therefore can establish nothing as true. And in the end, in context, there is nothing all that remarkable about Christianity's origin or success.[25] Dreams or visions are all we have first-hand accounts of as having happened. Mass ecstasies tell us nothing. And the history of Christianity itself is far too mundane to require an actual resurrection

---

24. See Carrier, *Historicity*, 73–83 and 137–43.

25. See my chapter "Christianity's Success Was Not Incredible," in *The End of Christianity*.

as the initial inspiration. This whole exchange between Craig Blomberg and Carl Stecher only confirms my own prior conclusion:

> If God Himself were really appearing to people, and really was on a compassionate mission to reform and save the world, there is hardly any credible reason [He] would appear to only one persecutor rather than to all of them. But if [the persecutor] Paul's experience was entirely natural, and not at all divine [*as in Acts, just a subjectively experienced light and voice*], then we should expect such an event to be rare, possibly even unique—and, lo and behold, that appears to be the case. Paul's conversion thus supports the conclusion that Christianity originated from natural phenomena, and not from any encounter with a walking corpse. A walking corpse—indeed a flying corpse (Luke 24:51 and Acts 1:9–11) or a teleporting corpse (Luke 24:31–37 and John 20:19–26)—could have visited Pilate, Herod, the Sanhedrin, the masses of Jerusalem, the Roman legions, even the emperor and senate of Rome. He could even have flown to America (as the Mormons actually believe he did), and even China, preaching in all the temples and courts of Asia. In fact, being God, he could have appeared to everyone on earth. He could visit me right now. Or you! And yet, instead, besides his [already-devoted] followers, just one odd fellow ever [reported seeing] him.
>
> If Jesus was a God and really wanted to save the world, [one would expect] he would have appeared and delivered his Gospel personally to the whole world. He would not appear only to one small group of believers and one lone outsider, in one tiny place, just one time, two thousand years ago, and then give up. But if Christianity originated as a natural movement inspired by ordinary hallucinations (real or pretended), then we would expect it to arise in only one small group, in one small place and time, and especially where, as in antiquity, regular hallucinators were often respected as holy and their hallucinations believed to be divine communications. And that's exactly when and where it began. The ordinary explanation thus predicts all we see, whereas the extraordinary explanation predicts things we don't see at all.[26]

---

26. "Christianity's Success Was Not Incredible," in *The End of Christianity*, 70–71.

This statement holds as well for every other scenario and combination of scenarios Carl proposes. There really isn't any way to get around this. And Craig has provided none. All he has are rationalizations and speculations. But what we need is *evidence*.

Evidence, Explanation, and Expectation

Peter S. Williams, M.Phil.

As we consider the debate between Professors Carl Stecher and Craig Blomberg on the purported resurrection of Jesus, it's important to understand how different historical methodologies lead them to embrace different sets of *evidence* to be explained, and how their competing *explanations* for what they consider to be the relevant evidence are not only shaped by that evidence, but by their different worldview *expectations*.

The importance of distinguishing between *evidence*, *explanations*, and *expectations* is apparent from Carl's misunderstanding of N. T. Wright's *The Resurrection of the Son of God*. Wright doesn't claim, as Carl states in his opening case: "that the physical resurrection of Jesus is as certain a historical fact as the destruction of the Jerusalem Temple by the Romans in 70 AD." Rather, it's the *evidence* of Jesus' postcrucifixion burial in a subsequently empty tomb and *apparent* resurrection appearances that Wright argues is on a par with the fall of Jerusalem's Temple.[1] This becomes clear if we quote Wright in context:

---

1. Carl Stecher, "Faith, Facts, and the Resurrection of Jesus: A Review of The Resurrection of the Son of God by N. T. Wright," *Skeptic Magazine* 11, no. 4 (2005): 73–78, likewise conflates Wright's assessment of *evidence* with his defense of the resurrection hypothesis as the best *explanation* thereof.

A further, more recent suggestion can also be ruled out: that, after his crucifixion, Jesus' body was not buried, but left instead for dogs and vultures to finish off. Had that happened, no matter how many 'visions' they had had, the disciples would not have concluded that he had been raised from the dead. We are left with the secure historical conclusion: the tomb was empty, and various 'meetings' took place not only between Jesus and his followers (including at least one initial sceptic) but also, in at least one case (that of Paul; possibly, too, that of James), between Jesus and people who had not been among his followers. I regard this conclusion as coming in the same sort of category, of historical probability so high as to be virtually certain, as the death of Augustus in AD 14 or the fall of Jerusalem in AD 70. This brings us to step 7 of the argument I outlined at the start of the chapter.[2]

Wright places "visions" and "meetings" in scare quotes to show that the question of Jesus' resurrection isn't being prejudged. He writes that "neither an empty tomb nor visual 'appearances'—however we categorize them—would be sufficient to generate the early Christian beliefs we have been studying."[3] When mentioning "meetings with the risen Jesus," Wright qualifies what he means as "stories about him appearing to people" and "sightings of an apparently alive Jesus."[4] In short, Wright *agrees* with Carl that (as Carl puts it) "an appearance of an appearance is not necessarily the reality of an appearance." Wright's point is that it's historically "virtually certain" that various people *subjectively experienced* meeting Jesus alive after his crucifixion.

Wright poses the question (with scare quotes): "How then can we explain these two facts, the empty tomb and the 'meetings'?"[5] It's only here, with step seven of his argument (set out on pages 686–87), that Wright moves from collecting *evidence* for the "empty tomb [and]

---

2. N. T. Wright, *The Resurrection of the Son of God* (Fortress, 2003), 709–10.

3. Ibid., 692.

4. Ibid.

5. Ibid., 710.

'appearances'"[6] to asking: "what *explanation* can be given for these two phenomena?"[7]

Wright concludes that the resurrection hypothesis "possesses unrivalled power to explain the historical data at the heart of early Christianity,"[8] but that's not the same as concluding, as Carl mistakenly says Wright concludes, that "the physical resurrection of Jesus is a historical certainty."

Whether or not one finds the explanatory power of the resurrection hypothesis "overwhelming"[9] (in the sense of providing reason to think it more probable than not that Jesus was resurrected) will depend, in part, upon the worldview expectations one brings to considering the arguments for the resurrection hypothesis and its implications as one understands them. As Wright comments: "Historical argument alone cannot force anyone to believe that Jesus was raised from the dead," but "historical argument is remarkably good at clearing away the undergrowth behind which scepticisms of various sorts have been hiding."[10]

So, let's review the *evidence*, *explanations*, and *expectations* in this debate.

Evidence

We should first consider the criteria our debaters use for deciding what counts as reliable *evidence*, to better understand the results at which they arrive.

Criteria for Establishing Evidence

I think Craig could have strengthened his case by explaining more about the "criteria of authenticity" to lay some methodological foundations upon which to establish the evidence he thinks is best explained by the

---

6. Ibid., 692.

7. Ibid., 687.

8. Ibid., 718.

9. Ibid.

10. Ibid.

resurrection.[11] Carl opens the debate by asserting, "What is lacking is any method for differentiating the historical from the legendary and fictional," genres he assumes are mixed together in the New Testament.[12] Carl nevertheless thinks he can make this differentiation, stating, "The gospels contain information that is probably historical—Jesus' execution by the Romans, for example—but also passages that are legendary embellishments and others that are fictionalizations." However, if there's no method for differentiating between historical and nonhistorical material, how can Carl justify asserting that the Gospels contain both types of material, or that the crucifixion is historical but that the empty tomb isn't?

Concerning the resurrection "appearances," Carl says: "there's no way of determining what if any of it is actually historical." However, since he concedes that Jesus was "an itinerant rabbi with local fame for teaching, healing, and miracle working [who] was crucified by the Romans during the rule of Pontius Pilate," and that "some of Jesus' disciples thought they saw Jesus raised from the dead," how can Carl maintain we lack any "way of determining" whether specific statements in the New Testament are "actually historical"?

The ways of "determining what if any of it is actually historical" are codified in the so-called criteria of authenticity:

---

11. See: Peter S. Williams, YouTube playlist, "Historical Criteria of Authenticity," www.youtube.com/playlist?list=PLQhh3qcwVEWg6gh7wSlE4EWoDtTHaq--5 (November 26, 2018); Robert H. Stein, "Criteria for the Gospel's Authenticity," in *Contending with Christianity's Critics*, ed. Paul Copan and William Lane Craig (B&H Academic, 2009).

12. Carl says the gospels were written by "anonymous authors who were not eyewitnesses" and that "The titles 'According to Matthew. . .' were assigned in the second century." There's no evidence the Gospels ever circulated without the traditional authorial attributions attached to them. Only Matthew and John are said to be by disciples, which is odd if the attributions were later inventions, but matters less than the questions of what sources were used by the Gospel writers and what evidence can be gleaned from them using the criteria of authenticity. See: Peter S. Williams, YouTube playlist, "Who Wrote the NT Gospels?" www.youtube.com/playlist?list=PLQhh3qcwVEWg2vHjaH7hwE3BdtZao15CS (May 29, 2018).

[W]hat the criteria really amount to are statements about the effect of certain types of evidence upon the probability of various sayings or events . . . all else being equal . . . the probability of some event or saying is greater given, for example, its multiple attestation than it would have been without it . . . these "criteria" . . . give evidence for thinking specific elements of Jesus' life to be historical, regardless of the general reliability of the document in which the particular saying or event is reported.[13]

In general, the more criteria of authenticity a saying or event passes, the more seriously we should take it (though some criteria are more telling than others). The criteria work best when combined so they "contribute to a cumulative argument about particular texts,"[14] such that *even if one thought the New Testament contained generally unreliable testimony about the historical Jesus*, testimony supported by the criteria should nevertheless be regarded as reliable.

Eyewitness Sources. Firsthand evidence is preferable to secondhand evidence, even for traumatic events: "recent research indicates that although some details of traumatic events may be forgotten or confused, the core of the memory—what actually happened—generally remains intact."[15]

Early Sources. John Dickson notes: "The less time there is between an event and its written description, the less the margin for error—for forgetting or adding."[16]

Independent Sources and/or Forms. Craig himself explains: "That which appears in . . . more than one Gospel source, or more than one

---

13. William Lane Craig, *Reasonable Faith*, 3rd ed. (Crossway, 2008), 298.

14. David Wenham and Steve Walton, *New Testament: Volume One—Exploring the New Testament: A Guide to the Gospels & Acts* (IVP, 2001), 139.

15. Susan A. Clancy, *Abducted: How People Come To Believe They Were Kidnapped by Aliens* (Harvard University Press, 2005), 13.

16. John Dickson, *Investigating Jesus: An Historian's Quest* (Lion, 2010), 124.

form stands a better chance of being authentic than that which is singly attested."[17]

Historical Verisimilitude. According to James A. Beverley and Craig A. Evans: "One of the most important indications of an ancient document's veracity is something historians call verisimilitude." That is, "do the contents of the document match with what we know of the place, people and period described in the document?"[18] Verisimilitude includes "linguistic and cultural features that fit what we know of first-century Palestine."[19] The New Testament exhibits "geographic and topological verisimilitude, cultural and archaeological verisimilitude, and religious, economic and social verisimilitude."[20]

Embarrassing Sources. Graham Stanton notes: "traditions which would have been an embarrassment to followers of Jesus in the post-Easter period are unlikely to have been invented."[21]

Unintentional Signs of History. This criterion "argues that particularly vivid details of an eyewitness can demonstrate accurate knowledge of the environment and the event. This contributes to the credibility of a text."[22]

---

17. Craig L. Blomberg, *Jesus and the Gospels* (Apollos, 1997), 186.

18. James A. Beverley and Craig A. Evans, *Getting Jesus Right: How Muslims Get Jesus and Islam Wrong* (Castle Quay Books, 2015), 22.

19. Thomas R. Yoder Neufeld, *Recovering Jesus: The Witness of the New Testament* (SPCK, 2007), 44. For example, "There are particular words in the Gospels, such as '*Abba*', '*talitha cum*', '*eloi, eloi, lama sabachthani*', which are Aramaic. . . (Mark 5:41; 14:36; 15:34). Their appearance in the Greek gospels is most simply explained in terms of Jesus' own usage" (Wenham and Walton, *New Testament*, 138).

20. Beverley and Evans, *Getting Jesus Right*, 23.

21. Graham Stanton, *The Gospels and Jesus* (Oxford University Press, 1993), 175.

22. Darrell L. Bock, *Studying the Historical Jesus* (Baker Academic, 2002), 201.

Memorability. Inherently memorable events have a better chance of being remembered. Much of Jesus' teaching was designed for memorization using mnemonic devices "such as rhyme, rhythm, alliteration and parallelism which aid the disciple to recall and pass on the teaching."[23] This point applies to the various creeds and hymns quoted by New Testament letters.

Historical Coherence. As an addendum to the other criteria: "If any of the other criteria enable us to identify some sayings or stories of Jesus that are probably historical, then we may . . . include other sayings and stories . . . which fit in with the emerging picture."[24]

Disconfirmation by Silence. Carl offers a methodological principle by which he seeks to rule *out* the historicity of various items of testimony: "when one source reports an event of transcendent importance but other sources, which should know of the event but make no mention of it." As Carl notes, this would usually be called an "argument from silence," although he calls it *"disconfirmation by silence."*

Carl's criterion is purely negative, so it fails to explain his positive judgments about certain New Testament claims. At the very least, this shows that *"disconfirmation by silence"* needs to be subsumed within a wider set of criteria:

> When a biography of a recent figure by Suetonius or Plutarch offers information that is not corroborated elsewhere, we do not for that reason dismiss its claims . . . We can corroborate these writers' accounts frequently enough from parallel sources to recognize that they are not simply wildly inventing stories . . . This pattern offers a sort of default expectation in the Gospels as well: although multiple attestation is helpful, we need not approach even unique accounts . . . with dismissive scepticism. Accounts in a writer who elsewhere normally depends on material the substance of which we can verify are themselves a form of evidence.[25]

---

23. Ibid., 144.

24. Wenham and Walton, *New Testament*, 139.

25. Craig S. Keener, "Introduction," in *Biographies and Jesus: What Does It*

Arguments from silence require care. The history of biblical criticism is strewn with long abandoned arguments from silence against biblical claims, arguments that were unseated by later discoveries.[26] That said, liberal theologian John Robinson used an argument from silence to convince many that the Synoptic Gospels should be dated before the destruction of the Temple, which Luke fails to mention in Luke–Acts.[27] In short, an absence of evidence can be reasonably treated as evidence of absence only if we have a reasonable expectation (a) that such evidence should have existed in the first place, (b) that it should have survived into the present, and (c) that it should have been discovered by now: "Absence of evidence is evidence of absence *when the evidence should be there and is not.*"[28]

Carl says, "there is no evidence that any first-century Jewish or Roman document ever noticed the small sect of Jews who were Jesus' disciples." I wonder what extant first-century document that demonstrably should mention Jesus and/or his followers, but that fails to do so, he has in mind? But even if there were a lack of expected evidence in this or that source, this wouldn't eliminate the need to consider the positive evidence we have from first-century sources such as Josephus[29] and those gathered into the New Testament (plus second-century sources such as Celsus, Ignatius, Lucian of Samosata, Pliny the Younger, Suetonius, and

---

Mean for the Gospels to be Biographies? ed. Craig S. Keener & Edward T. Wright (Emeth, 2016), 14–15.

26. See: Paul L. Maier, "Biblical History," equip.org/article/biblical-history-the-faulty-criticism-of-biblical-historicity.

27. See: John Robinson, *Redating the New Testament*, new ed. (SCM, 2012).

28. Victor J. Stenger, *The New Atheism: Taking a Stand for Science and Reason* (Prometheus, 2009), 58, my italics.

29. See: Peter S. Williams, YouTube playlist, "Josephus on Jesus," www.youtube.com/playlist?list=PLQhh3qcwVEWh-7X8CFtPpH8tPwEiVcnVW (last updated April 6, 2017); Gary J. Goldberg, "The Coincidences of the Emmaus Narrative of Luke and the Testimonium of Josephus," josephus.org/GoldbergJosephusLuke1995.pdf; Paul L. Maier, "Josephus and Jesus," 4truth.net/fourtruthpbjesus; Geza Vermes, "Jesus in the Eyes of Josephus," standpointmag.co.uk/node/2507/full; Alice Whealey, "The Testimonium Flavianum in Syriac and Arabic," khazarzar.skeptik.net/books/whealey2.pdf.

Tacitus[30]). Carl tacitly makes the false assumption that "*disconfirmation by silence*" will always outweigh even the strongest case using positive historical criteria.

Ancient History

Carl's critique of the canonical gospels often stems from an uncharitable and historically uninformed hermeneutic. For example, instead of concluding from Luke's extended portrait of Jesus' resurrection "appearances" in Acts that the presentation of the appearances in Luke's Gospel is selective (and so shouldn't be read as necessarily contradicting Matthew's account), Carl not only concludes that Luke contradicts Matthew, but that Luke contradicts himself!

Besides, historians are used to working with discrepant accounts. The three ancient "historians who narrate the Great Fire of Rome in AD 64 disagree about Nero's whereabouts during the fire and whether he 'fiddled' (played the lyre) or sang while the city burned . . . [but] no one doubts that Nero failed to show leadership while the city was being destroyed."[31] Likewise, the common and essential content of the New Testament reports pertaining to Jesus' death, burial, and resurrection can be established from the *early* testimonies contained within the *multiple forms* of (1) the (*memorable, Aramaic containing*) creed quoted by Paul in 1 Corinthians 15;[32] (2) the passion narrative used by Mark (with its *embarrassing* female witnesses); (3) Peter's *eyewitness* testimony recorded in Acts 2:23–32 (see also Acts 10); and (4) Paul's sermon

---

30. See: J. Warner Wallace, "Is There Any Evidence for Jesus Outside the Bible?" coldcasechristianity.com/2017/is-there-any-evidence-for-jesus-outside-the-bible; Robert E. Van Voorst, *Jesus Outside the New Testament: An Introduction to the Ancient Evidence* (Eerdmans, 2000).

31. Paul Barnett, *The Truth about Jesus*, 2nd ed. (Aquila, 2004), 136.

32. See: YouTube video of Gary R. Habermas's Veritas Forum lecture, "The Resurrection Argument That Changed a Generation of Scholars," www.youtube.com/watch?v=ay_Db4RwZ_M&feature=youtu.be; Peter May, "The Resurrection of Jesus and the Witness of Paul," www.bethinking.org/did-jesus-rise-from-the-dead/the-resurrection-of-jesus-and-the-witness-of-paul.

Table 1. Four Early Sources on the Resurrection

Acts 2:23–32 Peter's Pentecost sermon from AD 33.	1 Corinthians 15:3–5 Early Creed, c. AD 33–34.	Mark 15:37–16:7 Pre-Marcan passion narrative, c. AD 37.	Acts 13:28–31 Paul's Pisidian Antioch sermon, c. AD 45.
you . . . put him to death by nailing him to the cross.	Christ died . . .	Jesus breathed his last.	they asked Pilate to have him executed.
David died and was buried, and his tomb is here to this day [Peter thereby implies Jesus' empty tomb].	he was buried . . .	Joseph bought some linen cloth, took down the body, wrapped it in the linen, and placed it in a tomb . . .	they took him down from the tree and laid him in a tomb.
God has raised this Jesus to life . . . [which likewise implies an empty tomb]	he was raised . . . [which implies an empty grave or tomb]	He has risen! [The empty tomb is thereby implied]	But God raised him from the dead. . . [which implies the empty tomb]
we are all witnesses of the fact.	he appeared . . .	He is going ahead of you into Galilee. There you will see him . . .	for many days he was seen . . .

recorded in Acts 13:28–31 (see table 1).[33] Adding the passion-related materials from the Gospels according to Matthew, Luke, and John gives us *seven first-century sources* (see table 2). These early sources come in *multiple forms*, and include *embarrassing* testimony and several *eyewitness sources* (i.e., Peter, Paul, John, and Matthew).

Carl's complaint that "we don't even have a single case of a group encounter attested by any member of the group" is a red herring that presupposes a rejection of the traditional authorship of Matthew and John, refuses to count the experience of Saul and his traveling companions as a group encounter, and ignores Peter's testimony.

---

33. James D. G. Dunn explains: "Luke has sought out much earlier material and has incorporated it into the brief formalized expositions which he attributes to Peter, Stephen, Paul, etc.," in *Why Believe in Jesus' Resurrection?* (SPCK, 2016), 22.

Table 2. Seven First-Century Sources on the Resurrection

	Peter in Acts	1 Cor.	Mark's Passion Source	Paul in Acts & Letters	Luke	Matt.	John
Death	2:23 & 10:39	15:3	15:37	13:28–29	23:46	27:24	19:30
Burial		15:4	15:46	13:29; Rm. 6:4; Col. 2:13	23:53	. 27:64	19:42
Empty Tomb	Implied by 2:29–32		16:6		24:2, 10, 12, 23	28:6 & 12–13	20:2, 6
Appearances	2:32 &10:41	15:5–8	16:7	13:31, 22:6–9 & 26:13–14; 1 Cor. 9:1 & 15:8; Gl 1:13–17	24:12, 15 & 36	28:9– 10 & 16–17	21:14

The criteria of authenticity allow us to side-step questions like "Did Nero play the lyre, or sing, or both?" and "Was Jesus' first appearance to the male disciples in Jerusalem or Galilee?" whilst highlighting *specific* data that can be shown to be historically likely quite apart from debates about the *general* reliability of the New Testament. As Terry L. Miethe and Gary R. Habermas emphasize:

> Our arguments [for the resurrection are] based on a *limited number* of knowable historical facts and *verified by critical procedures.* Therefore, contemporary scholars should not spurn such evidence by referring to "discrepancies" in the New Testament texts or to its general "unreliability."[34]

Table 3 tabulates five criteria of authenticity that eight resurrection "appearances" pass (*in addition* to being *early*, historically *coherent* reports of intrinsically *memorable* events):

---

34. Terry L. Miethe and Gary R. Habermas, *Why Believe? God Exists!* (College Press, 1998), 273.

Table 3. Five Historical Criteria That Eight Resurrection Appearance Reports Pass *in Addition* to Being *Early*, Historically *Coherent Reports of Memorable Events*

Witnesses	Reported	Eyewitness Testimony	Multiple Literarily Independent Sources	Multiple Forms	Embarrassment	Verisimilitude
Mary Magdalene	John 20:11–18 (see Mark 16:9)				X	X
At least four other women (Joanna, Salome & Mary the mother of James)	Matt. 28:1–10; Luke 24:8–11				X	X
Cleopas & Mary	Luke 24:13–32 (see Mark 16:12)				X	X
Peter	1 Cor. 15:5; Luke 24:34		X	X		X
Ten disciples (& others)	John 20:19–23; Luke 24:36-49 (see Mark 16:14)	X	X			
Eleven disciples including Thomas	John 20:24–30 (see 1 Cor. 15:5)	X			X	
Seven disciples	John 21:1–25 (see Mark 16:7)	X				
Saul (& others)	1 Cor. 15:8 & Acts 9:1–19	X	X	X		

Evidential Results

Carl acknowledges as "bedrock facts" that "Jesus . . . was crucified by the Romans" and that "after his death some of his disciples had experiences that convinced them that Jesus had been miraculously resurrected." Indeed, he recognizes not only that (according to his rebuttal to Craig) "Jesus' disciples came to believe that Jesus had been miraculously resurrected from the dead," but also that (according to his opening case) "some of Jesus' disciples thought they saw Jesus raised from the dead."[35] That said, Carl contests several relevant historical claims.

Contested Evidence

1. Jesus' Burial.[36] In his rebuttal to Craig, Carl opines that "it's very unlikely that someone convicted and executed for sedition would be given an honorable burial," but since Jesus' burial wasn't in a family tomb, and the preceding rites were rushed, it wouldn't have counted as an "honorable burial." Moreover, the suggestion that the soldiers at the crucifixion could have been bribed to allow Jesus' burial, before returning to remove the evidence of their corruption, founders on the fact that Jesus' burial was otherwise by the book. According to Craig A. Evans, "Jews buried

---

35. See: Peter S. Williams, YouTube playlist, "The Resurrection Appearances of Jesus," www.youtube.com/playlist?list=PLQhh3qcwVEWgUZZO-MUpLJhm 7ZmscmAk6 (March 3, 2016); James Bishop, "45 Scholar Quotes on Jesus' Resurrection Appearances," jamesbishopblog.com/2015/06/29/jesus-really-did-appear-to-the-disciples-and-skeptics-after-his-death-40-quotes-by-scholars; William Lane Craig, "Dale Allison on Jesus' Empty Tomb, His Post-Mortem Appearances, and the Origin of the Disciples' Belief in His Resurrection," www.reasonablefaith.org/writings/scholarly-writings/historical-jesus/dale-allison-on-jesus-empty-tomb-his-post-mortem-appearances-and-the-origin; Gary R. Habermas, "Experiences of the Risen Jesus," www.garyhabermas.com/articles/dialog_rexperience/dialog_rexperiences.htm.

36. See: Peter S. Williams, YouTube playlist, "Jesus Was Buried in a Tomb," www.youtube.com/playlist?list=PLQhh3qcwVEWjOA69as_NWrHsBRBLY_ a3Y (October 28, 2015); Craig A. Evans, "Getting the Burial Traditions and Evidences Right," in *How God Became Jesus: The Real Origins Of Belief In Jesus' Divine Nature*, ed. Michael F. Bird (Zondervan, 2014); Craig A. Evans and Tom Wright, *Jesus: The Final Days* (SPCK, 2008).

all dead, including the executed, and the Romans complied with Jewish customs—at least during peacetime."[37] As Josephus commented, "Jews are so careful about funeral rights that even malefactors who have been sentenced to crucifixion are taken down and buried before sunset."[38] Jewish New Testament scholar Geza Vermes concedes the point with respect to Jesus: "The Bible orders that a person condemned to death by a court should be buried on the day of his execution before sunset, as happened to Jesus, too."[39]

Yehohanan, the Jewish victim of crucifixion whose ossuary contained a nail driven through the heel bone of his left foot, had been given a decent burial.[40] Archeologists have recently reassessed the skeletal materials and nails from the ossuary in Abba Cave in Jerusalem, concluding that the deceased—identified by an inscription as "Mattathias son of Judah"—was the man known in Greek as Aristobulus II, the last Hasmonean ruler, whom Marcus Antonius had crucified. Three nails, still bearing traces of human calcium, were recovered from his ossuary. Furthermore: "138 iron nails have been recovered from [Jewish] tombs and many of them have imbedded in the rust human bone and calcium . . . evidence probably of dozens of crucifixion victims who were properly buried."[41]

In sum, belief in Jesus' burial does *not* "require a suicidal Joseph of Arimathea" as Carl thinks. Atheist historian Michael Grant argues that the absence of Jesus' circle of male disciples from his burial is "too un-

37. Craig A. Evans, "The Christ of Faith is the Jesus of History," in *Debating Christian Theism*, ed. J. P. Moreland, Chad Meister, and Khaldoun A. Sweis (Oxford University Press, 2013), 464.

38. Josephus, *Jewish War*, quoted by Evans in "Jewish Burial Traditions and the Resurrection of Jesus," *Journal for the Study of the Historical Jesus* 3, no. 2 (2005): 233–48.

39. Geza Vermes, *The Resurrection* (Penguin, 2008), 22.

40. See: Biblical Archaeological Society Staff, "A Tomb in Jerusalem Reveals the History of Crucifixion and Roman Crucifixion Methods," www.biblicalarchaeology.org/daily/biblical-topics/crucifixion/a-tomb-in-jerusalem-reveals-the-history-of-crucifixion-and-roman-crucifixion-methods.

41. YouTube record of a Trinities Podcast discussion by Craig A. Evans, "The burial and empty tomb traditions" (tinyurl.com/yclutnjt).

fortunate, indeed disgraceful, to have been voluntarily invented by the evangelists."[42] As Robert J. Hutchinson observes:

> [M]any scholars, and not merely Christian ones, insist that Jesus' body was almost certainly taken down from the cross and buried, in deference to the Jewish holiday of Passover . . . contemporary historians and archaeologists—such as Shimon Gibson, Jodi Magness, James Dunn, N. T. Wright, Raymond Brown, E. P. Sanders, James Tabor, Michael Grant and Craig Evans—believe that Jesus was indeed given a proper burial.[43]

In any case, the bribery hypothesis is disconfirmed by the evidence that the authorities knew about Jesus' burial (see Mark 15:43; Matthew 27:57–66, 28:11; John 19:38–42). It also fails to explain why the tomb was left open, or why the expensive grave-clothes and spices were left behind.

2. Jesus' Empty Tomb.[44] Carl observes that:

> According to many proponents, the vast majority of New Testament scholars accept the empty tomb as established fact. The

---

42. Michael Grant, *Jesus: An Historian's Review of The Gospels* (Charles Scribner's Sons, 1977), 175.

43. Robert J. Hutchinson, *Searching for Jesus: New Discoveries in the Quest for Jesus of Nazareth—And How They Confirm the Gospel Accounts* (Nelson, 2015), 232–233.

44. See: Peter S. Williams, YouTube playlist, "Jesus' Tomb Was Empty," www.youtube.com/playlist?list=PLQhh3qcwVEWhqraAeJ8gVcSIbXhZR2R 6p (November 26, 2018); William Lane Craig, "The Historicity of the Empty Tomb of Jesus," reasonablefaith.org/the-historicity-of-the-empty-tomb-of-jesus, "The Disciples' Inspection of the Empty Tomb," reasonablefaith.org/the-disciples-inspection-of-the-empty-tomb, and "Reply to Evan Fales: On the Empty Tomb of Jesus," reasonablefaith.org/reply-to-evan-fales-on-the-empty-tomb-of-jesus; Gary R. Habermas, "The Empty Tomb of Jesus," www.namb.net/apologetics-blog/the-empty-tomb-of-jesus/?pageid=8589952861; Kristen Romey, "Unsealing of Christ's Reputed Tomb Turns Up New Revelations," news.nationalgeographic.com/2016/10/jesus-christ-tomb-burial-church-holy-sepulchre.

first question to be asked about this appeal to the authority of "the vast majority of New Testament scholars" is what proportion of these scholars are precommitted to biblical inerrancy and thus would have a confirmation bias in favor of anything that would bolster their argument for historicity.

This *ad hominem* argument assumes scholars who believe in inerrancy can't distinguish between what they believe on the basis of inerrancy and what they can demonstrate on the basis of historical scholarship. In fact, the appeal to scholarly consensus (though hard to quantify objectively) is made primarily to indicate that belief in the empty tomb is not the result of precisely the sort of bias Carl assumes; for "since the end of the twentieth century, studies of the historical Jesus and of the New Testament in general have been an ecumenical enterprise including Christian, Jewish and non-religious scholars."[45] As David Mishkin writes in his review of *Jewish Scholarship on the Resurrection of Jesus*:

> Many non-Jewish scholars already have a faith commitment to Jesus. This does not mean that their scholarship should summarily be discarded as biased. It should be evaluated on its own merit. Nevertheless, the reality is that presuppositions are influential. Jewish scholars begin with a different set of presuppositions. But, what is interesting to note is that the main historical events that make up this discussion are virtually the same for both groups: crucifixion, burial, disciples' belief, empty tomb, and Paul's dramatic turnaround.[46]

The empty tomb is verified by multiple criteria of authenticity and is consequently accepted by many New Testament scholars *irrespective of their worldview*. According to Vermes, "the women belonging to the entourage of Jesus discovered an empty tomb and were definite that it

---

45. Halvor Moxnes, *A Short History Of The New Testament* (I.B. Tauris, 2014), 181.

46. David Mishkin, *Jewish Scholarship on the Resurrection of Jesus* (Pickwick, 2017), 210.

was the tomb [in which Jesus had been placed]."[47] Contra Carl, in John it isn't "Mary alone" who goes to the tomb, as is clear from John 20:2. Vermes argues:

> The evidence furnished by female witnesses had no standing in a male-dominated Jewish society ... If the empty tomb story had been manufactured by the primitive Church to demonstrate the reality of the resurrection of Jesus, one would have expected a uniform and foolproof account attributed to patently reliable witnesses.[48]

Grant concludes: "The historian cannot justifiably deny the empty tomb ... the evidence necessitates the conclusion the tomb was found empty."[49]

3. On the Road to Damascus.[50] Carl says Paul's experience on the road to Damascus shows that "an 'appearance' may be nothing beyond a blinding light and a voice from the sky that only one person can hear." For the sake of argument, suppose that's right. The thought seems to be that this would lessen the import of detail-free "appearance" reports, including the 1 Corinthians 15 creed. Of course, any attempt to downplay the "appearances" only increases the mystery as to why the disciples came to believe Jesus had been *resurrected*. However, the context of Paul's discussion in 1 Corinthians makes it clear that everyone understood the "appearances" to be of a *resurrected* Jesus. Moreover, the correlations between the creedal "appearances" and the "appearances" described in the Gospels indicate that we have multiple witnesses to the same events.

Paul claims that *he is himself an eyewitness to the resurrected Jesus*

---

47. Geza Vermes, *Jesus the Jew* (Collins, 1973), 40.

48. Geza Vermes, *The Resurrection* (Penguin, 2008), 142.

49. Grant, *Jesus*, 176.

50. See: Peter S. Williams, YouTube playlist: "From Saul to Paul," www.youtube.com/playlist?list=PLQhh3qcwVEWgxr-o_wjk56gosqehDX-x7 (January 9, 2017).

(see 1 Corinthians 9:1, 15:8). This claim is corroborated in chapters 22 and 26 of Acts, where Paul's some-time traveling companion, Luke, summarizes speeches *made by Paul.*

William Lane Craig notes that:

> when Paul speaks of his "visions and revelations of the Lord" (II Cor 12.1–7) he does *not* include Jesus's appearance to him. Paul and the early Christian community as a whole were familiar with religious visions and sharply differentiated between these and an appearance of the risen Lord.[51]

Contra Carl, Both Paul (as related by Luke) and Luke make it clear Paul's Damascus road experience wasn't merely a private experience. Paul's companions not only saw the bright light but also heard a voice/sound (*phóné*).[52] It wasn't just Saul who fell prostrate to the ground, but his companions as well: "I saw a light from heaven, brighter than the sun, blazing around me and my companions. We all fell [prostrate] to the ground" (Acts 26:13–14, NIV). Perhaps Saul's companions stood up before he did: "The men who were traveling with him stood speechless, hearing the voice but seeing no one" (Acts 9:7, ESV). According to some translations of Acts 22:9, Paul says: "those who were with me saw the light, but they did not hear the voice of the One who was speaking to me" (HSBC). So, did Luke fail to notice contradictions between the reports he recorded? That seems unlikely (though one might accept that the "contradictions" between the various Lucan accounts of Paul's conversion are real whilst concluding that they fall within the acceptable limits of variation in secondary detail accorded by first-century historiography):

> [It] is over-interpretation to suggest that Acts 9:7 says that they did not see the light whereas here it says they did. All that is said

51. William Lane Craig, "The Bodily Resurrection of Jesus," www.reasonablefaith.org/writings/scholarly-writings/historical-jesus/the-bodily-resurrection-of-jesus/.

52. See: biblehub.com/greek/5456.htm.

here is that they did not see anyone. For those with Saul, there was neither an appearance nor a revelation. The point is that the others knew something happened and that Saul did not have a merely inner, psychological experience.[53]

The Greek for "hearing/hear" is ambiguous, referring to "hearing" plain and simple or to "hearing with understanding" (see Matthew 13:13). A charitable reader would conclude that Paul's companions heard the voice but didn't understand it.[54] In Acts 26:14 Paul notes that Jesus spoke to him "in the Aramaic dialect," so the lack of understanding on the part of Paul's companions may have been due to their not speaking Aramaic. Alternatively, they may have heard Jesus' voice without being able to make out what he said (perhaps because they were further away than Saul).

Only Paul saw a figure in the light, suffered temporary blindness as a result of the encounter (perhaps because only Paul looked *into* the light to see Jesus), and understood what Jesus said to him (perhaps because only Paul was close enough to hear it clearly, or because his companions didn't speak Aramaic). Luke's point "is that the others knew something happened and that Saul did not have a merely inner, psychological experience. Those with Paul, however, did not know exactly what took place."[55] The differences between the experiences of Paul and his companions fit Paul's claim that the resurrected Jesus' intent was to reveal himself to Paul in order to appoint him as an apostle (see Acts 26:16). Paul's eyewitness testimony must be taken seriously.

---

53. Darrell L. Bock, *Acts* (Baker Academic, 2007), 660.

54. See: Rob Bowman, "Did they hear what Paul heard? Acts 9:7 and 22:9 Revisited," www.academia.edu/19770469/Heard_but_Not_Understood_Acts_9_7_and_22_9_and_Differing_Views_of_Biblical_Inerrancy.

55. Darrell L. Bock, "Precision and Accuracy: Making Distinctions in the Cultural Context," in *Do Historical Matters Matter to Faith? A Critical Appraisal of Modern and Postmodern Approaches to Scripture*, ed. James K. Hoffmeier and Dennis R. Magary (Crossway, 2012), 370.

4. Raised Up and/or Resurrected? Carl seems to accept or reject the historicity of Jesus' predictions about his "rising" and being "resurrected" as it suits his argument. The disciples shared the messianic expectations of their culture: "The Jews believed in a general bodily resurrection at the end of time ... before the judgment (Isa. 66; Dan 12:1–2; 2 Macc. 7) but did not have an expectation of an earlier, immediate, special resurrection for anyone."[56] Joachim Jeremias confirms: "Ancient Judaism did not know of an anticipated resurrection as an event of history."[57] If Jesus' contemporaries made anything of his elliptical predictions about the Son of Man (i.e., himself) "rising" (Jesus uses cognates of *ēgerthē*, meaning "raise up," in Mark 14:28 and Matthew 26:32; whereas in Mark 8:31, 9:9 and 10:34, and Luke 18:33, 24:7 and 24:46, he uses words such as *anastēsetai* and *anastēnai* that literally mean "stand up again"—the semantic range of both terms coincide with that of the English "resurrection"),[58] they'd have thought in terms of (a) the resurrection of the righteous dead *at the last judgment* (see Mark 12:25; John 11:24), (b) resurrection in the lesser sense of a miraculous *revivification* to earthly life, as with Lazarus (though they'd probably assume a dead man couldn't revive *himself*), or (c) the Old Testament story of Elijah being "raised up" to heaven.

The dominance of these cultural assumptions is seen in the Sanhedrin's reason for having Jesus' tomb guarded: "lest his disciples go and steal him away and tell the people, 'He has risen from the dead'" (Matthew 27:64, ESV). The Greek translated as "risen from the dead" here isn't *anastēsetai* (resurrected), but *ēgerthē* (raised up). The Jewish *Toledot Yeshu* places this interpretation of events on the disciples' own lips: "On the first day of the week his bold followers came to Queen Helene with the report that he who was slain was truly the Messiah and that he

56. Bock, *Acts*, 125.

57. Joachim Jeremias, "Die alteste Schicht der Osterüberlieferung," in *Resurrexit*, ed. Edouard Dhanis (Editrice Libreria Vaticana, 1974), 194.

58. See: Mark 12:25 (biblehub.com/text/mark/12-25.htm) and John 11:24 (biblehub.com/text/john/11-24.htm).

was not in his grave; *he had ascended to heaven as he prophesied.*"[59] The Sanhedrin's concern was "that the disciples would steal the body and claim it had ascended to heaven."[60]

5. Was Jesus a False Prophet? Carl says the resurrection "appearances" convinced the disciples that Jesus "was in fact Messiah . . . who would return within their generation to rule over the newly established Kingdom of God." Carl thinks Jesus' failure to return within this time frame poses a problem for belief in the resurrection, presumably because it shows Jesus to have been a false prophet. However:

> Certain gospel passages speak of the 'coming [*erchomenon*]' of the Son of Man to the Father ('the Ancient of Days')—a reference to Daniel 7—within his generation. Most New Testament scholars take passages such as Matthew 16:28 and Mark 14:62/Matthew 26:64 and Luke 22:69 as references to AD 70—not some distant 'second coming.'[61]

That Jesus didn't believe his public vindication over against the Temple—his "coming" (*erchomenon*) to God for enthronement—would coincide with the end of earthly history is indicated by his (hyperbolic) assertion that in those days "there will be great tribulation, such as has not been from the beginning of the world until now, no, and never will be" (Matthew 24:21, ESV),[62] which implies that history would continue. That Jesus is predicting a passing historical event is likewise clear from his comment, "If those days had not been cut short, no one would survive" (Matthew 24:22, NIV), and his warnings not to believe anyone

59. My italics, see J. Warner Wallace, "Is There Any Evidence for Jesus Outside the Bible?" coldcasechristianity.com/2017/is-there-any-evidence-for-jesus-outside-the-bible.

60. J. P. Holding, "Hallucinations and Expectations," in *Defending the Resurrection* (Xulon, 2010), 269.

61. Paul Copan, *When God Goes to Starbucks* (Baker, 2009), 173. See also: R. T. France, *Tyndale New Testament Commentary: Matthew* (IVP, 2008).

62. See: biblehub.com/text/matthew/24-21.htm.

claiming "at that time" (Matthew 24:23, NIV) that the Messiah has appeared here or there: "For as the lightning comes from the east and shines as far as the west, so will be the coming [*parousia*—presence] of the Son of Man" (Matthew 24:27, ESV). We see here a distinction between Jesus' temple-related *erchomenon* within a generation on the one hand and his later but otherwise unspecified *parousia* or "second coming" on the other hand: "A close look at Matthew 24 shows that Jesus was answering two questions [see verse 3]. Jesus knew the answer to the first [see Matthew 24:34]. But he didn't know the answer to the second [see Matthew 24:36, 42–44]."[63] When Jesus predicts the destruction of the Temple, signifying the *erchomenon* of the Son of Man to God the Father *à la* Daniel 7, he says, "this generation will certainly not pass away until all these things have happened" (Matthew 24:34, ESV). When he discusses his *parousia* (his "second coming"), he says, "But about that day or hour no one knows, not even the angels in heaven, nor the Son, but only the Father . . . you do not know on what day your Lord will come . . . the Son of Man will come at an hour when you do not expect him" (Matthew 24:36–44, ESV).[64] There's every reason to think Jesus was an accurate prophet.[65]

Explanations

Having assessed the evidence, we need to search for the best (simplest, most adequate) explanation thereof. The adequacy of a historical explanation depends on several factors, including its *explanatory scope* (whether it encompasses the relevant facts), *explanatory power* (whether it raises the probability of the relevant facts), *explanatory plausibility* (how far our background knowledge implies the hypothesis), degree of *explanatory disconfirmation* (conflict with our background knowledge), and degree of *explanatory ad hoc-ness* (the fewer contrived, un-

---

63. Copan, *When God Goes to Starbucks*, 168.

64. Ibid.,162–190.

65. See: Peter S. Williams, "Jesus the Prophesied Prophet," peterswilliams. podbean.com/mf/feed/ew2qjf/N_Ireland_Jesus_Prophecied_Prophet.mp3.

evidenced hypotheses, the better).

The resurrection hypothesis offers a relatively *simple*[66] and wholly *adequate* explanation of the relevant historical evidence, an explanation that combines excellent explanatory scope (i.e., *if* the resurrection happened, it would explain "why the tomb was found empty, why the disciples saw post-mortem appearances of Jesus, and why the Christian faith came into being"[67]) and power (i.e., *if* God chose to resurrect Jesus from the dead, *then* the empty tomb, postmortem appearances of Jesus and the origin of belief in Jesus' resurrection all become highly probable) with a *fair* degree of plausibility and *low* degrees of *disconfirmation* and *ad hoc–ness* (especially if one already accepts theism).

Although the resurrection hypothesis posits an explanation that's miraculous—and therefore unusual, and on that account unlikely *a priori*—the hypothesis gains plausibility from our background knowledge about the case for theism, [68] about Jesus' claims in the context of his character,[69] about his reported miracles,[70] and his fulfillment of prophecy.[71]

The degree to which one finds the resurrection hypothesis as *ad hoc* and/or *disconfirmed* by what one counts as background knowledge ultimately depends upon the worldview expectations one brings to considering the arguments for the resurrection (and its implications as one

---

66. See: Jay Wesley Richards, "Divine Simplicity: The Good, the Bad, and the Ugly," in *For Faith and Clarity: Philosophical Contributions to Christian Theology*, ed. James K. Beilby (Baker Academic, 2006).

67. Craig, "Bodily Resurrection."

68. See footnote 8 in my "Horizons" chapter.

69. See: Peter S. Williams, YouTube playlist, "The 'Lunatic, Liar or Lord' Argument," www.youtube.com/playlist?list=PLQhh3qcwVEWiCA7mwy67RLgGt_2n4jzra (February 1, 2017); Peter S. Williams, *Getting at Jesus* and *Understanding Jesus*.

70. See: Williams, *Understanding Jesus*.

71. See: Norman L. Geisler, "Miraculous Bible Prophecy Fulfilments," philosophical11.wordpress.com/2012/09/12/miraculous-bible-prophecy-fulfillments/#more-151; Williams, *Understanding Jesus* and "Jesus the Prophesied Prophet," peterswilliams.podbean.com/mf/feed/ew2qjf/N_Ireland_Jesus_Prophecied_Prophet.mp3.

understands them), most especially the degree to which one thinks our background knowledge supports belief in a God who might choose to raise Jesus from the dead so that "given the historical context of Jesus' own unparalleled life and claims, the resurrection serves as divine confirmation of those radical claims."[72]

The question isn't whether the resurrection hypothesis *can* explain the relevant evidences, but whether any other hypothesis does *a better job.*

Carl's Explanations

Carl suggests that there are

> plausible natural explanations for the genesis of this belief—grief hallucinations, mistaken identity, dreams mistaken for reality, misheard or misinterpreted testimony, unconscious appropriation of another's experience, memory distortion, disciple rivalry. No one of these would likely be sufficient for the sincere belief of some of the disciples that Jesus had been resurrected. But ... [t] hese quite natural, understandable beginnings could have easily led to a belief that Jesus had been miraculously resurrected, and to all the Gospel stories, with their fundamental contradictions and fictional and legendary embellishments. No miraculous resurrection required.

Carl's explanations possess some *plausibility*, because they appeal to events which are implied, to some degree, by our background knowledge. However, Carl asserts that some combination or other of the factors he lists has the *explanatory power* to account for the origin of the "belief that Jesus had been miraculously resurrected" and that these factors could likewise "have easily led ... to all the Gospel stories" about Jesus' resurrection. I think not only that Carl's factors have *limited explanatory power* but also that they suffer from problems of *disconfirmation, ad hoc–ness,* and *insufficient explanatory scope.*

---

72. William Lane Craig, "The Resurrection of Jesus," www.reasonablefaith. org/the-resurrection-of-jesus. See: Williams, *Getting at Jesus.*

I think Carl should accommodate the historicity of Jesus' empty tomb. However, his theories regarding the "appearances" don't explain an empty tomb, whilst his explanation for an empty tomb (i.e., corrupt soldiers) doesn't explain the "appearances." To buy sufficient explanatory scope Carl must combine these independent theories, increasing the *ad hoc* complexity of his hypothesis. Indeed, of his explanation for an empty tomb, Carl comments: "Is there any evidence that this happened? No." Yet part of what determines if an explanation is a good one is the degree to which it is *ad hoc*.

Secondary Factors. As Craig observes, "rivalry between Jesus' disciples" isn't an explanation, but a motivation. Carl appeals to "cognitive dissonance reduction," but concedes this "might not by itself explain the disciples' belief."[73] Indeed not, for the disciples didn't double down on their existing beliefs despite the crucifixion, but embraced a radical new belief on the basis of the "appearances" and the empty tomb.[74]

I don't think "mistaken identity" has much to offer: since the disciples probably knew grief tends to make the departed "appear" in every crowd, experiences that can be explained in such terms don't convincingly explain their belief that Jesus was alive, let alone *resurrected*. Moreover, Carl's observation that "in several of the appearances reported in the Gospels . . . there were problems recognizing [Jesus]" counts *against* the mistaken-identification theory; as does his observation that "Jesus' disciples were terrified and in hiding." Not only would hiding have "made it very difficult to find Jesus' *Doppelgänger*," it would have made it difficult to see him in the first place.

Primary Factors: Dreams and Co-opted Memories.[75] Carl asks us to

---

73. On this problem see N. T. Wright, *The Resurrection of the Son of God* (SPCK, 2003), 697–700.

74. See: William Lane Craig, "Doubting the Resurrection," www.reasonablefaith. org/media/reasonable-faith-podcast/doubting-the-resurrection/; N. T. Wright, *The Resurrection of the Son of God* (SPCK, 2003), 697–702.

75. See: Peter S. Williams, YouTube playlist, "Memory Implantation," www. youtube.com/playlist?list=PLQhh3qcwVEWjoBnrBC8UZrQuIoMR5Hsq7&dis

"consider the possibility of a dream experience being mistaken for an actual experience." He imagines Andrew reporting a vivid dream of Jesus speaking to him and (motivated by rivalry) Peter lying about having had a similar dream, and then: "Years later, because of memory distortion, Peter fully believes that Jesus appeared to him. And that it wasn't a dream."

It's not clear if Andrew supposedly dreamt of a *resurrected* Jesus, or if Peter is meant to have added this innovation. Either way, the hypothesis lacks explanatory power because it doesn't address belief in Jesus' *resurrection*.

Carl gives his theory time to work that the evidence doesn't permit (the faster the naturalistic mechanisms Carl suggests are required to work to produce belief in Jesus' resurrection, the less plausible they become). The disciples' resurrection experiences turned their world upside-down from the morning of Easter Sunday. Peter didn't come to believe in the resurrection "years later." He risked his life by proclaiming Jesus' resurrection in Jerusalem *within weeks* of the crucifixion (see Acts 2:14–40). Multiple individual and group appearances were codified in creedal form by the Jerusalem church *within a few years or even months* of the crucifixion.

Saul wasn't part of the rivalry between disciples (nor were the women). While Saul had no doubt heard about the disciples' belief in Jesus' resurrection, (a) he obviously didn't believe it until his road to Damascus experience, and (b) he'd probably have heard about Jesus' purported ascension, which would have likely seemed to one and all to preclude Jesus appearing to anyone before the second coming (see Acts 1:11; 1 Corinthians 15:8).

Carl's familial example of how people can "co-opt memories" includes a gap of "several years." Did his wife mistakenly co-opt the memory from the *Reader's Digest* story as her own (if this is what happened) by later that day, that week, or even that month? As noted above, Peter and the other disciples didn't come to think they'd encountered the resurrected Jesus "years later."

able_polymer=true (March 19, 2017).

Although someone may misremember an event they heard about having happened to someone else as having happened to them, in such a case the event in question still *happened to someone!* Besides, Mrs. Stecher's supposed appropriation of an experience happened in a context far removed from one in which the originating experience is being repeatedly discussed, including by the person who had that original experience. Would she have co-opted the story if Carl had read it to her not just the once, but on a regular basis? Moreover, in the case Carl relates, we have conflicting accounts of who had the experience in question. When it comes to the resurrection we find no disputes over who had which experience.

Carl references a study in which patients "received a false suggestion" about experiences from previously reported dreams being on a list of real experiences and adopting those beliefs. However, unlike belief in the resurrection, the beliefs in question weren't contrary to the subject's cultural expectation.

Professor of psychology Robyn Fivush confirms it's possible to "introduce error into memory," but cautions this can be done "only under certain conditions with certain people in certain ways."[76] As Fivush notes, experiments conducted by cognitive psychologist Elizabeth Loftus found that only c. 25 percent of subjects could be induced to develop a false memory of an event they hadn't experienced (e.g., being lost in a shopping mall as a small child[77]). Other researchers have found that "at least some kind of false memory could be implanted in between 20 percent and 40 percent of participants."[78] That leaves 60–80% of people whose memories are *not* co-opted. Indeed, under a stringent definition

---

76. Amy Wilson, "War & Remembrance: Controversy is a Constant for Memory Researcher Elizabeth Loftus, Newly Installed at UCI," *Orange County Register*, williamcalvin.com/2002/OrangeCtyRegister.htm.

77. To make this suggestion plausible, relatives of the subjects provided researchers with details of shopping malls that they could have been, but were not, lost in as children. See: K.A. Wade et al., "Implanting False Memories: Lost in the Mall & Paul Ingram," www.spring.org.uk/2008/02/implanting-false-memories-lost-in-mall.php.

78. Denyse O'Leary, "Unravelling 'recovered memory'," mercatornet.com/conjugality/view/unravelling-recovered-memories/18887.

of memory (one that excludes images not experienced as memories), the percentage of participants in memory studies who falsely came to believe they could recall an event from childhood "ranged from 0% for events selected for being implausible (Pezdek et al., 1997, Study 2, receiving an enema) to 65% (Lindsay et al., 2004, put slime in teacher's desk)."[79]

Memory implantation experiments involve "authority figures conniving over multiple sessions to persuade a participant that an event really happened in their childhood"[80] and are thus dis-analogous to the experience of the resurrection witnesses:

> false memory paradigms can shift how we evaluate past events, and can for a minority of participants provoke memory-like experiences. But the rates are very low and the effects variable, and the one that produces the strongest effect—memory implantation—is also the most invasive, and least likely to match the experiences of people in normal life.[81]

Positing the *deliberate* inculcation of false memories in the resurrection witnesses would produce *an ad hoc conspiracy theory*.

In their own systematic review, Chris R. Brewin and Bernice Andrews conclude that "susceptibility to false memories of childhood events appears more limited than has been suggested."[82] They note that even when "some recollective experience for the suggested events is induced" in memory implantation studies, "only in 15% [of study subjects] are these experiences likely to be rated as full memories." Accord-

---

79. Ibid.

80. Ibid.

81. Alex Fradera, "It's Easy to Implant False Childhood Memories, Right? Wrong, Says a New Review," *Readers Digest*, May 26, 2016, digest.bps.org.uk/2016/05/26/its-easy-to-implant-false-childhood-memories-right-wrong-says-a-new-review.

82. Chris R. Brewin and Bernice Andrews, "Creating Memories for False Autobiographical Events in Childhood: A Systematic Review," *Applied Cognitive Studies* (April 8, 2016), onlinelibrary.wiley.com/doi/10.1002/acp.3220/full.

ing to memory researcher Elizabeth Loftus, one experiment:

> asked 27 highly hypnotizable individuals during hypnosis to choose
> a night from the previous week and to describe their activities
> during the half hour before going to sleep. The subjects were then
> instructed to relive that night, and a suggestion was implanted that
> they had heard some loud noises and had awakened. Almost one
> half (13) of the 27 subjects accepted the suggestion and stated *after*
> hypnosis that the suggested event had actually taken place. Of the
> 13, 6 were unequivocal in their certainty.[83]

Hence, even with a group of "highly hypnotizable individuals,"
most subjects rejected the hypnotist's suggestion, and below a quarter
of subjects were subjectively certain about the false memory. Indeed:
"average scores on measures of recollective experience and confidence
in memory for false events all fell at or below the midpoint of the scales
used. Even when clear memories were identified by the investigators,
participants' confidence in them was below the scale midpoint."[84] This
evidence *disconfirms* the hypothesis that the disciples' claim that Jesus
had been resurrected—a claim about which they were so confident they
were willing to suffer anything, and for which several clearly suffered
martyrdom (including Peter, James, and Paul)—was grounded in co-
opted memories.

Multiple studies have shown that even in the most successful cases,
false memories are *not* co-opted by a large percentage of subjects: "most
participants in these studies disbelieve the childhood event ever happened, and they doubt any apparently new memories that arise, despite
the pressure to think otherwise."[85] As Ross Pomeroy warns, "implanting
a false memory in a person, and having them fully believe it, takes some
doing. Even in the lab, researchers succeed less than half of the time."[86]

---

83. Elizabeth Loftus, "The Reality of Repressed Memories," faculty.
washington.edu/eloftus/Articles/lof93.htm.

84. Brewin and Andrews, "Creating Memories."

85. Ibid.

86. Ross Pomeroy, "How to Install False Memories," *Scientific American*

It's especially hard to implant false memories of events people judge to be unlikely: "Pre-existing beliefs play a causal role in the acceptance of potential false memories as authentic."[87] If it's hard to get people to believe they put slime in their teacher's desk as a child, it would be harder to convince first-century Jews that they recently met a crucified friend who'd been resurrected.

Primary Factors: Hallucinations.[88] A hallucination is an apparent perception via the physical senses lacking a corresponding external physical stimulus. Carl suggests the resurrection appearances could be bereavement "grief hallucinations." However, if the disciples had hallucinations, why didn't they hallucinate that Jesus had been vindicated in terms of the culturally established concept of having ascended to be with Abraham in paradise? And why would the grieving disciples hallucinate *a Jesus that they didn't recognize* (see Luke 24:13–31; John 20:15, 21:4)? Besides, Saul wasn't grieving Jesus' death.

Expectations play a major role in hallucinations,[89] but as Vermes writes, "The cross and the resurrection were unexpected, perplexing, indeed, incomprehensible for the apostles . . . As for the resurrection,

---

Guest Blog, February 9, 2013, blogs.scientificamerican.com/guest-blog/how-to-instill-false-memories/#.

87. Christopher C. French, "Fantastic Memories: The Relevance of Research into eyewitness Testimony and False Memories for Reports of Anomalous Experience," in *PSI Wars: Getting to Grips with the Paranormal*, ed. James Alcock et al. (Imprint Academic, 2003), 169.

88. See: Peter S. Williams, YouTube playlist, "Can Hallucinations Explain the Resurrection?" www.youtube.com/playlist?list=PLQhh3qcwVEWgVNLsZO UCB5i64lC51Zsji (November 28, 2018); Joseph W. Bergeron MD and Gary R. Habermas, "The Resurrection of Jesus: A Clinical Review of Psychiatric Hypotheses for the Biblical Story of Easter," www.garyhabermas.com/articles/irish-theological-quarterly/Habermas_Resurrection%20of%20Jesus.pdf; Jake O'Connell, "Jesus' Resurrection and Collective Hallucinations" *Tyndale Bulletin* 60, no. 1 (2009): 69–105, legacy.tyndalehouse.com/Bulletin/60=2009/5%20 O'Connell.pdf, and *Jesus' Resurrection and Apparitions: A Bayesian Analysis* (Resource, 2016), 85–91.

89. See: Rujuta Pradhan, "Why Do We Hallucinate?" www.scienceabc.com/humans/why-do-we-hallucinate.html.

no one was awaiting it, nor were the apostle's willing to believe the good news brought to them by the women who had visited the tomb of Jesus."[90]

Carl's references to the legend of the "Angels of Mons"[91] and to the illusion at Fatima[92] are red herrings when the subject is the purported reality of collective hallucinations:

> the concept of collective-hallucination is not found in peer reviewed medical and psychological literature ... and there is no mention of such phenomena in the Diagnostic and Statistical Manuel of Mental Disorders. As such, the concept of collective hallucinations is not part of current psychiatric understanding or accepted pathology.[93]

Psychologist Gary A. Sibey writes, "I have surveyed the professional literature (peer reviewed journal articles and books) written by psychologists, psychiatrists, and other relevant healthcare professionals during the past two decades and have yet to find a single documented case of a group hallucination."[94] Carl E. Olson concludes that "group hallucinations are, at best, incredibly rare."[95]

---

90. Vermes, *Resurrection*, 86.

91. See: Dr. Alan S. Coulson & Michael E. Hanlon, "The Legends and Traditions of the Great War: The Case of the Elusive Angel of Mons," www.worldwar1.com/heritage/angel.htm; David Clarke, *The Angel of Mons: Phantom Soldiers and Ghostly Guardians* (Wiley, 2005).

92. See: Benjamin Radford, "The Lady of Fátima & the Miracle of the Sun," www.livescience.com/29290-fatima-miracle.html.

93. Joseph W. Bergeron MD and Gary R. Habermas PhD, "The Resurrection of Jesus: A Clinical Review of Psychiatric Hypotheses for the Biblical Story of Easter," www.garyhabermas.com/articles/irish-theological-quarterly/Habermas_Resurrection%20of%20Jesus.pdf.

94. Gary A. Sibey quoted by Michael Licona, *The Resurrection of Jesus* (Apollos, 2010), 484.

95. Carl E. Olson, *Did Jesus Really Rise from The Dead?* (Ignatius Press/Augustine Institute, 2016), 108.

A 1971 survey of widows experiencing grief hallucinations showed that "the longer the marriage, the more likely it was for the living spouse to have bereavement experiences."[96] Most of the disciples would have known Jesus for around three years. Moreover, 46 percent of widows merely reported "feeling the presence" of the deceased. Visual experiences (more common in those over 40) made up 14 percent of such experiences, speaking with the spouse (more common in those over 60) 11.6 percent, and tactile experiences just 2.7 percent.[97] According to independent early reports, the disciples touched Jesus on multiple occasions (see John 20:27, 17, 24–30; Matthew 28:9; Luke 24:39). According to the 1971 study, "If the spouse attempted to speak with the apparition, the vision would dissipate."[98] The resurrected Jesus held extended conversations in the presence of multiple individuals and groups (see Luke 24:13–32, 24:36–49; John 20:11–18, 20:19–23, 21:1–25; Acts 1:3, 9:1–19).

A 2011 survey of recently bereaved individuals found that visual experiences of the deceased had a prevalence of just 4 percent.[99] A 2016 study found that 80 percent of elderly people experienced a hallucination shortly after the death of a spouse. Half of the study participants said they "felt a presence." Only one in three said they either heard or saw their departed spouse. None of these experiences were taken to indicate that the deceased was alive, let alone that they'd been resurrected!

Bereavement hallucinations usually recur over years, not the limited period reported by the New Testament. While hallucinations come from within and draw upon what we already know, "the resurrection of Jesus involved ideas utterly foreign to the disciples' minds."[100] Hallucinations don't consume food. According to independent early reports,

---

96. Ibid.

97. Ibid.

98. Bergeron and Habermas, "Resurrection."

99. Naomi M. Simon et al., "Informing the Symptoms Profile of Complicated Grief," *Depression and Anxiety* 28 (2011): 118–26.

100. William Lane Craig, *The Son Rises: Historical Evidence for the Resurrection of Jesus* (Wipf & Stock, 1981), 121.

including reports from two eyewitnesses, the resurrected Jesus ate on at least two separate occasions (see Luke 24:42–43, John 21:1–14, and Peter in Acts 10:41). Finally: "hallucinations rarely produce longstanding convictions or radical lifestyle changes. But belief in the resurrection of Jesus did both."[101]

Even if the disciples suffered from multiple hallucinations around the same time, it's astronomically unlikely that they'd have all *seen* Jesus, let alone *an unexpectedly resurrected Jesus*, let alone *talked with* him, let alone *touched* him, let alone *seen and talked with and touched* him, and clearly not *over an extended length of time*, let alone *in a group setting*, let alone *on multiple occasions*, let alone *sharing food with him*, and let alone *with life-changing results!*

Jake O'Connell points out that in the rare *claimed* cases of collective hallucinations "not all present see the vision;"[102] whereas the evidence suggests that everyone present saw the resurrected Jesus. Again, in claimed cases of collective hallucination, "Those who do see the vision see it differently";[103] whereas the resurrection experiences were coordinated (e.g., *neither* disciple on the road to Emmaus recognized Jesus until he broke bread with them, whereupon they *both* recognized him, etc.). In particular, O'Connell argues that "while expectation seems theoretically capable of accounting for collective visual hallucinations, it would not be able to give rise to a collective hallucinatory conversation."[104] O'Connell concludes, "the [resurrection] narratives are inconsistent with collective hallucinations."[105]

Pick and Mix. The most interesting hypothesis advanced by Carl is that a combination of psychological factors might explain the resurrection

---

101. Stephen T. Davis, *Rational Faith: A Philosopher's Defence of Christianity* (Lion, 2017), 76.

102. Jake O'Connell, "Jesus' Resurrection and Collective Hallucinations," *Tyndale Bulletin* 60, no. 1 (2009): 69–105 (quote: p. 85), legacy.tyndalehouse.com/Bulletin/60=2009/5%20O'Connell.pdf.

103. Ibid.

104. Ibid., 86.

105. Ibid., 88.

"appearances." Suppose one person had a dream or hallucination that they mistook for an experience of a resurrected Jesus. Mightn't their delusion have been co-opted by the other disciples? Such a combination of theories still requires the concept of a *resurrected* Jesus to emerge in the absence of a plausible horizon of expectation, but it has the merit of only requiring this to happen once.

However, the hypothesis of a chain of delusion transmitted via false memories has difficulty accounting for the fact that the resurrection "appearances" reported by the New Testament vary significantly. The "appearances" cannot be arranged in a sequence of "common descent" through which one person's delusion could be co-opted by all the others. Indeed, the suggestion that Mary Magdalene's belief in the resurrection was produced by a misleading psychological mechanism (hallucination, co-opted memory, etc.) stands in tension with the testimony that she clearly didn't expect her encounter with Jesus (she thought his tomb was empty because his *corpse* had been moved); that far from mistaking the gardener for Jesus, she mistook Jesus for the gardener; and that she recognized Jesus at close quarters during an extended conversation in an encounter that was integrated into her unique circumstances that Easter morning.

The appearance to Cleopas and his wife Mary (see John 19:25) on the Emmaus road happened before they heard about the appearances to Mary Magdalene and the other women. The other women (a second group experience) didn't know about Mary Magdalene's encounter, or the later events in Emmaus. While the male disciples (a third group experience) had heard the women's report, "they did not believe the women, because their words seemed to them like nonsense" (Luke 24:11). Their rejection of the women's testimony (which is culturally understandable but still embarrassing in light of their later beliefs) adds to the implausibility of the suggestion that they co-opted the women's experience as their own.

The documented experiences of Jesus as resurrected aren't *generic* experiences (analogous to being lost in a shopping mall as a child) that could easily be "transmitted" from one person to another. The "appearances" had features that made them specific to the individual or individuals that had them. For example, the male disciples couldn't have co-opted the women's experience of going to tend to Jesus' corpse, or of reporting *to the male disciples* (and even if they did co-opt the women's memory, you'd think someone would point out that the women claimed to have exactly the same experience, only without any male disciples being involved)! Likewise, Thomas didn't believe in the resurrection until he thought he saw for himself. When he did, his (*embarrassing*) experience was unique. Moreover, the experience of the other disciples when Thomas met the resurrected Jesus for the first time was clearly distinct from their previous group meeting with Jesus when Thomas wasn't with them. Again, although Saul had likely heard claims about Jesus' resurrection, he clearly didn't believe them. Neither Saul nor his companions on the road to Damascus were co-opting anyone's memory, since (a) Saul's resurrection experience was unique and (b) Saul's companions didn't experience the resurrected Jesus (although they did experience a light and a voice/sound).

In sum, the appeal to co-opted memories can't eliminate the appeal to *multiple* hallucinations, including *multiple group hallucinations*.

Expectations

The resurrection hypothesis "*outstrips any of its rival hypotheses* . . . alternative explanations . . . have been almost universally rejected by contemporary scholarship."[106] However, as previously noted, how convincing one finds the resurrection hypothesis partially depends upon the worldview expectations one brings to considering both the arguments for the resurrection and its implications as one understands them. We inevitably assess the "fit" between the explanation offered for the evidence (and the implications of that explanation as we understand them) and our current worldview. However, this process should be a two-way street: "everyone generally operates within his or her own concept of reality . . . having said this, however . . . We do need to be informed by the data we receive. And sometimes . . . the evidence on a subject

---

106. Craig, "Resurrection of Jesus."

convinces us against our indecisiveness or even contrary to our former position."[107]

Miracles[108]

Carl rightly looks for natural explanations before miraculous ones, but the correct basis for this bias is that miracles are by definition the exception rather than the rule. The resulting preference for natural explanations cannot preclude accepting a miracle *regardless of the evidence* as "contrary to nature" after the manner of David Hume's tendentious definition of miracles as "violations" of natural law:

> Miracles are not "violations" of the laws of nature at all. The laws . . . describe what objects in nature are capable of producing in light of the powers that they have . . . Thus . . . believing in events having supernatural causes needn't saddle one with believing that there are *false laws of nature*, laws having exceptions. Miracles are . . . occurrences having causes about which laws of nature are simply silent. The laws are true, but simply don't speak to events caused by divine intervention.[109]

In other words: "miracles do not violate the laws of nature. They threaten not our understanding of how nature works when not intervened upon by something other than itself, but rather the insistence that nature is never affected by supernatural agency."[110] Whether or not a miracle is the best explanation for a given set of data is thus a judgment that must be made *a posteriori*.

---

107. Gary R. Habermas, "Did Jesus Perform Miracles?" in *Jesus Under Fire*, ed. Michael J. Wilkins and J.P. Moreland (Paternoster, 1996), 126.

108. See: R. Douglas Geivett & Gary R. Habermas, eds., *In Defence of Miracles: A Comprehensive Case for God's Action in History* (Apollos, 1997); Robert A. Larmer, *The Legitimacy of Miracle* (Lexington, 2014); Williams, *Getting at Jesus*.

109. J. A. Cover, "Miracles and Christian Theism," in *Reason for the Hope Within*, ed. Michael J. Murray (Eerdmans, 1999), 362.

110. Robert A. Larmer, *The Legitimacy of Miracle* (Lexington, 2014), 86.

The God Question

Carl's overriding reason for rejecting the resurrection is that it entails a belief in God, even a specifically Christian God.[111] Carl prefers his aggregate naturalistic explanation because, he says, "this account does not require the existence of God" or "a specifically Christian God to provide a miracle." However, these points will obviously weigh differently with different people, depending upon how they evaluate the question of God's existence and nature apart from the evidence for the resurrection.

Carl states, "The case for the resurrection as an historic fact . . . opens up myriad problems suitable for other debates, none of which exist in the simpler and more plausible natural explanations [for the resurrection]." However, that naturalistic explanations of the "appearances," etc., avoid raising questions suited to other debates doesn't necessarily mean that the resurrection isn't the best explanation of the evidence. Nor does it necessarily mean naturalism is a better worldview than Christianity.[112]

Problems with Evil[113]

The problem of evil isn't an argument for atheism or naturalism. The

---

111. See: Thomas V. Morris, *Our Idea of God: An Introduction to Philosophical Theology* (University of Notre Dame, 1991); Peter S. Williams, "Understanding the Trinity," www.bethinking.org/god/understanding-the-trinity.

112. After all, the fact that theory *x* raises theoretical questions that theory *y* avoids doesn't automatically mean theory *y* is better than theory *x*, because theory *y* might raise theoretical questions more troublesome than those faced by *x* (e.g., there might be better answers to the questions raised by *x* than by *y*).

113. See: Peter S. Williams, YouTube playlist, "The Problem of Evil," www.youtube.com/playlist?list=PLQhh3qcwVEWjSOz8xsGXuS_VahByzSzhe (February 15, 2018); Kelly James Clark, "I Believe in God the Father, Almighty," calvin.edu/academic/philosophy/writings/ibig.htm; Gregory E. Ganssle, "God and Evil," in *The Rationality of Theism*, ed. Paul Copan and Paul K. Moser (Routledge, 2003); Daniel Howard-Snyder, "God, Evil, and Suffering," in *Reason for the Hope Within*, ed. Michael J. Murray (Eerdmans, 1999); Chad Meister and James K. Drew Jr., eds., *God and Evil* (IVP, 2013); Williams, *A Faithful Guide to Philosophy*.

traditional "logical problem of evil" claims to deduce the nonexistence of a creator who has maximal goodness, maximal power, *and* a maximal capacity for knowledge, from the premise that objective evils exist. Robin Le Poidevan's careful phrasing of the argument makes this explicit:

> If [God] is all-knowing, he will be aware of suffering; if he is all-powerful, he will be able to prevent suffering; and if he is perfectly good, he will desire to prevent suffering. But, clearly, he does not prevent suffering, so either there is no such deity, or, if there is, he is not all-knowing, all-powerful and perfectly good, though he may be one or two of these.[114]

The conclusion of the "logical" argument is consistent with belief in a creator lacking one or more of the great-making properties of maximal power, etc. The significance of the "logical" argument lies in its claim to exclude the existence of precisely the sort of deity that Christians accept.

According to Christian orthodoxy, God was free not to create.[115] It follows, *contra* Craig Blomberg, that God's choice to create means he is indirectly responsible for the existence of evil. However, I don't think this affirmation is detrimental. For one thing, "philosophers of religion, theists and atheists alike have agreed in recent years that [the logical] problem of evil has been decisively rebutted and is therefore unsuccessful."[116] As atheist William L. Rowe observes,

> Some philosophers have contended that the existence of evil is *logically inconsistent* with the existence of the theistic God. No one, I think, has succeeded in establishing such an extravagant claim.

---

114. Robin Le Poidevin, *Arguing for Atheism* (Routledge, 1996), 88.

115. See: James Beilby, "Divine Aseity, Divine Freedom: A Conceptual Problem for Edwardsian-Calvinism," www.etsjets.org/files/JETS-PDFs/47/47-4/47-4-pp647-658_JETS.pdf; Thomas D. Senor, "Defending Divine Freedom," philpapers.org/archive/SENDDF.

116. Chad Meister, "God, Evil and Morality," in *God Is Great, God Is Good*, ed. William Lane Craig and Chad Meister (IVP, 2009), 108.

Indeed, granted incompatibilism, there is a fairly compelling argument for the view that the existence of evil is logically consistent with the existence of the theistic God.[117]

The typical claim made by informed atheists today isn't that evil *disproves* theism, but that it *counts against the rationality of theism*. However, atheist Michael Tooley, a leading advocate of this "evidential" form of the argument from evil, acknowledges that it is "highly controversial"[118] and concludes:

> even if it can be shown that the evils that are found in the world render the existence of God unlikely, it might still be the case that the existence of God is not unlikely *all things considered*. For perhaps the argument from evil can be overcome by appealing either to positive arguments in support of the existence of God, or to the idea that belief in the existence of God is properly basic.[119]

The resurrection may raise problems about evil, but so does naturalism, and the problems raised by naturalism are at least as serious as the problems raised by the resurrection. For example, I agree with those naturalists who argue that naturalism is inconsistent with the existence of objective evil. The thing is, as plenty of other naturalists argue, some things really are objectively evil. In other words, the existence of objective evil is inconsistent with naturalism;[120] and the question of how to account for objective evil leads to the metaethical argument for theism.[121] As H. P. Owen argues,

---

117. William L. Rowe, "The Problem of Evil and Some Varieties of Atheism," *American Philosophical Quarterly* 16 (1979). See also: Alvin Plantinga, *God, Freedom, and Evil* (Eerdmans, 1974).

118. Michael Tooley, *Knowledge of God* (Wiley-Blackwell, 2008), 70.

119. Ibid. See: Peter S. Williams, "Problems with the Problem of Evil" (Trondheim University, 2018), peterswilliams.podbean.com/mf/feed/jpz78a/ Trondheim_2018_Problems_With_Evil.mp3; Alvin Plantinga, *Warranted Christian Belief* (Oxford, 2000).

120. See: J. P. Moreland, *Scaling the Secular City* (Baker, 1987), 112–113.

121. See: Peter S. Williams, YouTube playlist, "The Moral Argument for God,"

The dictates of society cannot explain the absoluteness of the categorical imperative; but in so far as they are personal they have a superficial credibility. . . bare belief in an impersonal order of claims . . . does not provide the personal basis which their imperatival quality requires . . . On the one hand [objective moral] claims transcend every human person . . . On the other hand . . . it is contradictory to assert that impersonal claims are entitled to the allegiance of our wills. The only solution to this paradox is to suppose that the order of [objective moral] claims . . . is in fact rooted in the personality of God.[122]

The Truth That Would Save

Carl's major theological concern is "why this God, supposedly the loving father of all mankind, has revealed himself [in such a way as to leave] billions of humans with no hope of salvation." According to Carl, believing in the resurrection means believing God excludes billions from salvation. Craig disagrees, as do I.[123]

Peter affirms, "The Lord is not willing that any should perish but [desires] that all should reach repentance" (2 Peter 3:9, NIV). John states, "God did not send his Son into the world to condemn the world, but to save the world through him" (John 3:17, NIV). Paul writes that God "desires all men to be saved and to come to a knowledge of the

---

www.youtube.com/playlist?list=PLQhh3qcwVEWhOfs_uQrFceuBRfMF1asf4 (August 18, 2018); Peter S. Williams, "Can Moral Objectivism Do Without God?" www.bethinking.org/morality/can-moral-objectivism-do-without-god; Paul Copan, "The Moral Argument," in *The Rationality of Theism*, ed. Paul Copan and Paul K. Moser (Routledge, 2003); Robert K Garcia and Nathan L King, eds., *Is Goodness Without God Good Enough?* (AltaMira Press, 2009); Stuart C. Hackett, "The Value Dimension in the Cosmos: A Moral Argument," in *Philosophy of Religion*, ed. William Lane Craig (Edinburgh University Press, 2002); H. P. Owen, "Why Morality Implies the Existence of God," in *Philosophy of Religion*, ed. Brian Davies (Oxford, 2000); Peter S. Williams, *C. S. Lewis vs the New Atheists* (Paternoster, 2013).

122. H. P. Owen, "Why Morality Implies the Existence of God," in *Philosophy of Religion: A Guide and Anthology*, ed. Brian Davies (Oxford, 2000), 647–648.

123. See: Peter S. Williams, "The Particular and Exclusive Christ," peterswilliams.podbean.com/mf/feed/zr36r9/Exclusivism_2017.mp3.

truth" (1 Timothy 2:4, NIV). He also makes it clear that God doesn't condemn anyone for *ignorance*, but only for a *culpable refusal* to welcome "the truth that would save them" (2 Thessalonians 2:9–10, ISV). Those who will "come under judgment" are people "who have refused to believe the truth and have taken pleasure in unrighteousness" (2 Thessalonians 2:12, Weymouth NT). If our understanding of the "good news" contradicts these apostolic affirmations, our understanding must be improved![124]

Whilst the *fullest* expression and experience of "the truth that would save" is found "in Christ" (see Acts 19:1–6; Romans 10:1–21; 2 Thessalonians 2:13), as Nicky Gumbel observes,

> Abraham and David . . . were justified by faith. Jesus tells us in the parable of the Pharisee and the tax collector that the tax collector who said "God, have mercy on me, a sinner," went home justified before God (Luke 18:9–14).[125]

Moreover, I believe that everyone saved by faith will ultimately receive salvation "in Christ" (see John 8:56; Acts 10:1–48; Romans 11:23–24; Hebrews 11:39–40). This jives with the venerable theory that salvation is possible postmortem.[126] Finally, given divine middle-knowledge, we may reckon that people who refuse salvation are people who would

---

124. See: William Lane Craig, *On Guard for Students* (David C. Cook, 2015); Clark H. Pinnock, ed., *The Grace of God and the Will of Man* (Bethany House, 1989); Jerry L. Walls, *Heaven: The Logic of Eternal Joy* (Oxford University Press, 2002); Jerry L. Walls and Joseph R. Dongell, *Why I Am Not A Calvinist* (IVP, 2004); Dallas Willard, *Knowing Christ Today* (HarperOne, 2009).

125. Nicky Gumbel, *Searching Issues* (Kingsway, 1995), 36.

126. Jewish belief in the possibility of postmortem forgiveness is seen in *2 Maccabees* (12:38–45). The "Harrowing of Hades" was taught by many theologians of the early church (including Ambrose, Athanasius, Clement of Alexandria, Origen, John of Damascus, and Tertullian). Belief in postmortem evangelism has been supported by modern scholars such as G. R. Beasley-Murray, Donald Bloesch, C. E. B. Cranfield, Stephen T. Davis, Brian Hebblethwaite, Richard Swinburne, and Jerry L. Walls. See: John Sanders, *No Other Name: Can Only Christians Be Saved?* (SPCK, 1994); Jerry L. Walls, *Heaven: The Logic of Eternal Joy* (Oxford University Press, 2002).

make the same choice in any possible world wherein it's feasible for God to create them.[127]

Conclusion

The debate between Carl and Craig on the resurrection certainly raises questions that merit further consideration. Jesus' resurrection is only one piece of the Christian jigsaw, albeit a key piece. This key piece integrates with other pieces, and the picture one thinks they form, one's assessment of that picture and of the reasons for and against trusting it, will influence one's view of the matter at hand.[128] That is, what one makes of the resurrection depends not only upon one's methodology in the gathering of *evidence* and the assessment of competing *explanations*, but also upon an open and critical dialogue with one's philosophical *expectations*.

---

127. See: William Lane Craig, *On Guard for Students* (David C. Cook, 2015) and *The Only Wise God: The Compatibility of Divine Foreknowledge and Human Freedom* (Wipf & Stock, 2000); William Lane Craig and Joseph E. Gorra, *A Reasonable Response: Answers to Tough Questions* (Moody, 2013).

128. See: Paul Copan and Paul K. Moser, eds., *The Rationality of Theism* (Routledge, 2003); C. Stephen Evans, *Why Believe?: Reason and Mystery as Pointers to God* (Eerdmans, 1996); Thomas V. Morris, *Making Sense of It All: Pascal and the Meaning of Life* (Eerdmans, 1998); Keith Ward, *Christianity: A Short Introduction* (OneWorld, 2000); Dallas Willard, *Knowing Christ Today* (HarperOne, 2009); Ravi Zacharias, *Can Man Live Without God?* (Nelson, 1994).

PART FIVE: FINAL THOUGHTS

Miracle Not Required

Carl Stecher, Ph.D.

Professor Williams challenges the case that I have made against the historicity of Jesus' resurrection. Because of the long and collegial relationship we have had, I will subsequently refer to Professor Williams as Peter. Peter writes:

> Stecher opens the debate by asserting, "What is lacking is any method for differentiating the historical from the legendary and fictional," genres he assumes are mixed together in the New Testament. Carl nevertheless thinks he can make this differentiation . . . However, if there's no method for differentiating between historical and nonhistorical material, how can Carl justify asserting that the Gospels contain both types of material, or that the crucifixion is historical but the empty tomb isn't?

Peter's challenge is justified; at the very least my point needs clarification. My statement reflects a position of skepticism and the rejection of Christian biblical literalism and infallibility. Some of the scholars that Peter quotes often—Norman Geisler is a good example—believe in biblical inerrancy: that whatever the Bible says is simple truth. Geisler holds that Jesus taught that God created Adam and Eve and that Jonah was swallowed by a great fish. Geisler certainly is not suggesting we disbelieve Jesus! Geisler further believes that Noah's flood happened.

This biblical literalism has often put Christian scholars, even those who agree on many issues, at odds with each other. Geisler, for example, has pretty much read Craig Blomberg out of the faith because Craig has expressed doubt that the passage in Matthew 27, with its account of the Jewish saints coming out of their graves and parading around Jerusalem—or, as I like to call it, the parade of zombies—portrays an actual event in history.

I am not attributing this belief in biblical infallibility to Peter, but I'm not clear, from what he has written here, what his position on the authority and historical accuracy of the Bible is. This is, after all, a pivotal issue in any consideration of the historicity of the New Testament accounts of Jesus' resurrection.

Before proceeding further, I will first respond to several statements made by Peter in his chapter to which I find fault. Peter writes, "Carl tacitly makes the false assumption that '*disconfirmation by silence*' will always outweigh even the strongest case using positive historical criteria." I have never taken this position. I would prefer that Peter address statements that I have actually made, not tell me what he thinks I am thinking. Shortly after, Peter writes, "Carl not only concludes that Luke contradicts Matthew, but that Luke contradicts himself!" This is correct, and I have already cited the evidence. Peter does nothing to refute my analysis; an exclamation point is neither argument nor evidence.

Later, Peter writes, "Carl's complaint that 'we don't have a single case of a group encounter attested by any member of the group' . . . refuses to count the experience of Saul and his traveling companions as a group encounter." In this context, Peter approvingly quotes Darrel Bock, "The point is that [Paul's traveling companions] knew something happened and that Saul did not have a merely inner, psychological experience." As I see it, that Paul's anonymous companions "knew something had happened" is hardly the equivalent of a shared group experience of Jesus. And do we really think that Paul's companions would have had a modern understanding of psychological experiences?

Peter then writes, "in John, it isn't 'Mary alone' who goes to the tomb, as is clear from John 20:2." But John, which Peter does not quote, portrays Mary as being alone when she goes to the tomb, not in the company of other women. This clearly contradicts the reports in Mark (16:1-8), Matthew (28:1–10), and Luke (24:1–10).

As evidence for the empty tomb, Peter cites the Jewish *Toledot Yeshu*. My guess is that readers will be unfamiliar with this document. According to classical Judaism scholar Mika Ahuvia, "Toledot Yeshu is a decidedly non-rabbinic counter-narrative and satire of the foundational story of Christianity, which likely originated in the late antique or early medieval period . . . in the genre of the folk story, no two manuscripts are identical and storytellers likely embellished it with every recounting."[1] Peter's citing of this obscure and certainly unreliable document signals to me how thin and fraught with problems the actual evidence is.

Finally, in his discussion of Jesus as a prophet, Peter writes, "There's every reason to think Jesus was an accurate prophet." But Peter has done nothing to refute the evidence to the contrary that I have already cited. For example, what of Jesus' failure to return as promised within the generation of those living then? Consider Jesus' words in Mark when challenged by the high priest: "'Are you the Messiah, the Son of the blessed One?' 'I am,' said Jesus, 'and you will see the Son of Man seated at the right hand of the Almighty and coming with the clouds of heaven'" (14:61–62). Clearly this is a claim by Jesus that his return will be witnessed by the priests interrogating him.

My position is that the historicity of the resurrection accounts is undermined by passages in the Gospels and in Paul's epistles that (*pace* Geisler) are *clearly* legends or fictionalizations. I place in these categories the birth legends in Matthew and Luke (which contradict each other and are in conflict with known facts about the period); the opening of John, with its portrayal of Jesus' role in the creation about six thousand years ago; those passages in which the voice of God comes out of the sky (Matthew 3:16–17 and many others); conversations recorded verbatim and at length for which there were no plausible witnesses (Judas and the Temple priests in Matthew 27:3–6); the guards

---

1. "An Introduction to Toledot Yeshu," *Ancient Jew Review*, December 25, 2014, www.ancientjewreview.com/articles/2014/12/25/a-quick-introduction-to-toledot-yeshu.

and the temple priests plotting false testimony in Matthew 28:12–13); Pilate questioning Jesus in a private interview in John 18:28–38, despite our being told, "It was now early morning, and the Jews themselves stayed outside the headquarters to avoid defilement, so that they could eat the Passover Meal" (18:28).

I am not claiming infallibility in my categorizing these passages as unhistorical and thus evidence that much in the New Testament accounts of the resurrection should be treated with skepticism. Peter and Craig refer to some of the same passages and, it seems, consider them to be history, not legend or fiction, and thus supportive of the historicity of Jesus' resurrection. A voice out of the sky announcing, "This is my beloved Son, in whom I take delight"? For Craig and Peter, nothing here but history; a voice coming out of the sky is not to be considered unhistorical. After all, Craig's mother had direct experience of this phenomenon, so for Craig there is no need of confirmation.

I, however, have never heard the voice of God, nor has any family member or friend reported such an experience. Nor have I encountered any report of such an event from a respected news source—say, the *New York Times*, the *Washington Post*, or *PBS News* (*pace* Donald Trump). If there were confirmation from such a source of a voice from the sky that could only be the voice of God, or of a person ascending into the sky and disappearing into a cloud, I would need to reconsider my world view, my impulse to assume that such events are either mistaken reports or they have a natural, nonmiraculous explanation. First, I would check the date to make sure it was not April 1st.

This takes us back to our "Horizons" chapters, revelatory of our differing senses of reality. So too, it should remind the four contributing authors that our goal is not to "win the debate," whatever that might mean, but to lay out as clearly as possible the positive and negative cases for the resurrection of Jesus as a fact of history. In doing this, at the very least we can clarify where we are in accord, and where our different perceptions of reality cannot be reconciled. We hope that our readers will find our efforts to achieve this helpful in their own effort to find useful truth about this powerfully significant question of Jesus' resurrection.

Turning to some interesting arguments that Peter has made, Peter writes, "In general, the more criteria of authenticity a saying or event passes, the more seriously we should take it." This seems reasonable to me. But I would like to suggest a corollary: *The fewer and weaker the evidence for any alleged "fact," the weaker the case for accepting it.* In this regard another general rule might be *the greater the importance of an event involving the eternal fate of billions of people, the more compelling should be the evidence that this event actually happened.*

Applying this to the event we are debating, the alleged resurrection of Jesus, if Peter and Craig are not mistaken, having the correct interpretation of this alleged event is determinative of whether upon dying one ascends to heaven to experience eternal joy with God, or whether one ceases to exist or descends to hell, there to spend all eternity because of a failure to believe in Jesus and his resurrection.

There is certainly biblical evidence to support this teaching: "This Jesus is the stone, rejected by you the builders, which has become the corner-stone. There is no salvation through anyone else; in all the world no other name has been granted to mankind by which we can be saved" (Acts 4:11–12). "No one can come to me unless he is drawn by the Father . . . In very truth I tell you, whoever believes has eternal life" (John 6:43–47). "[B]ut the unbeliever has already been judged because he has not put his trust in God's only son" (John 3:18). At least for someone who has read the Bible, and specifically Matthew 25:41, information is given about the fate of those who do not make the cut, who are consigned to hell: "A curse is on you; go from my sight to the eternal fire that is ready for the devil and his angels."

What is rather strange and confusing is that Jesus' words in this passage (and in others, like Luke 16:19–31) indicate that God's judgment, and his division of all humanity into sheep and goats, has nothing to do with what one believes, but instead is determined by the supplicant's behavior: those who will be blessed with an eternal life in heaven fed the poor, clothed the naked, gave hospitality to strangers; those who did not take care of their less fortunate neighbors are to be rejected and punished. Such passages stand in contrast to many others in which Jesus is portrayed as teaching that the determinative factor for whether someone is rewarded or punished in the afterlife is whether one believes in Jesus, not one's treatment of neighbors or strangers.

My only problem with the equity of judgment based upon behavior, rather than on belief, is that the sins indicated in the Matthew 25 passage are almost entirely sins of omission—failure to visit a friend in hospital, or to feed the poor. But very few people, even what I would think of as essentially good people—will do as much as might be done in these situations. Need one impoverish oneself and one's family to provide for strangers? Does one have family obligations (charity begins at home) that might compete with one's charitable impulses? Is enough ever enough? Does any such failure justify the consignment of anyone to eternal torment in hell?

Given the transcendent importance of belief in Jesus' resurrection according to traditional Christian teaching, one would expect very compelling evidence assessable by everyone that Jesus' resurrection actually occurred. But we do not have such evidence. Even Luke acknowledges the limitations of the evidence provided by God. "God raised him to life on the third day, and allowed him to be clearly seen, not by the whole people, but by witnesses whom God had chosen in advance— by us, who ate and drank with him after he rose from the dead" (Acts 10:40–41).

Given that, according to Christian teaching, the eternal fate of billions of human beings rests upon their becoming Christian believers, it seems to me uncharitable that many Christian apologists, Peter and Craig included, argue that God has given ample evidence of Jesus' resurrection in that Jesus appeared to Paul, an avowed enemy, and perhaps to James, the unbelieving brother of Jesus. (The New Testament does not make clear that this appearance actually happened and made James a believer.)

Peter examines my *disconfirmations by silence* argument and, quoting physicist Victor J. Stenger, comments, "Absence of evidence is evidence of absence *when the evidence should be there and is not.*" I agree. I've argued on this basis that the report of Jesus' final words and his physical and visible ascension into heaven clearly meet this criteria. Yet this event, alleged by the author of Acts, is nowhere confirmed or even hinted at by Paul or the authors of Mark, Matthew, or John, our only first-century sources for the stories of Jesus' resurrection. These documents have not a hint that their authors have ever heard the story told by Luke of Jesus' final words and ascension. Craig suggests that all the other first-century accounts do not mention Jesus' last words and ascension because Luke has saved this for the "sequel" to his Gospel, the Acts of the Apostles. This, however, fails to account for the other Gospel accounts not completing the story with its natural climax. Peter also does not explain their silence.

Peter writes, "Stecher's critique of the canonical gospels often stems from an uncharitable and historically uninformed hermeneutic," hermeneutic defined as the rules for interpretation.

I'm sorry to be characterized as "uncharitable" in my analysis of the Gospel accounts, but I'm unclear on what role charity should have in the understanding of these texts. The charge, however, is telling, because Peter and like-minded Christian scholars have no case to make at all without considerable charity. To illustrate this point, let's examine what a more charitable interpretation of the canonical gospels might look like in practice by briefly considering the work of apologist Michael Licona. Licona writes, "The evangelists occasionally displace an event from its original context and transplant it in another either to raise tension in the narrative or to link it with another story involving the same characters."[2] Drawing attention to similarities in the descriptions of the appearance accounts in Matthew 28:16–17 and Luke 24:36–49, Licona argues that these passages are "describing the same event."[3] This appearance, he says, probably occurred in Jerusalem as Luke and John independently report, but Matthew "displaces" it to Galilee, *and this was acceptable by the genre standards of first-century biography.* Hence, Licona argues, "We can't dismiss the gospels as historical sources on the basis that Matthew appears to disagree with Luke and John about the location of this 'appearance.'"

---

2. Michael Licona, *Why Are There Differences in the Gospels? What We Can Learn from Ancient Biography* (Oxford University Press, 2017), 183.

3. Ibid., 180.

But is it conceivable that these two passages are describing the same event, with Matthew simply displacing the Luke account to Galilee? In the Matthew account, Jesus at the tomb instructs his female disciples to tell his male disciples to "Go and take word to my brothers that they are to leave for Galilee. They will see me there." And then, "The eleven disciples made their way to Galilee, to the mountain where Jesus had told them to meet him. When they saw him, they knelt in worship, though some were doubtful." And then, "Jesus came near and said to them: '. . .Go therefore to all nations and make them my disciples; baptize them in the name of the Father and the Son and the Holy Spirit, and despatch them to observe all that I have commanded you. I will be with you always, to the end of time" (Matt. 28:10–20).

In the parallel passage in Luke's Gospel, Jesus does not appear at the empty tomb, so he cannot instruct anyone that his disciples are to meet him in Galilee. The disciples obey Luke's risen Jesus and stay in Jerusalem and its environs, an exhausting three-day journey from Galilee. According to Luke, Cleopas and an unidentified disciple encountered Jesus as they walked to Emmaus, a nearby village. They do not for some time recognize Jesus, but they tell the stranger how some of the female disciples who had gone to Jesus' tomb had "returned with a story that they had seen a vision of angels who told them that he was alive. Then some of our people went to the tomb and found things just as they women had said; but him they did not see" (24:24). The stranger is about to share lunch with the two disciples, but suddenly reveals himself to be Jesus and disappears. The two disciples return to Jerusalem, rejoining the eleven disciples in hiding, when suddenly Jesus appears to them. Jesus shows the frightened disciples the wounds on his hands and feet, shares a fish lunch with them, then explains how the scriptures foretell the sufferings of the Messiah and his rising from the dead on the third day. He instructs them, "*wait here in this city until you are armed with power from above*" (my italics), a seeming reference to the day of Pentecost, forty days in the future (Luke 24:49). Jesus' instructions are repeated in the opening verses of Acts, with explicit reference to Pentecost: "To these men [the eleven apostles] he showed himself after his death . . . over a period of forty days . . . he directed them not to leave Jerusalem" (1:3–4).

What might Peter say of this argument that Matthew and Luke are describing the same event? Might he approvingly call it charitable? The fact is Matthew and Luke conflict in nearly every possible way—to assert that they differ only in the displacement of the appearances from Jerusalem to Galilee simply ignores the actual texts, which I have specifically shown. Is this the type of charity Peter asks of me?

Peter places considerable emphasis on the alleged empty tomb. For Christian scholars, the discovery of Jesus' empty tomb, which can only be explained by his having risen from the dead, is a major piece of evidence. But in my case against the historicity of the resurrection accounts, I referred to the many plausible arguments for natural explanations detailed in Price and Lowder's *Jesus Beyond the Grave;* Peter does not respond to any of these possibilities.

Peter has an interesting response to the question of whether Jesus was a false prophet, promising his Second Coming during the lifetime of some of his disciples (Peter refers to Jesus' words on this subject as "elliptical predictions"; I do not know what he means by this). According to Peter, Jesus' words refer to the events that would happen in 70 C.E. But what happened then was the violent repression of those Jews who thought to establish God's Kingdom on earth and the destruction of Jerusalem and the sacred Temple. This was probably the worst defeat of Jewish hopes for the Kingdom of God being established on earth until the holocaust many centuries later. Peter writes, quoting Paul Copan, "Most New Testament scholars take passages such as Matthew 16:28 and Mark 14:62/Matthew 26:64 and Luke 22:69 as references to AD 70—not some distant 'second coming.'" But is this interpretation plausible?

Matthew 16:28 quotes Jesus, "Truly I tell you: there are some of those standing here who will not taste death before they have seen the Son of Man coming in his kingdom." Matthew 26:64, also quoting Jesus, reads, "from now on you will see the Son of Man seated at the right hand of the Almighty and coming on the clouds of heaven." I am unable to see the connection between these passages and the events of 70 C.E.

Note the similarities of these passages with passages that Peter does not quote, passages that make clear Jesus' promise to return during the present generation. Jesus is responding to this question from his disciples: "Tell us, they said, . . . what will be the sign of your coming and the end of the age?" (Matthew 24:3). After describing to his disciples the disasters, both natural and man-made that are about to happen, Jesus tells his disciples:

> Then they will see the Son of Man coming in the clouds with great power and glory, and he will send out the angels and gather his chosen from the four winds, from the farthest bounds of earth to the farthest bounds of heaven. Learn the lesson from the fig tree. When its tender shoots appear and are breaking into leaf, you know that summer is near. In the same way, when you see all this happening, you may know that the end is near, at the very door. *Truly I tell you: the present generation will live to see it all.* Yet about that day or hour no one knows, not even the angels in heaven, not even the Son; no one but the Father. (Mark 13:26–32)

Jesus' words could hardly be clearer: he promised his disciples that he would return during the lifetime of at least some of them. Jesus does not know the hour nor the day of his return, but if they have lamps, he says, make sure the lamps have enough oil to last through the night (Luke 12:35–40).

About the alleged empty tomb, which is not clearly referenced until Mark's Gospel written decades later, Peter writes that my questioning of the conclusions cited by a conservative Christian study group committed to a literalist interpretation of the Bible is an *ad hominem* argument, assuming that "scholars who believe in inerrancy can't distinguish between what they believe on the basis of inerrancy and what they can demonstrate on the basis of historical scholarship." But this suggests that such believers are not subject, as we all are, to confirmation bias. I certainly do not mean to question the character of these scholars, but given that membership in this group might well be viewed as an honor, and a negative finding about the evidence for the empty tomb might lead members to feel they have to resign from the organization, a finding confirming historicity is hardly surprising. None of us achieve complete objectivity.

My most compelling argument against the empty tomb is the complete lack of evidence that Jesus' tomb ever became a holy shrine in the first century. Peter does not respond to this argument.

Reading Peter's critique of the case I make that the disciples' belief that Jesus had been miraculously resurrected could be attributed to a variety of purely natural causes, all of them part of universal human experience, well-documented, and the study of university studies and experiments, I notice that Peter constantly assumes the historicity of every detail of the New Testament accounts. For the reasons I have previously given, I do not make this assumption. I wonder if Peter recognizes anything in the New Testament (or the Old Testament, for that matter) that is not historically accurate, but legend or fiction?

Peter writes:

> Saul wasn't part of the rivalry between disciples . . . While Saul had no doubt heard about heard about the disciples' belief in Jesus' resurrection, (a) he obviously didn't believe it until his road to Damascus experience, and (b) he'd probably have heard about Jesus' purported ascension, which would have likely seemed to one and all to preclude Jesus appearing to anyone before the second coming.

But Peter here is forgetting or ignoring the dispute between Saul and Peter recorded in Galatians:

> But when Cephas [*another name for Peter*] came to Antioch, I opposed him to his face, because he was clearly in the wrong . . . he was taking his meals with gentile Christians; but after they came he drew back and began to hold aloof, because he was afraid of the Jews. The other Jewish Christians showed the same lack of principle . . . But when I saw that their conduct did not square with the truth of the gospel, I said to Cephas in front of the whole congregation, "If you, a Jew born and bred, live like a Gentile, and not like a Jew, how can you insist that Gentiles must live like Jews?" (Galatians 2:11–14)

Note also that Peter Williams here is basing his argument on speculation ("... probably ... would have likely ..."). Peter simply ignores Paul's invective: "You stupid Galatians! ... can you really be so stupid?" (Galatians 3:1–3). The New Testament text shows that the bitter divisions that have beset Christianity through the centuries began with the very first generation of Christians. This inability of Christians through the centuries to agree upon the true faith undermines the claims of contemporary Christians that salvation or damnation is consequent on correct belief in Jesus' reported resurrection (or indeed anything Jesus taught).

Peter examines my contention that false memories might be a source of the disciples' belief that Jesus had risen from the grave, citing a great deal of modern research on the topic. But the research he cites and the conclusion that he reaches do not match. Peter writes, "Multiple studies have shown that even in the most successful cases [of implanting a false memory], false memories are not co-opted by a large percentage of subjects ... Even in the lab, researchers succeed less than half of the time." Peter's conclusion is: "This evidence *disconfirms* the hypothesis that the disciples' claim that Jesus had been resurrected ... was grounded in co-opted memories." But I never made such a claim. I did argue that co-opted memories might be one of many plausible explanations for the disciples' belief—in fact, I listed eight such natural explanations. I certainly do not believe that co-opted memories alone could account for the resurrection belief. But Peter has confirmed that this does happen, even if only for a minority of the population.

I would have made a stronger case for this if I had reversed Peter (the disciple) and Andrew in my speculation on how the resurrection belief might have begun—one of many ways—since so much more is known of Peter's life. So let's imagine that Peter reports a dream experience of the risen Jesus to the disciples. Andrew, arriving late, doesn't realize that Peter is relating a dream, and claims a similar encounter with the risen Jesus. This would be only human—and the Gospels make clear there was disciple rivalry. Several years later Andrew remembers the occasion very imperfectly: in his recollection, he had an encounter with the risen Lord—and it wasn't a dream!

Is this what happened? We have no way of knowing two thousand years later. But it is just one of the many possible natural explanations that I have suggested for the disciples' belief they had encountered Jesus after his execution by the Romans.

Here I offer a final thought—a perspective on this whole question. As Craig has agreed, the greatest significance of this debate on Jesus' alleged resurrection is the place this event has in the closely related questions of God and his supposed plan for the world and for all who live in it. As conservative Christian scholars Gary Habermas and J. P. Moreland correctly note, "Often a particular belief is part of a larger system of beliefs, and it gains rational support from its role in that system."[4] But I would suggest a corollary to this observation: "When a particular belief is part of a system which lacks coherence or is contradicted by indisputable evidence, that belief lacks credibility."

In his reply to my case against the resurrection, Craig hints at this same kind of observation, when he suggests that my own conclusions are based on something other than the merits of the case at hand:

> It is . . . interesting that at at the end of Carl's chapter he makes reference to the problem of evil. He did this briefly in the two live debates I had with him in recent years at Oregon State University that spawned our friendship and dialogue. He has done so in email exchanges with me more recently. I suspect that this is the real nub of the problem. There can't be an all-powerful and all-loving God because of the amount of evil in the universe. If there is no God, then there are no miracles. If there are no miracles, there is no resurrection. I suspect that for all of Carl's more sophisticated arguments this is really the reasoning that has led him to his conclusions. If this is the case, then the real issue to be debated is not the resurrection but the problem of evil. And that, of course, would take a different and separate volume.

My response is we live in a world that is beset by lethal natural disasters: in 2004, an earthquake in the Indian Ocean created a tsunami that killed 228,000; in 2008, a cyclone and storm surge in Myanmar

---

4. Gary Habermas and J. P. Moreland, *Beyond Death* (Crossway, 1998), 16.

killed 138,000; in 2010, 159,000 people died when an earthquake hit Haiti. Such disasters are termed "Acts of God" by insurance companies. Given that we poor humans can do nothing to stop these forces of nature, but that an all-powerful God could do so without any effort, the label seems justified.

Reading the *Boston Globe* the other day, on an inner page I came across a story that left me stricken, appalled. The headline was, "Toddler Hit, Killed by Car Driven by Her Mother." According to the story, the 27-year-old mother was backing out of a parking space at their apartment when the accident happened.

Millions of Christians believe in a God who is supposedly everywhere, all-powerful, all-knowing, loving of all his children, morally perfect. I cannot share this belief.

Summing It All Up

Craig Blomberg, Ph.D.

No one will be surprised that an evangelical Christian and an atheist assessing our debate would side heavily with the participants in the debate who share the same convictions as they. Of course, a poor participant on either side should draw critique from anyone, so it is to Carl's credit that Richard Carrier has next to nothing to criticize in his work. I am similarly grateful that Peter Williams found only a couple of minor points in my sections of this book that he feels could have been strengthened. I am likewise appreciative that we have had two very capable and thoughtful assessments of the debate as Carrier and Williams have given us. Again, no one will be surprised that I find Williams far more convincing than Carrier. My natural inclination is to try to do what we all have been doing to varying degrees throughout this volume and reply to Carrier more or less point by point, but our self-imposed space limitations in these final remarks preclude such an approach. Instead, I will focus on some key methodological issues and give only select illustrations.

Let me begin with one where I am in complete agreement with Carrier. He takes me to task for arguing for the credibility of the Gospels' resurrection accounts from various internal details, such as the disciples locking themselves in the Upper Room after Jesus' crucifixion, showing that they were in no psychological state to expect a resurrection, or Thomas's skepticism that had to be countered with very empirical evidence that an embodied Jesus had appeared. If the resurrection narratives were invented out of whole cloth, with no historical details in them whatsoever, then whoever put them in the form we have them could have invented these details as well. If they were particularly sophisticated, they might have even invented them to give the narratives greater appearance of credibility or plausibility. I was very much aware in my reply to Carl that a different participant in the debate might make this very point; I have certainly heard it repeatedly throughout my life. I also knew that Carrier thinks that Jesus probably never existed,[1] so I wouldn't have expected him to leave room for any core of historical detail about Jesus in the Gospels and certainly not in the resurrection narratives.

But Carl wasn't arguing along those lines. He was willing to accept many things about the historical Jesus that did not involve the resurrection or the miraculous. So it was appropriate for me to point to these very human and lifelike details—the disciples' fear that they would be the Roman authorities' targets next and Thomas's unwillingness to believe the disciples' stories about a resurrected Jesus without firsthand proof. These are the kinds of details that the standard criteria of authenticity legitimate even when scholars question numerous other details in these passages. It is ironic that Carrier charges me with misrepresenting Carl's argument (which in fact I don't!) when he himself distorts Carl's argument by claiming that Carl is holding the identical position that he does.[2] His restatement of Carl's perspective is an excellent restatement

---

1. Richard Carrier, *On the Historicity of Jesus: Why We Might Have Reason to Doubt* (Sheffield Phoenix, 2014).

2. There are numerous inaccuracies in Carrier's representations of what I wrote, so that he can knock down the straw man he accuses me of pushing over. For example, he claims I misrepresent Carl by imagining an "impostor" trying to convince the apostles he was Jesus. I nowhere say anything of the kind. There are plenty of inaccuracies at other points, too. To cite just two examples, (1) Mormonism does not claim that Jesus flew to America, merely that he appeared here; and (2) the evidence for the angel Moroni and the magical gold plates is not stronger than the evidence for Jesus' resurrection. No one besides Joseph Smith ever claimed to have seen Moroni, whereas

of his own views, articulated elsewhere, but in several places it goes well beyond what Carl actually argues, as the careful reader of our volume may well have already noticed.

This becomes clearest when we come to the issue of the supernatural. Carl explicitly denies that he is arguing from antisupernaturalist presuppositions. I wonder if he *has* successfully bracketed these to the extent he has claimed to, but I have given him the benefit of the doubt and therefore responded to his arguments as he presented them. But Carrier repeatedly rehearses David Hume's famous line of reasoning from eighteenth-century Scottish philosophy, though without actually mentioning him. Hume stopped a hair's breadth short of explicitly affirming antisupernaturalism, but his approach was the de facto equivalent, as we have already discussed (in previous entries in this volume). What we did not point out earlier is that Hume's reasoning logically excluded free human agency as well. Human beings are regularly inventing, creating, and experimenting with activities that are unlike what people have done before. Indeed, "everything is unprecedented until it happens for the first time!"[3] Hume himself would no doubt have dismissed accounts of the possibility of the Internet, space flight, or holo-

---

hundreds are said to have seen Jesus. The witnesses who testified to having seen the golden plates, including two who later renounced their religion but continued to insist they had seen them, were unable to read anything on them. It is possible that there were some kind of plates that Joseph found or created, but who knows what was on them? No one else has ever seen them since, if they did exist. In the case of the written accounts of the resurrection of Jesus, anyone who can read Hellenistic Greek, or any of the reliable translations into hundreds of the world's languages, can learn for themselves what they claim.

3. In 1819, Richard Whatley (*Historical Doubts Relative to Napoleon Buonaparte*) demonstrated this by applying Hume's approach to evidence for the then living Napoleon, showing how a case could be made that he did not exist! The quotation is taken from the script of the film, *Sully*, based on the true story of the pilot who successfully landed a commercial plane on the Hudson River with no loss of life but then had to face interrogation over whether such extreme measures were necessary. It was initially doubted that the plane experienced a double bird strike disabling the engines on both sides of the aircraft because such an event had never occurred before in the history of aviation.

grams had someone been able to describe these later inventions to him, viewing them as just as laughable as a resurrection. Of course, today we understand that such inventions can be explained scientifically.

Every generation too often yields to the temptation to believe that what is presently viewed to be possible or impossible according to the majority of scientists is somehow completely (or at least largely) accurate, when the history of science suggests that the "knowledge" about which we so confidently pontificate today may be shown in another two or three hundred years to have been embarrassingly inaccurate. C. S. Lewis's famous defense of miracles drew on this observation as he pointed out plausible ways that many of the biblical miracles could be seen as scientific processes sped up beyond any of our current abilities to comprehend them.[4] I am not necessarily arguing for Lewis's perspective, just reminding us of how little we may indeed actually know about the nature of the universe, with or without God.

Carrier's regular reasoning about arguments from silence merit significant scrutiny as well. Over and over again, he tells us that unless we have evidence of something existing at a certain period of history we cannot say that we know it. But he employs this form of reasoning highly selectively. When the actual evidence does not support his case, then he appeals to how little we know from the ancient world and rejects the evidence that we have.

Take, for example, the case of the shorter and most likely original ending of Mark. If what we call Mark 16:8 is where this Gospel originally ended, then Carrier is absolutely correct that there is no resurrection narrative per se in this, the earliest known Gospel. But that cannot be where discussion stops. For whom was this document written? Scholars may speculate all they want, but the actual evidence that Carrier so longs for comes from multiple second-century Christian sources and their uniform answer is: persecuted Christians in Rome while the apostle Peter was still alive and passed on his memoirs to John Mark.[5] Mark

---

4. C. S. Lewis, *Miracles: A Preliminary Study* (Macmillan, 1947).

5. For references and discussion, see Craig L. Blomberg, *The Historical Reliability of the New Testament* (B & H, 2016), 7–13, and the literature there cited.

was not written to evangelize but to encourage believers in a context of severe attacks on them for their faith. But how did they become believers in the first place? Every known ancient source that *is* in existence that even remotely addresses this question, both inside and outside of the New Testament, focuses on the cross of Christ and his resurrection as the heart of early Christian preaching. That is the evidence. One can speculate that at some earlier date it was something different but that is an argument from silence. The actual evidence that we have suggests that Mark's audience already knew well the stories of the resurrection. Carrier does not follow his own ground rules.

But there is more. Mark three times narrates Jesus' own predictions about his coming resurrection (Mark 8:31, 9:31, 10:34). He narrates Jesus' prediction that Peter would deny him and then describes the fulfillment of that prediction (14:30, 66–72). He narrates Jesus' prediction that Judas would betray him and then describes the fulfillment of that prediction (14:18–21; 43–46). He narrates the young man dressed in white announcing to the women who discovered the empty tomb that Christ was risen and that the women should tell the disciples that he would meet them in Galilee (16:5–7). The author of Mark's Gospel has portrayed Jesus and those speaking on his behalf as reliable predictors. Even if someone who did not know the tradition of the resurrection got a hold of Mark's Gospel and read it carefully, they would have every reason to expect that Mark believed Jesus to be risen even though he did not include an actual resurrection appearance in his narrative.[6] He ended his Gospel with the fear and silence of the women not because that was the end of the story as he knew it, but as part of his recurring theme of highlighting the fear and failure of Jesus' followers (as a precursor to their subsequent restoration, without which there would have been no Roman church to receive this document), to encourage those who were afraid or felt like failures in the midst of Roman persecution that God could still use them mightily.[7]

---

6. A. T. Lincoln, "The Promise and the Failure: Mark 16:7, 8," *Journal of Biblical Literature* 108 (1989): 288–90.

7. See, e.g., Douglas W. Geyer, *Fear, Anomaly, and Uncertainty in the Gospel of Mark* (Scarecrow Press, 2000).

Or consider the question of what Paul knew about the resurrection of Jesus when he penned 1 Corinthians 15:3–8. Carrier maintains that because Paul does not tell us any details about any of the appearances to the various people that he itemizes, we cannot infer that he knew anything about them. This is highly improbable. As has been pointed out, these verses take a creedal or confessional form of tightly packed, condensed doctrinal teachings deemed to be important. They are something Paul says he "received" and "passed on," using technical terms for the careful transmission of oral tradition. The very nature of the genre of a creed is that it leaves out much that is known and presupposed. If it didn't, it would no longer be succinct and memorably phrased. Although some scholars still claim that there is little evidence that Paul knew about the traditions of Jesus' teachings and deeds, the evidence continues to mount and the body of literature to grow that makes it highly likely Paul knew quite a bit about the historical Jesus.[8]

Thus Paul can cite Jesus' teaching at his Last Supper in detail (1 Corinthians 11:23–26; Luke 22:17–20). He knows Jesus' views on divorce, remarriage, and celibacy, and even distinguished between what he knows the historical Jesus taught and what he believes God was more directly revealing to him (cf. 1 Corinthians 7:10 with v. 12; cf. vv. 25, 40). He reiterates Jesus' countercultural teachings on taxes (Romans 13:7; Mark 12:13–17) and on blessing the persecutor, loving one's enemies and overcoming evil with good (12:14, 20–21; Luke 6:35, Matthew 5:42–43). He reuses Jesus' striking metaphor of him coming like a thief in the night (1 Thessalonians 5:2; Matthew 24:43), which no Christian was likely to have invented without precedent, as potentially unflattering as it would be for someone who misunderstood the analogy and thought that Jesus was coming to steal something! In fact, Paul knows considerable details from Jesus' "eschatological discourse" (Matthew 24–25 and parallels), and quite a few teachings from the Sermon on the

---

8. The fullest study in the past generation was David Wenham, *Paul: Follower of Jesus or Founder of Christianity* (Eerdmans, 1995). For a recent update, see Craig L. Blomberg, "Quotations, Allusions, and Echoes of Jesus in Paul," in *Studies in the Pauline Epistles: Festschrift for Douglas J. Moo*, ed. Matt Harmon and Jay Smith (Zondervan, 2014), 129–43.

Mount/Plain (Matthew 5–7/Luke 6:20–49). Precisely because, as Carrier observes, Paul's epistles predated the written Gospels, this information must have come from an oral tradition that preceded Paul. We have already seen that Paul met with key apostles a mere three years after his conversion (Galatians 1:15–18), when he would have learned much more about Jesus' life, death, and resurrection. So, it is not the case that the evidence Carrier asks for is lacking. But, of course, for him to admit this evidence he would have to admit that Jesus most likely existed!

So Carrier's protests that I too often argue from silence rather than on actual evidence appear to be special pleading. That he is inclined elsewhere to dismiss all the ancient evidence that points to the existence of a historical Jesus as the founder of Christianity shows just how reluctant he is to accept the actual evidence that exists (completely apart from the issue of the miraculous), which convinces the vast majority of biblical scholars (believers and unbelievers alike) that there was such a person. If one looks hard enough, one can always find some reason to doubt almost every historical claim. But it is good to admit what one is doing, rather than claiming to be following just what the hard evidence points to.

It would have been nice, for example, for Carrier to be transparent about what the ancient stories about Inanna, Zalmoxis, Bacchus, Romulus, and Osiris actually contained. A resurrection, as narrated in Scripture, is the restoration to full, healthy, embodied life of a genuine human being after that person was undeniably dead. It is extraordinary that Carrier can call my accounts of his alleged pagan parallels "not factually correct," when I gave no accounts of them! But I can supply them here: Inanna was an ancient Sumerian goddess from more than two millennia before the time of Jesus who was a goddess of love, sensuality, fertility, and also war. Like many ancient gods and goddesses in various cultures, she was believed to descend to the underworld every winter and return every spring, accounting for the seasonal cycles of vegetation. She was never a human being and never had a bodily resurrection.[9] Zalmoxis was an obscure individual that the pre-Christian

---

9. Joshua J. Mark, "Innana," *Ancient History Encyclopedia* (2010), www.ancient.eu/Innana/.

Greek historian Herodotus made brief mention of as someone who centuries earlier had hidden for years in an underground chamber so that people thought he was dead only to reappear to them and convince them he was alive again. No real death, so no resurrection.[10]

Bacchus was the Roman name for the Greek god of wine, Dionysus, son of Zeus and Hera, the chief god and goddess of the Olympic pantheon. One myth recounted how the infant Dionysus was torn to pieces, cooked, and eaten by evil Titans. But Zeus reassembled and reanimated him. No human being, no bodily resurrection.[11] Romulus and his twin brother, Remus, may or may not have been real people, but they became the legendary founders of Rome, seven centuries before Christ. Romulus, after his death, underwent apotheosis, so the story goes, and his spirit ascended to heaven. Still no bodily resurrection.[12] The god Osiris was the brother-husband of the famous Egyptian goddess Isis. Killed by his enemies, with his dead body hacked into pieces, Isis was able to reassemble him enough for him to come back to some form of existence as lord of the underworld. But he was never completely whole again or able to leave the realm of the dead. No real human and no resurrection.[13]

Carrier puts these examples forward as the best of some unspecified larger number of supposed parallels. If they are this irrelevant, one can only imagine how poor the rest of his "evidence" is. If one wants to ascribe the resurrection appearances of Jesus to humanly invented fiction, the only potentially credible way would be to do so in a Palestinian Jewish context based on Old Testament texts like Daniel 12:1–4 that predicts the bodily resurrection of all people at the end of human history. New Testament origins are consistently and overwhelmingly rooted in Jewish backgrounds. But of course that provides no precedent

10. Herodotus, *Persian Wars* 4.94–96.

11. "Dionysus: Greek Mythology," *Encyclopaedia Britannica*, www.britannica.com/topic/Dionysus.

12. Brittany Garcia, "Romulus and Remus," *Ancient History Encyclopedia* (2013), www.ancient.eu/Romulus_and_Remus/.

13. "Osiris: Egyptian God," *Encyclopaedia Britannica*, www.britannica.com/topic/Osiris-Egyptian-god.

for a resurrected Messiah separate from and prior to the resurrection of the rest of humanity. That is the state of the actual evidence. But it all works against Carrier's views. In sum, there are no known accounts anywhere in the ancient world, except for those about Jesus, of an individual who was known to be a real, live human being with followers still alive who wrote (or narrated to those who wrote) things about him that even make the claim of a bodily resurrection from an undisputed death.[14] That is the real evidence. Everything else is "fake news." Of course, if one has decided *a priori* that the Gospels' accounts cannot under any considerations be accepted as historical, then one will reject them. But the speculation that Carrier resorts to in order to try to explain the genesis of those accounts flies in the face of all his appeals to follow actual evidence.

So where does all this leave us? Are believers and atheists doomed to talk past each other and to take seriously only that which supports their presuppositions? The conversions of atheists to a robust belief in historic Christianity and vice-versa suggest that not everyone is so predestined. But the accounts of the conversions of atheists to Christianity and of Christians to atheism typically show that the process involved a much longer period of time and many more elements than reading just one book containing a debate on the resurrection and being convinced by one side in that debate.[15] On the other hand, books and debates have been one of the many elements that have influenced some, so we can hope that our writing has not just reinforced the beliefs of those who already agree with us, but also may lead some people to change their minds.

I would like to suggest, in closing, that a topic that gets too little

---

14. Cf. further N. T. Wright, *The Resurrection of the Son of God* (Fortress Press, 2003); Stanley E. Porter, Michael A. Hayes and David Tombs, ed., *Resurrection* (Sheffield Academic Press, 1999); Murray Harris, *From Grave to Glory: Resurrection in the New Testament* (Zondervan, 1990); Stefan Alkier, *The Reality of the Resurrection* (Baylor University Press, 2013).

15. Scot McKnight and Hauna Ondrey, *Finding Faith, Losing Faith: Stories of Conversion and Apostasy* (Baylor University Press, 2008); John W. Loftus, *Why I Became an Atheist: A Former Preacher Rejects Christianity,* rev. ed. (Prometheus, 2012).

attention in this and similar debates involves what philosophers and students of historiography call the burden of proof. My very first publication examined the "the burden of proof" in matters of historical investigation. The criteria of authenticity also very much come into play.[16] The Keith and Le Donne volume to which Carrier refers does not reject all use of the criteria; the majority of the contributors point out ways in which the criteria can be abused and ways to use them and newer criteria better.[17]

What is often overlooked, however, is that one's starting point—where one assigns the burden of proof—makes a huge difference in one's outcomes. There are three logical possibilities: (1) one assumes that an ancient source, presented in what by the conventions of the day would have been viewed as a historical or biographical genre, is reliable until there is repeated and good evidence for becoming more suspicious; (2) one assumes that an ancient source of this same kind is unreliable until there is repeated and good evidence for becoming less suspicious; (3) whatever case one intends to make, one assumes the opposite until there is repeated and good evidence for overturning that assumption. More succinctly, and applied to the debate concerning the resurrection, these three options boil down, respectively, to: the burden of proof is on the skeptic; the burden of proof is on the believer; and the burden of proof is on whoever wants to make a case in either direction.

Skeptical criticism of Scripture has almost uniformly adopted position (2). Classical historians have traditionally adopted position (1), though in a postmodern age there is greater diversity today. Position (3) sounds like the most objective of all, yet if applied to areas where we have far less information than we do for the origins of Christianity, much that is routinely accepted in world civilizations textbooks and standard encyclopedias would have to be rejected. Of course, this

---

16. Stewart C. Goetz and Craig L. Blomberg, "The Burden of Proof," *Journal for the Study of the New Testament* 11 (1981): 39–63.

17. Chris Keith and Anthony Le Donne, eds., *Jesus, Criteria and the Demise of Authenticity* (T&T Clark, 2012). Only Keith and Scot McKnight, among the contributors, have given up on the criteria. The other seven, like all the other scholars Carrier lists, are not this pessimistic.

brings us right back to the problem of the miraculous. If one excludes the supernatural *a priori*, then the pervasiveness of miracles in the Jewish and Christian Scriptures will be precisely the evidence that a person needs for becoming suspicious of the biographies of Jesus. Apart from this single issue, the amount of corroborating information for the Gospels' accounts is overwhelming. But then, if one closely examines the miracles of Scripture, including the resurrection, one sees that they are consistently used, in context, to support the conviction that God's royal reign over this cosmos is advancing in ways designed to bring wholeness of all kinds to human beings. No other collection of miracles in the world's literature consistently functions in this fashion, though certain isolated individual accounts may do so here and there.[18]

Carrier repeats what Carl earlier quoted him as saying, that if there were a God who wanted to save everyone he would disclose himself unequivocally to every human being. One wonders if this is his real bottom line. Neither of the two men has ever personally experienced a miracle; therefore they will never believe in any report of a miracle. But such assertions are quite removed from an approach that relies on actual evidence. Evidence can come from many sources, not just personal experience. And, as I said earlier, if God does exist and values freely given love relationships with human beings so much that he is willing to permit many to reject him so that others might freely accept him, then he cannot disclose himself in ways that preclude all doubt. Rather, he would leave behind enough evidence to make faith rational but not the only plausible response to that evidence. It would appear this is exactly what has occurred.

---

18. See Craig L. Blomberg, *Can We Still Believe the Bible? An Evangelical Engagement with Contemporary Questions* (Brazos, 2014), 179–211.

RECOMMENDED READING
FOR FURTHER UNDERSTANDING

Book Recommendations by Carl Stecher, Ph.D.

Karen Armstrong, *The Case for God* (Knopf, 2009)

Dan Barker, *Losing Faith in Faith* (FFRF, 1992)

Howard Bloom, *The God Problem: How a Godless Cosmos Creates* (Prometheus Books, 2016)

Yuval Noah Harari, *Sapiens: A Brief History of Humankind* (Harper Perennial, 2015)*

John Loftus, *Why I Became an Atheist* (Prometheus, 2012)

Michael Martin, *The Case Against Christianity* (Temple University Press, 1991)

Robert M. Price and Jeffery Jay Lowder, eds., *The Empty Tomb: Jesus Beyond the Grave* (Prometheus, 2005)

Michael Shermer, *How We Believe* (W.W. Freeman, 2000)

Carl Stecher and Peter S. Williams, *God Questions*, http://bethinking. org

Gary Wills, *Head and Heart: American Christianities* (Penguin, 2007)

* especially recommended

Book Recommendations by Craig Blomberg, Ph.D.

Stefan Alkier, *The Reality of the Resurrection: The New Testament Witness* (Baylor University Press, 2013).

Christopher Bryan, *The Resurrection of the Messiah* (Oxford University Press, 2011).

Paul Copan and Ronald K. Tacelli, eds., *Jesus' Resurrection: Fact or Figment? A Debate Between William Lane Craig and Gerd Lüdemann* (IVP, 2000).

Gary Habermas and Michael Licona, *The Case for the Resurrection of Jesus* (Kregel, 2004).

Murray J. Harris, *From Grave to Glory: Resurrection in the New Testament* (Zondervan, 1990).

George E. Ladd, *I Believe in the Resurrection of Jesus* (Eerdmans, 1975).

Michael Licona, *The Resurrection of Jesus: A New Historiographical Approach* (IVP, 2010).

John Wenham, *Easter Enigma: Are the Resurrection Accounts in Conflict?* (Zondervan, 1984; Wipf & Stock, 2005).

N. T. Wright, *Surprised by Hope: Rethinking Heaven, the Resurrection and the Mission of the Church* (HarperOne, 2008).

N. T. Wright, *The Resurrection of the Son of God* (Fortress, 2003).

Book Recommendations by Peter S. Williams, M.Phil.

Paul Copan and Paul K. Moser, eds., *The Rationality of Theism* (Routledge, 2003).

William Lane Craig, *On Guard for Students: A Thinker's Guide to the Christian Faith* (David C. Cook, 2015).

William Lane Craig and J. P. Moreland, eds., *Naturalism: A Critical Analysis* (Routledge, 2014).

Stephen C. Evans, *Why Believe? Reason and Mystery as Pointers to God* (Eerdmans, 1996).

Andreas J. Köstenberger and Justin Taylor, *The Final Days of Jesus* (Crossway, 2014).

Robert A. Larmer, *The Legitimacy of Miracle* (Lexington, 2014).

Troy A. Miller, ed., *Jesus: The Final Days* (SPCK, 2008).

Peter S. Williams, *Getting at Jesus: A Comprehensive Critique of Neo-Atheist Nonsense about the Jesus of History* (Wipf & Stock, 2019).

Peter S. Williams, *A Faithful Guide to Philosophy: A Christian Introduction to the Love of Wisdom* (Wipf & Stock, 2019).

Peter S. Williams, *Understanding Jesus: Five Ways to Spiritual Enlightenment* (Paternoster, 2011).

Book Recommendations by Richard Carrier, Ph.D.

Richard Carrier, *On the Historicity of Jesus: Why We Might Have Reason for Doubt* (Sheffield Phoenix, 2014).

Richard Carrier, *Why I Am Not a Christian* (Philosophy, 2011).

Richard Carrier, *Not the Impossible Faith: Why Christianity Didn't Need a Miracle to Succeed* (Lulu, 2009).

Richard Carrier, *Sense and Goodness Without God: A Defense of Metaphysical Naturalism* (AuthorHouse, 2005).

Chris Hallquist, *UFOs, Ghosts, and a Rising God* (Reasonable, 2009).

Kris Komarnitsky, *Doubting Jesus' Resurrection*, 2nd ed. (Stone Arrow, 2014).

John Loftus, ed., *The End of Christianity* (Prometheus, 2011).

John Loftus, ed., *The Christian Delusion* (Prometheus, 2010).

Matthew McCormick, *Atheism and the Case Against Christ* (Prometheus, 2012).

Robert M. Price and Jeffery Jay Lowder, eds., *The Empty Tomb* (Prometheus, 2005).

About the Authors

Carl Stecher, Ph.D., is a professor emeritus at Salem State University, a recipient of a Woodrow Wilson Fellowship, and a frequently published voice on the topics of educational policy and religion.

Craig Blomberg, Ph.D., is Distinguished Professor of New Testament at Denver Seminary in Littleton, Colorado and author of twenty-five books.

Richard Carrier, Ph.D., is the author of *Sense and Goodness Without God, On the Historicity of Jesus, The Scientist in the Early Roman Empire,* and many other works.

Peter S. Williams, M.Phil., is an assistant professor at Gimlekollen School of Journalism and Communication, NLA University, Norway.